GRANT LAWRENCE

THE
Lonely
END
of the
RINK

★★★

Douglas and McIntyre (2013) Ltd.
P.O. Box 219, Madeira Park, BC, VON 2H0
www.douglas-mcintyre.com

Edited by Silas White
Copyediting by Derek Fairbridge
Cover and text design by Naomi MacDougall
Cover compositing by Andrew Hogan
Illustrations by Christy Nyiri
Photographs from the author's collection unless otherwise noted
Printed and bound in Canada

Cataloguing data available from Library and Archives Canada
ISBN 978-1-77100-077-2 (paper)
ISBN 978-1-77100-078-9 (ebook)

Douglas & McIntyre (2013) Ltd. gratefully acknowledges
financial support from the Government of Canada through the
Canada Book Fund and the Canada Council for the Arts,
and from the Province of British Columbia through the
BC Arts Council and the Book Publishing Tax Credit.

FOR
Mom
★ ★ ★

Contents

★ ★ ★

PROLOGUE

PING! IN A painfully close, gut-churning championship hockey game, there is no better sound to a goalie's ears. It is a sound as sweet as a church bell in the French countryside. And it can be heard from about as far. You could be in the last row of the nosebleeds of the largest hockey arena in the world—if the puck hits the post you'll hear the *PING*. You could be at home on your couch with the commentators yakking and the crowd going wild—if the puck hits the post you'll still hear the *PING*. I love that sound, because I am a goalie.

There were under three minutes left in the third period of our championship final when the puck defiantly whizzed past my outstretched glove in the blink of my eye, only to sharply and loudly hit the scarred red goalpost and deflect into the corner of the rink. The score was a perilous 2–1 for our team, the Vancouver Flying Vees, a beer-league hockey club, extra old stocked with various members and friends from the local arts and music scene.

I stood in my crease shuddering from the near miss, the *PING* still ringing in my ears. My shoulders relaxed slightly as I watched one of our most dependable defencemen "Young" Greg, tall, blond and mulleted like Bo Duke in Bauers, skate the puck safely across our blue line into the neutral zone. He made it to centre and shot the puck into the far corner of our opponent's zone, killing off vital time on the clock. The seconds ticked down in agonizing lethargy, a stark contrast to the scrambled action on the ice. The puck pin-balled back into the neutral zone.

My eyes twitched and my hand gripped my goalie stick tightly as an enemy player pounced on the puck in suddenly way-too-wide-open ice and hurtled back toward me, crazy-eyed and drooling like Jon Voight in *Runaway Train*. My heart slammed against the inside of my stinky chest protector like it was trying to escape, while salty sweat streamed the length of my body, filling my stunted goalie skates. I stole a glance up at the clock: 1:46 to go. That's a lifetime for a goalie like me in a 2–1 hockey game. As the opposing player slashed his way back into our zone I hunched into what I had always hoped was the right position: knees together, feet apart, out beyond the edge of my crease. I stuck out my chin and my glove and put the blade of my goalie stick on the ice, trying to stay with the puck carrier, swivelling awkwardly backward on my skates as he drew closer far too quickly for my liking, legs pumping like pistons, skate blades barely touching ice. Our only defensive hope was our last man back, Chris "Nitzy" Mizzoni.

Nitzy was a diehard Toronto Maple Leafs fan, so much so that he had the original Leafs logo tattooed on his shoulder. It somewhat bothered Nitzy to play on the Vees, a skating tribute to the Vancouver Canucks' history and lore. But Nitzy loved hockey and when he moved out from Toronto, he had to play. Nitzy was the author of the bestselling children's hockey book *Clancy with the Puck*, looked like Alfalfa from *Our Gang* when he took his helmet off after the game, and was an exceptional hockey player. And he was the last man back in the championship final with less than two minutes to go.

Nitzy knew he was beat and couldn't allow the play to develop any further so late in the game, so he did what he had to do: he

xii

dove forward and jammed his Sidney Crosby–pattern Reebok stick into the opposing player's skates, causing the attacker to collapse, bellyflopping onto the ice, sliding toward me with his arms and legs up in the air like a kid on a Slip 'n Slide. I was able to whack the puck into the corner with my paddle before the opposing forward crashed into the net and me.

Tina the Referee's arm shot straight up into the air. Her whistle's screech brought us all to a halt. Tina leaned down, dragged one arm across the shins of her black pants and pointed at Nitzy. She was calling Nitzy for a two-minute tripping penalty in the championship game with only 1:38 left. I stared in horror through the metal grate of my mask, my breath steaming out in front of my face like the smokestack of the *Royal Hudson* as I untangled myself from the mess of limbs and sticks in the net. Would Tina twist the dagger and call a penalty shot? Nitzy complained bitterly all the way to the penalty box.

"You're giving me two minutes for tripping?" Nitzy panted. "What are you giving that prick for his swan dive, Tina? 8.1 maybe?"

"Shut up, Nitzy!" I barked from behind my mask, fearful that at any second Tina the Referee would furiously point to centre ice, the unmistakeable signal for a penalty shot and something I was doubtful my racing heart could take. But bless her stripes, she never did.

After failing to convince Tina that they deserved a penalty shot, the opposing team determinedly took to the ice for the power play, pulling their goalie for six skaters against four, a titanic advantage. I hoped my whimpering in the crease wasn't audible. I needed the game to be over. The other team won the faceoff deep in our zone. They managed to shovel the puck directly behind our net along the boards, where their centre was able to set up in "The Office," so named for Wayne Gretzky sealing deals and assuring future contracts with crisp passes for easy one-timers past hapless goalies. If the pass wasn't available, Gretzky would take it himself, jumping out for his own shot, jamming in a wraparound, or even lofting it over the net and ingloriously bouncing it in off the goalie's butt. Hence, "The Office" is incredibly difficult to defend from the goalie's position, because it is the one place on the ice where the goalie must turn his back to the puck, and can completely lose sight of it, relying on the sounds of skates and teammates' warnings as to exactly which side of the net the puck will emerge.

Sure enough, the enemy centre controlling the play in "The Office" put a tape-to-tape pass onto the blade of one of his teammates rushing into the slot, directly in front of my crease. As soon as he felt the puck on his stick he let it rip. I heard the CLACK of the puck making contact with a stick, but I never saw the shot. Desperately, I kicked out my left goalie pad, threw my glove up in the air, and slammed the paddle of my stick down on the ice. Their players broke into a wild celebration directly in front of me. I couldn't move. From my collapsed, frozen position on the goal line, I looked up at the clock: 1:21. Then I looked over my shoulder at Tina the Referee.

The

LONELY END

of the RINK

"The only job worse than goalie is being a javelin catcher at a track-and-field meet."

GUMP WORSLEY, *NHL goaltender, 1952–1974*

First
PERIOD
★ ★ ★

THAT BOSTON DANDY

MOM WAS ONE of those people who always maintained that she never won anything. The massive exception was in the summer of 1972, when she became one of the luckiest hockey fans in Canada. Canadians from coast to coast were caught up in a frenzy of anticipation for a hockey event like nothing the country had seen before or since, scheduled for that September. It was a tournament that would become one of the defining moments of our nation's history: the eight-game international "Summit Series" that for the first time ever pitted the USSR's most elite, disciplined, mysterious players from behind the Iron Curtain up against our brutish, long-haired Canadian NHL all-stars. It was the Canadians against the Communists.

There would be four games held in Canada—Montreal, Toronto, Winnipeg and Vancouver, each rink holding between fifteen thousand and eighteen thousand fans—followed by four games in Russia for a best-of-eight series. In 1972, the population of Canada was just over twenty-two million. And it appeared that there were just over twenty million requests for the seventy thousand tickets that were available. Because of the unprecedented demand, organizers devised a lottery system as a way to sell tickets to Canadians as fairly as possible. Ticket hopefuls would enter their names into the lottery for one of the four cities. If entrants' names were drawn, they'd be eligible to purchase the tickets for the specific game they selected. There was such fervent interest that many Canadians entered into the draw for all four cities to spread their odds, willing to travel great distances to see a Summit Series game if need be.

My parents realized they would be visiting my dad's family the day the Summit Series game was scheduled for Winnipeg, his hometown. On a whim, Mom entered the ticket lottery. No one was more shocked and delighted when Mom and Dad were informed by letter that they had won the right to purchase tickets for Game 3 in Winnipeg.

Pretty much every Canadian hockey player, fan and pundit, including Mom and Dad, thought the eight-game series would be a butter-tart walk for the Canadians. When the series finally began on September 2, 1972, Mom's birthday, the country was collectively stunned to see our shaggy, swaggering, bladed heroes not only lose Game 1 in Montreal to the surprisingly lethal and precise Soviet machine, but also lose badly by the embarrassing score of 7–3. The series would culminate in an eventual moment in time, a freeze-framed snapshot of victory, a moment many Canadians who were alive in 1972 would never forget. I was indeed alive, but I was barely one year old, and completely oblivious. By my parents' account I was a happy, curious baby, smiling and laughing most of the time, adorned with ridiculously long Shirley Temple–like blond ringlet curls that bounced up and down on my head like a bouquet of Slinkys. I was cute, and still several years away from full-blown nerdom.

On the morning of September 5, 1972, my parents and I were at the Toronto International Airport, domestic departures, waiting to board our plane to Winnipeg. To my parents' shock and delight, who did they see surrounding us at the boarding gate but a gathering of the very men they were jet-setting across the Canadian Shield to see, the most famous men in Canada: hockey players. The mustachioed, long-haired, gap-toothed, broad-shouldered and barrel-chested members of that first-ever squad known as *Team Canada*. They were dressed in loud checkered jackets, open-collared shirts and flared polyester pants. They smelled like cologne and cigarettes. Team Canada was flying coach, just like everybody else.

On that morning, the members of Team Canada—as well as everyone else in the airport and across the country—were in a great mood. The night before, our Canadian boys had bounced back in Game 2 to beat up the geeky, gangly, helmeted Russians 4–1 at Maple Leaf Gardens, the hallowed hall of hockey, evening the series at one win apiece. Americans must have wondered what that warm gale from the north that reeked of beer was: it was Canadian hockey fans breathing a massive sigh of relief. For the moment, everything seemed right in the hockey world again.

We boarded our plane. A friendly stewardess led our young family to our seats, where we found ourselves surrounded by Team Canada hockey royalty. Strolling down the aisle toward us was the charming architect of the entire series, Alan Eagleson, one of the most famous behind-the-scenes figures in hockey. He stopped and chatted with my star-struck parents, charming them and mussing up my little blond curls with his big hand. In the row directly in front of us sat Montreal Canadien Yvan "The Roadrunner" Cournoyer in the aisle seat. Sitting by the window was Boston Bruin Wayne Cashman (who would eventually be forced to leave the series after a bizarre tongue injury requiring over forty stitches). Squeezed ingloriously into the middle seat was the most famous person on the plane, one of the most famous Canadians ever and easily hockey's greatest star: Canada's sweetheart, Bobby Orr.

Bobby Orr was injured. He was recovering from knee surgery and therefore was not playing in the tournament, but he had insisted on going along with the team while in Canada for the moral support. Orr and Cashman were both fresh from winning the Stanley Cup with the Bruins that spring and had been partying all summer long. They looked healthy, tanned and relaxed. They were joking about finally seeing their recently engraved Stanley Cup, and how the engraver managed to outrageously misspell their Original Six team name using 'Q's instead of 'O's: BQSTQN BRUINS. In the rows behind and across from our family were Bobby Clarke, the wild, young, toothless turk from the Philadelphia Flyers; Frank "The Big M" Mahovlich and beside him his little brother Peter, both from the Montreal Canadiens; as well as Ron Ellis, long-time member of the Toronto Maple Leafs.

Mom was ever gregarious, immediately engaging the surrounding hockey players in conversation, boasting that she and Dad had coincidentally grown up with Stanley Cup-winning teammates on the big, bad Boston Bruins. Mom was close high school friends with Bruins' star winger Ken Hodge when they both attended Alderwood Collegiate in Etobicoke, Ontario. Dad played on the same peewee team in Winnipeg with "Terrible" Ted Green, the Bruins' ferocious Métis enforcer on the blue line. With connections made and conversation flowing, once the plane was in flight those big, brawny players were showering attention on her little blond baby with the Shirley Temple ringlet curls.

Bobby Orr poked his famous, friendly face over the seat, his warm smile framed by his wavy brown hair, and asked my parents if he could hold me. Without hesitation, Mom tossed me like a bag of pucks into the softest hands in hockey. I ended up cuddled and cooing in the lap of the greatest player of his generation, and possibly of all time, for most of the flight. That year alone, Bobby Orr had won the Hart Trophy for the NHL's most valuable player of the regular season, the Norris Trophy for best defenceman, the Conn Smythe Trophy for most valuable player of the playoffs, and the Stanley Cup.

When the plane landed in Winnipeg, my parents walked into Winnipeg's bright, modernist airport amongst the players, Bobby

6

Mom and Dad loved to skate, Mom in her white figure skates and Dad in his tough leather hockey skates. They'd take to any outdoor frozen surface they could find in Canada and they always took me with them whether I wanted to be there or not, even in a pram.

Orr leading the way until he stopped suddenly. Through the glass, the players could look down to the arrivals area and the baggage carousel, where they saw a huge throng of reporters waiting to grill them like bison burgers on their shaky start to the series. Bobby Orr turned on a dime, not wanting to face the media. The rest of the players followed, escaping through a side door further down the hall and away from the press. Orr must have sensed the impending fate facing Team Canada. In Winnipeg, they blew 3–1 and 4–2 leads to wind up with a final score of 4–4, thanks to the speedy Russians scoring two short-handed goals. In Vancouver, Team Canada was greeted by booing at the Pacific Coliseum before the drop of the puck. They went on to lose the game 5–3.

Team Canada would eventually turn the series around in violent, controversial fashion while in Russia, winning the whole thing at the very last minute, literally, with just thirty-four seconds to go in Game 8. Needless to say, despite having to witness the

7

tie in Winnipeg, my parents were ecstatic about our close encounter with Team Canada. It has forever remained one of the favourite stories around our family dinner table. For my hockey-loving parents, having their baby coddled by Bobby Orr was the equivalent of a Roman Catholic couple having their child baptized by the Pope. Surely, such a fortuitous blessing by a Canadian hockey god would have foreshadowed a life of dizzying athletic achievement for that blond little baby with the ringlet curls . . . right?

CANADIAN
WINTERS

WRONG.

I was not athletic. Not even in the slightest, but somehow I was born into a highly competitive, sporting family, which reached professional proportions in the sport of golf on Dad's side. Dad grew up in Winnipeg, my mom in Toronto, both cities winter wonderlands for cold-weather sports enthusiasts in the 1950s and '60s. As a kid, Dad played hockey from October to April on the frozen Red River half a block from his family home in the Norwood neighbourhood, then on that peewee team with "Terrible" Ted Green. Dad naturally played right wing, predicting his future political leanings. Mom spent her winters skating on any available public ice surface in Etobicoke and Toronto, and has fond memories playing a skating game called "Crack the Whip" with Green's future teammate Ken Hodge. Big Ken would lead a long chain of skaters holding hands, forming a "whip." Ken would skate around the rink in random directions, twisting and turning, usually causing the last player in the "whip" to let go and fly headlong into the boards or a snowbank. Apparently this was fun.

9

In the warm comfort of our living room on Christmas morning, I was delighted to discover what Santa brought me at age two: my first pair of skates. I would soon have a different outlook on that gift once they were crammed onto my feet in the frosty outdoors and I was left to my own devices on all those rinks my parents loved to carve up all winter long.

As a Canadian kid with fully winterized parents, I was expected to learn how to skate soon after I learned how to walk. At age two, I received my first pair of hockey skates for Christmas. Thus, many of my earliest childhood memories involved freezing temperatures and foot pain. My parents would balance me on the cold bench alongside various outdoor rinks, Mom on her knee trying to shove my tiny foot into an unforgiving, unbending stiff little black leather boot with a shiny three-inch blade of steel running lengthwise along the bottom. I'd scream as she kept shoving, a Canadian rite of passage for which there is no equal. Then I'd hit the ice. Usually face-first.

My parents looked like winter Olympians, flying down the frozen white sheet as if propelled by invisible jetpacks: twirling around, skating backward and twisting their feet into impossible positions like a frosty Fred Astaire and Ginger Rogers. Dad always wore his black, well-worn, tough hockey skates, Mom in her pretty white leather figure skates. They'd carve back around with big smiles on their faces, holding hands, the cold, fresh, dry air of the Canadian winter whipping through their hair. They'd laugh when they found me floundering face down on the ice, helpless as a baby seal. They would lift me to my feet and I would stand there in my puffy one-piece navy blue snowsuit with a bright red maple leaf over the heart and knit scarf.

My ankles were caving in upon themselves as I tried to keep my balance by flailing my arms like a chicken trying to take flight, inching toward them, the cold cutting through the nylon snowsuit straight to my little two-year-old bones. Dad would show me the moves, bending his knees and sticking his bum out, explaining to me that the secret to *all* sports was to keep your knees bent, have a low centre of gravity and position your body like a coiled spring. Eventually Mom spoke my language: "Just pretend you're sitting on the toilet." Little did they know how close I was to shitting my snowsuit from the pure anxiety of being in skates. I couldn't bend my knees. I was stiff as a board, the top-heavy weight of my head causing me to topple backward repeatedly.

My parents snapped this photo of me actually upright in my new skates. The Christmas morning smile has been wiped clean, replaced by an anxiety-ridden frown, as the cold and discomfort seeped in. It didn't help that all the other toddlers my age whizzed about me like bladed bumblebees.

Dad propped me back up, patted me on the hood and took off for a speed skate. As I stood there, older toddlers with hockey sticks waddled past me, taking very short but effective strides. They were skating in a flock as if someone were fast-forwarding *March of the Penguins*. All were chasing a heavy black puck. As the last boy skated by me his elbow caught my shoulder and spun me like a top, sending me to the ice one more time. I'm pretty sure the rangy toddler did it on purpose, since he looked back and laughed. From the ice, curled in the fetal position, I looked back longingly to where our warm boots sat under the bench.

After about ten minutes my feet would feel like blocks of ice. This was followed by an intense burning sensation; then after about half an hour, very little feeling at all. Finally my parents would return, laughing and breathless from an invigorating skate. I would be scooped up from hell frozen over. I would then discover that removing a tiny skate from a frozen foot is even more painful than forcing it on. I would lie flat on my back in the snow as Mom yanked and tugged on the frigid little boot, eventually wrenching it free and taking my Toronto Maple Leafs sock with it, leaving my little naked pink foot twisting in the elements.

Finally back upright, the feeling of taking a step on solid ground with my flat-soled snow boots was a bizarrely comforting and natural sensation after spending thirty minutes in skates. I could propel myself forward again without pain and public ridicule. I felt like a tiny, sure-footed gazelle leaping in the direction of the hot chocolate machine, which automatically dispensed a little paper cup with handle. The machine then furiously filled it with its steaming beverage, the reward for my frozen ordeal. I quickly learned that skating was my parents' number one winter pastime; and I would slowly learn to eventually and reluctantly skate, thanks to them.

3

TRUE PATRIOT LOVE

B Y THE TIME my family settled in Vancouver, the Vancouver Canucks had been in the NHL for a couple of seasons and were generally terrible, having started off on the wrong skate entirely. The Buffalo Sabres were the expansion cousins of the Vancouver Canucks, both teams having entered the NHL in 1970. To decide which team would get the first pick of all eligible amateur players that year, the NHL had spun an actual roulette wheel at the draft, Vegas-style. The Canucks had numbers one through ten, and the Sabres eleven through twenty. The stakes were formidable for the brand new teams: the entire NHL knew the number one pick would be a young French-Canadian scoring sensation named Gilbert Perreault.

The wheel of sporting fortune was spun and the hockey world waited with bated breath. The wheel slowly *click-click-clicked* to a stop. Men in suits, wide ties and bushy sideburns strained to see. Then NHL president Clarence Campbell leaned in, took a look and shouted, "Number one. Vancouver selects first!" The Canucks management group was instantly on their feet, ecstatic, cheering, until they heard the Buffalo Sabres' general manager, none other than the legendary hall of famer Punch Imlach, also on his feet, yelling and pointing at the roulette wheel: "No, goddamit! That's not number one... It's number eleven!"

It was true. President Campbell had blown the call; the roulette wheel had stopped at number eleven. Buffalo won the first pick and selected Gilbert Perreault, who would wear #11 throughout his playing career as a salute to that roulette wheel. Perreault would go on to become a perennial NHL all-star, leading the team in scoring for years and becoming the key figure in Buffalo's famed "French Connection" line of the 1970s. At number two the Canucks picked Dale Tallon, who arrived to a chilly reception, Vancouver fans basically blaming him for the roulette wheel misfortune. That first stroke of bad luck ushered the Canucks into a decade of futility and disappointment.

Nonetheless, as new and proud Vancouverites my parents became season ticket holders. For birthdays and Christmases, I would receive various pieces of early Canucks merchandise, everything from toques and scarves to a large felt pennant for my bedroom wall to a weird, life-sized inflatable Canucks doll: a smiling boy in dark blue Canucks uniform named "Chuck Canuck." The only problem was that I wasn't interested in the Vancouver Canucks or hockey in the slightest. I was into art and reading and staying inside wearing slippers.

On Saturday nights, Dad would lie on the couch with his feet up at one end, our cat asleep on his stomach, a Labatt stubby in one hand, as *Hockey Night in Canada* blared out of our TV. I would often sit cross-legged on the carpet between Dad and the TV, ignoring the game, deeply involved in the pages of *The Adventures of Tintin*. The cacophony of the commentators, fans, sticks and commercials was all an urgent white noise washing over me. It was a comforting white noise, however. It made me feel safe and sound.

My loving mom was also nearby, in the kitchen getting dinner ready, which we were allowed to eat in front of the TV on Saturday nights because of hockey. It was a bittersweet luxury, my only real

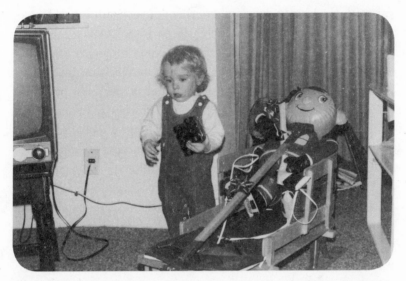

If I had only known then what an ultra-rare, boy-sized "Chuck The Canuck" inflatable mascot doll would have fetched on eBay in 35 years, I would have treated him with so much more love, respect and dignity.

entertainment coming when Dad would let out a "WHOOO!" after the Canucks scored, causing our cat to jump from him in panic. I'd look up at the TV and see several hairy, happy men hugging and celebrating in front of a fallen goaltender. For reasons I didn't understand, I'd stare at the goaltender and wonder how he felt at that moment, with his shoulders drooped and head hung low, scooping the puck out of his net.

When Mom and Dad asked me to go to games at the Pacific Coliseum, I'd adamantly shake my head and say no, and my parents didn't force me. I'm sure my anti-hockey stance disappointed them, but they never showed it. Even though my dad's family was extremely athletic, a few of his siblings had bad knees that would violently dislocate, disconnecting femur and tibia, causing a collapse to the ground in a torrid flood of pain. Both my sister and I had the misfortune of inheriting this wicked bodily malfunction. I first discovered my malady when I was playing kick the

15

can with the kids in our neighbourhood. I was running as fast as I could for the can in our neighbour's parking lot when I stepped in a small divot. My kneecap wrenched out of its socket like a popping champagne cork, sending me crashing face-first into gravel and screaming in agony. I looked down at my leg, now bent into the shape of an ostrich leg. I had to reach down with my hand and, while screaming, force my kneecap back into the socket so I could regain my footing and limp home to my parents in tears. Knee braces with squeaky hinges were soon to follow.

On weekends, Dad and I would take endlessly long drives into areas of BC wilderness for his real estate business. Dad and I would play various games to pass the time between my bursts of projectile vomiting due to uncontrollable carsickness. Always included was the licence plate alphabet game. We'd start by spotting an "A" on a licence plate and just keep moving up the alphabet. On one particularly long, puke-ridden drive, we were halfway up the Sunshine Coast Highway and halfway through the alphabet, looking for the letter "M." Dad often let me find them first. "Oh, what's this coming up?" he'd say, alerting me to a plate ahead.

I'd focus my eyes as hard as I could, pressing my face against the windshield as we'd close in on the car. "Uhhh... I can't see it yet," I'd complain.

"You can't see the letters on that licence plate?" Dad asked, concern in his voice.

"Uhhh... no, not yet," I answered, squinting like Clint Eastwood in a gunfight.

Yes, at age seven, already small for my age and shackled with hinged knee braces, I needed Coke-bottle glasses to see more than ten feet in front of me. With crystal clarity I remember the first time I exposed my glasses to my grade two classmates. We sat in pairs at our desks, and I was in the back row. Each morning at 9 a.m., before we started our lessons, my grade two class would all stand and sing "O Canada" to the accompanying music that would bleed through the single-speaker PA system above the chalkboard.

16

As we all shrilly hit the lyrics of the second verse—*With glowing hearts...*—I nonchalantly slipped on my brand new, wire-rimmed, oversized *Breaking Bad*-esque science-teacher glasses for the first time in public, desperately hoping none of my classmates would notice. No other kid in my class wore glasses. The world went from the soft and fuzzy view I was used to, to a sharpened, high-definition, three-dimensional classroom vista full of tiny details. For the first time in months I could read the chalkboard. It was awesome. For three seconds.

...we see thee rise, the true north strong and free... Jessie, the little freckled girl who sat beside me, noticed my glasses immediately. She turned and gasped aloud with shock and wonderment. *From far and wide, O Canada...* Other classmates spun to see what was so remarkable. When they saw what had become of me, giant new glasses over a crimson red face, they too joined the switch from the chorus of song to outcries of fascination and disgust, some pointing outstretched index fingers toward my face... *we stand on guard for thee!*

Soon it felt like I was the only child still singing, my knees shaking, my face as red as the Maple Leaf, my brand new glasses that covered most of my tiny face fogging up, as if the inanimate object itself was embarrassed for me. *God keep our land, glorious and free...* Mrs. Mulberry tried to regain the attention of the kids, smacking her pointer on the surface of her desk with a crack. All my classmates now had their backs to the flag at the front of the classroom, which hung as limply as my arms. *O Canada...*

Buck was the biggest boy in our class, already extremely adept at two things: bullying and hockey. To me, even at that age, bullies and hockey seemed to go hand in hand. Buck was adorned with a perfect Adam Rich chestnut-brown bowl cut and cold, lupine eyes the colour of slate. He was always rocking a cool Canadian tuxedo (jeans and jean jacket combo). He was a grade two tough guy just like Kelly from *The Bad News Bears*—if Kelly had worn a Philadelphia Flyers T-shirt.

Buck was my enemy. He was the largest boy and I was the smallest boy. It was elementary school Darwinism: the alpha dog picking out the prey of least resistance. He, like the majority of the boys in our class, liked Hot Wheels, *Batman* comics and Luke Skywalker. I liked my dad's lead toy farm animals from the 1940s, *The Adventures of Tintin* and R2-D2. Buck's favourite hockey player was Guy Lafleur, because he scored the most goals in the NHL. I liked the goalies best because they seemed like the most sympathetic and solitary characters in a hockey game. On a TV screen, the goalies looked and acted so differently than the rest of the players, who all seemed to look and act the same. The goalie was the weirdo at the lonely end of the rink. I was the weirdo at the lonely end of the classroom. Buck knew it and seemed to take every opportunity he could to let me know.

The moment Buck spotted the new geek goggles on my face, he saw a chance before him in his perfectly natural twenty-twenty vision and seized it, the breakaway pass for a sure scoring opportunity. He leapt from his desk like a jaguar from a tree branch and dashed down the aisle until he was directly in front of me. He peered at me in marvelling excitement, as if he were Indiana Jones finally discovering the most hideous and elusive idol.

Buck's eyes widened. He had already rained down a hailstorm of humiliation months earlier when I showed up, hobbling along in my knee braces. New glasses on the smallest boy was a grade two bullying miracle served up on a platter before his cold slate eyes, which narrowed as his smile grew. He straightened to his full height, equal to that of a kid in grade five. He pointed at me, the tip of his naturally tanned index finger an inch away from my face. He took a deep breath. Then he yelled, "FOUR . . . EYED . . . FREAK!"

"Take your seat this instant!" shouted Mrs. Mulberry.

O Canada, we stand on guard . . . for . . . THEE! As the final, usually triumphant notes of "O Canada" rang out, Buck turned to the rest of the class with one fist clenched in the air like General Aldo, the defiant gorilla from *Battle for the Planet of the Apes,* and started up the chant. Many joined in—some of Buck's young jock wannabes maliciously gleeful, other survivalist lemmings simply relieved Buck's attention wasn't on them.

The voices rose in unison as little fists pounded on desktops: "FOUR-EYED FREAK! FOUR-EYED FREAK! FOUR-EYED FREAK!" Still standing from the anthem, I broke into a squeaky dash, running from the classroom in tears, blinded by my foggy lenses. I staggered into the hall to escape the chant, the attention, the embarrassment. Mrs. Mulberry followed me, trying to calm me down, grabbing me by the sleeve of my *Mr. Dressup* turtleneck, spinning me around to face her. I threw up on her. She gave me my reprieve and sent me to the nurse's office. I cursed my glasses that day, and would curse them on many other days for the rest of my life.

For whatever ridiculous societal reason, the minute *anyone*, male or female, puts on a pair of glasses there is an immediate stigma attached to that gesture. There is an assumed physical weakness that stretches well beyond poor eyesight. In large groups of people, those wearing glasses are often considered to be the most passive and feeble. They might also be considered the smartest, the geekiest, the most likely to be a librarian or simply the ugliest, because they are wearing glasses. They are Piggy from *Lord of the Flies* in any social situation. It's no coincidence that Clark Kent literally hid behind a large, clunky pair of glasses, masking his alter ego. When he removed his glasses, he became Superman, *the greatest man on Earth*. When he put his glasses back on, Superman became a bumbling nerd/idiot/fool. And so what does that say to the kids who *can't* whip off their glasses to become Superman? It says that they are branded as perma-nerds.

Somehow I managed to get through the rest of that day, recovering in the fetal position on the vinyl bed in the nurse's office during recess. For the noon hour, I retreated to our elementary school's sanctuary for wearers of glasses: the library. When I got home from school that day, I wailed to Mom and Dad about the reception my glasses had received. Dad, never a glasses-wearer in

The Nerd Cometh. Behold, my first pair of glasses at age seven. From the moment I put them on in grade two, I've felt the stigma of being a lifelong glasses-wearer. And were my cheeks near-sighted? Why did these glasses have to be so huge? Why did jocks never have to wear glasses?

his life with perfect twenty-twenty vision, swept me up in his muscular arms and hugged me tightly, explaining softly that there was nothing to be done about it, that if I wanted to see, I had to wear them. I had to admit that the world was a much clearer, sharper place with my glasses on, but I wasn't sure if I could withstand the negative attention at school.

Dad then asked me if I knew who Ken Dryden was. "No..." I sniffed, wiping tears and snot onto my sleeve. Dad then told me "Ken Dryden plays hockey for the Montreal Canadiens, possibly one of the greatest teams ever assembled in the history of sports. The Montreal Canadiens have won six Stanley Cups with Ken Dryden, and you know what? Ken Dryden wears glasses."

I looked up at Dad, pushing my fogging glasses up the bridge of my nose. "What position does he play?"

"Ken Dryden is the goalie."

BLOOD ON THE ICE

IN AN EFFORT to survive at school, I began to slowly pay more attention to *Hockey Night in Canada* with Mom and Dad. Dad explained which teams were the powerhouses (Montreal and Philadelphia) and which teams were not (Vancouver and Toronto). I'd pay the most attention during the Philadelphia Flyers games, because I was riveted with fear and awe at how much blood, gore and violence there could be in a hockey game. Penalty boxes over-flowed with curly-haired, toothless, helmetless, mustachioed thugs, many of them reminding me of Animal from *The Muppet Show* as they sat panting, glaring through the glass, wanting more. The minute one was freed he'd mercilessly hunt down the opposi-tion and pounce like an attacking lion dragging down a panicked springbok. The Flyer's fists would jackhammer into the face of his prey, and once the on-ice officials finally intervened, he was taken straight back to the box—where, if harassed by spectators, he would try to get at the fans, too. It reminded me of a warning sign on the glass of the gorilla enclosure at the zoo that said, "Avoid making direct eye contact with the gorilla." The same sign could have been placed on the glass of the Flyers' penalty box.

21

Philadelphia's players had nicknames like "The Hammer," "Cowboy," "The Riverton Rifle," "Mad Dog," "Thundermouth," "Bedrock" and "Moose." Together they terrorized the NHL for years, known throughout the league as the "Mean Machine," the "Mad Squad," the "Blue Line Banditos" and, eventually, the nickname that stuck: the "Broad Street Bullies," a title that caused my glasses to fog every time I heard Bob Cole on *Hockey Night in Canada* excitedly squawk it out when a new bout of all-encompassing brawling erupted on our fuzzy TV screen on Saturday night.

The Philadelphia Flyers were the barbarians at the gate, the Philistines of Philadelphia, the team that no other in the NHL ever wanted to face. And the brutal intimidation factor worked, as the Broad Street Bullies (so named because their home rink, the Philadelphia Spectrum, was located on South Broad Street) won back-to-back Stanley Cups in 1974 and 1975. *Time* magazine put the Philadelphia Flyers on their cover in February of 1975, with the article title, "War on Ice: Courage and Fear in a Vortex of Violence." There were Flyers games that were so blood-drenched and one-sided that a strange malady known as "The Philly Flu" developed within the NHL whenever opposing teams were within a day or two of facing the Broad Street Bullies. It was also said that, just before the game, the visiting team's dressing room at the Philadelphia Spectrum was the quietest in professional sports. Big Canucks defenceman Jack McIlhargey knew first-hand how tough the Flyers were, having been traded from Philadelphia to Vancouver. On a Canucks road trip, the team bus pulled into the bowels of the dreaded Philadelphia Spectrum. The driver turned off the ignition, which caused the entire bus to shake and backfire, rattling the players on the inside. Jack couldn't help but play up the reputation of his former team shouting out "even the bus is scared shitless!" Looking back, it amazed me that I was allowed to watch the brutal real-life violence of NHL hockey in the 1970s, but was forbidden to watch *The Incredible Hulk* because my parents thought it was too violent.

22

At school, kids wore hockey sweaters of all types, including Philadelphia's. After the glasses incident I was continuously looking for ways to fit in and not get picked on as much, so for my next birthday I asked my parents if I could get my own hockey sweater. Mom did a spit-take of her Earl Grey. Dad was also startled. "You want a hockey sweater?" he asked. "Does that mean you want to play hockey?"

"No," I replied. "I just want my own hockey sweater." A few days before my birthday, Dad and I drove downtown to the towering white pillars of the Hudson's Bay Company. We pushed open its glass doors framed with fingerprinted brass to be greeted by a waft of overpowering ladies' perfume from the ground floor women's section. We rode three sets of escalators to the boys clothing department.

I still wasn't interested in the Vancouver Canucks despite my parents' rampant fandom. The Canucks had just revealed a bizarre new jersey, totally overhauling their original, classic stick-in-rink logo that formed a conceptual "C" for Canucks using the West Coast-friendly colours of green, blue, and white (representing forest, sky and mountaintop). Regarded as too passive, the Canucks went rogue, introducing the short-lived but infamous "flying V" jersey, arguably the NHL's most profoundly shocking jersey of all time. The "flying V" featured blazon stripes of orange, red, yellow and black, which filled the entire front of the jersey, boldly creating a letter "V" for "Vancouver" that started at the shoulders and came to a point just above the waist. It was, and remains, the only NHL jersey ever that wasn't based on a central image, logo or word; it was based on a *concept*, that concept being the jersey was so audacious that it would strike fear into the hearts of all comers.

Sadly, out of the gate, this crazy jersey did the opposite. The "flying V" design quickly became the laughingstock of the league, causing more confusion, catcalls and guffaws than anything else. Sports psychologists would later reveal that the hockey teams that won the most had red as the predominant colour on their

23

jerseys (Montreal Canadiens, New Jersey Devils, Detroit Red Wings, Team Canada), not the colours of Halloween. To hockey sweater historians it seemed to matter little that it was in this outrageously ugly outfit that the Canucks would make their first improbable push to the Stanley Cup Final in the spring of 1982, led by the scorpion-like goaltending of "King" Richard Brodeur.

Like almost everyone else, I thought the "flying V" sweaters were dreadful. Dad suggested either the Toronto Maple Leafs or the Montreal Canadiens, by far the most popular at our school. I looked at both, but had no allegiance to either.

"Dad, shouldn't the Maple Leaf be red like on the Canadian flag?"

"All the big teams from Toronto wear blue and white, Grant. Football, baseball and hockey. Blue sky, white snow."

"Mrs. Mulberry says 'Leafs' is spelled wrong."

"Well, technically she's right, but the Toronto Maple Leafs were named after a regiment of the Canadian army called the Maple Leaf, so by adding an 's' to it, that's okay." I slid the sweater past me on the rack.

The Montreal jersey was even weirder to me: a big red "C" that, inexplicably, had an "H" inside of it.

"What does this 'H' mean?" I asked, holding the bright red jersey up to Dad.

Dad smiled at the jersey. "Good trivia! Everyone thinks it stands for the Canadiens nickname, 'Les Habitants' or 'The Habs,' but it actually just stands for 'hockey.' *Club de hockey Canadien.*"

24 I'd remember the trivia, but I slid the sweater past me.

Next on the rack was the very popular orange, white and black Philadelphia Flyers sweater, the mark of the bully, the very sight of which caused me to shudder. Almost afraid to touch it, I slid the sweater past me.

At my impressionable young age, I was really into animals, so eventually I insisted on a hockey sweater with an animal on it. Dad sighed and showed me a few. The first was from a team called the

California Golden Seals of Oakland—a team that no longer existed by that name or in that place. The Golden Seals jersey interested me slightly despite the team being defunct; however, the animal depicted on the crest hardly looked like a seal at all, but more like a crude stick-figure drawing of a spawning salmon. Then there was the Pittsburgh Penguins, which featured a cartoon of a very determined-looking, chubby penguin skating hard, wearing hockey gloves and holding a stick. It was not quite for me. Doomed hockey player Brian "Spinner" Spencer had recently been traded from Buffalo to Pittsburgh, and in a bout of frustration after a series of losses, raged that penguins were "incompetent little birds that can't even fly, they just waddle!" I slid the Penguins sweater past, too.

Many times during my youth, our family would travel back to Dad's home province of Manitoba to visit family at the summer resort of Clear Lake in Riding Mountain National Park. Each time

My beloved Buffalo Sabres sweater, chosen by me on my birthday because the buffalo was my favourite animal. How was I supposed to know the Buffalo Sabres entered the league at the exact same time as the Vancouver Canucks, scooping the number one draft pick out from under the Canucks, which fans were intensely bitter about since the Sabres soared and the Canucks crashed?

25

we'd visit, I would always be taken aback by the imagery of the buffalo. A huge and majestic creature with its shaggy head, massive hump and intense burning eyes, the tough and sturdy animal was the very symbol of Manitoba and the rugged Canadian Prairies. My grandfather took me to see buffalo in Riding Mountain National Park. I was stunned to view a herd up close, separated only by the car's bug-splattered windshield.

And that's why, when I saw the Buffalo Sabres jersey glowing at me like the briefcase in *Pulp Fiction*, I knew it was the hockey sweater for me. It featured a hard-charging buffalo leaping over two awesome swords. The crest had action, excitement, weapons and my choice animal. It was also blue, my favourite colour. Dad tried to dissuade me, saying that if I wanted to pay homage to Manitoba, we could try to find a sweater for the Winnipeg Jets, a team on the verge of joining the NHL. As much as Dad tried to explain it to me, I didn't understand the long-standing inferiority complex that the Canucks felt in relation to their sister team the Buffalo Sabres. The Buffalo Sabres hockey sweater was mine. Wrong choice.

5

THE BUFFALO JUMP

I FELT EMPOWERED WEARING the Buffalo Sabres hockey sweater. I was proud that I hadn't sold out to the Leafs/Canadiens/Flyers sweater lowest common denominator. I could wear a sweater that showed off my favourite animal but also happened to represent a hockey team, making life easier for me. It all made sense. I wore the Buffalo Sabres sweater on my birthday and around the house for a while, but hadn't yet revealed it in public. Every Saturday at the West Vancouver Ice Arena there was open skating, which my family attended regularly. I knew that's when and where I would debut the sweater, hoping it would not only increase my cool factor but also make the pain of wearing skates hurt a little less by upping my pride.

In the gentle Vancouver winter, my parents could never get over the sensation of the air inside the rink being colder than the mild West Coast winter temperatures outside. The West Vancouver Ice Arena was always busy on Saturday. The well-worn chipped blue paint of the skate-rental counter was on one side, the busy concession counter was on the other, the steaming hot chocolate trade always brisk. I would immediately be hit by the manufactured chill in the air that tingled in my nostrils—that ice rink smell,

THEY WOULD BE ODOURLESS!

one of the most distinct stenches of my childhood, like sticking your face in the freezer and taking a whiff—if you kept your dirty socks in there. Hot breath streamed from the wide-open mouths of bundled-up kids, their voices cacophonously bouncing around the rink, as they eagerly stumbled in their skates atop thick black rubber mats. Several of the kids pressed their faces against the glass, hypnotized by the Zamboni methodically making its rounds, magically cleaning the ice after a minor hockey game had chewed it to shreds.

My family found some empty space on the benches, took off our shoes and stowed them in the cubbyholes provided beneath. I was always careful not to dip my stocking feet into the cold puddles of melted ice on the floor around us, because as I found out the hard way, wet socks could make a family skate even more miserable than usual. Mom forced my skates onto my feet then crammed my sister Heather's feet into hers, painful for both of us as always. As soon as mine were tightly laced, I stood up to unzip and remove my puffy ski jacket, exposing my new Buffalo Sabres sweater. A loud buzzer sounded, the huge wooden door at the rounded corner of the rink rolled open, and kids poured through the opening in a stampede of tiny steel blades, many wiping out the second they touched the ice. Other kids were off in a flash, bent over, arms pumping, skate blades gleaming, down the boards and back again. My sister and I would hold on tightly to the boards as we took to the ice, gingerly stepping down onto its slippery surface as if we could fall through the ice at any moment, then pinwheeling our arms until we found our balance.

We skated and skated in an endless loop to popular songs reverberating through the rink. I gained confidence and quickness with each loop, my new Buffalo Sabres sweater flapping gloriously in the miniature jet stream I created on the straightaways. I carved the ice like a Christmas ham to songs like "Crazy Little Thing Called Love," "It's Still Rock 'n' Roll to Me" and "Call Me." After about a half an hour of skating, I found my parents, gliding hand in hand, and told them I needed to go to the bathroom.

When I carefully stepped off the ice, I realized my feet were still frozen blocks of pain in my skates. Turning from the main rink into the corridor and walking stiffly in my skates, I came face to face with Buck and his budding jock buddies. They were leaving the rink, having just played their afternoon minor hockey game before the family skate. His brown bob was slightly mussed up and sweaty from the hockey helmet he had been wearing. He had on his usual denim-on-denim Canadian tuxedo, but had already changed out of his skates and was wearing an outrageous pair of thick wooden clogs, this apparently being the one era in the history of the planet that this footwear was cool, crossing over from little Dutch maidens to little elementary school jocks with Dutch heritage. Underneath his denim jacket, Buck wore his Philadelphia Flyers T-shirt. My teeth began to chatter.

Buck towered over me, glaring at my new sweater with utter contempt. He reached down and grabbed at my Buffalo crest with his fist, scrunching it up and pulling me in close, sneering like a wolverine. He gave me a hard, two-handed shove that easily knocked me off balance from my skates and down into the icy puddles on the rubber floor mat. He leaned down toward me. "BUFFALO SABRES SUCK, *WIMP!*" His budding jock buddies all broke into an instant chorus of peer pressure–approved laughter as they stepped over me. Buck was last and gave me a swift kick with his wooden clog.

Dad had warned me. When I eventually got back onto the rink, I had removed the Buffalo Sabres sweater, shoving it into our cubbyhole. I urged my parents that we should leave right away, even wanting to skip our hot chocolate–reward ritual. I was too ashamed to tell them what had happened. When we pushed open the doors of the rink to go home, the misty, wet West Coast winter air felt like a warm blanket of relief. I had tried to assimilate myself into elementary school hockey culture and I screwed it up. I never wore the Buffalo Sabres sweater again. It didn't seem to matter.

6

(I'M GONNA) RUN AWAY

GYM CLASS, NATURALLY, was my most detested subject in school. I loved playing games at recess and lunch in the playground, knee braces and glasses be damned, but I feared and loathed the unforgiving social torture of gym class. Gym was regimented, controlled and dictated by gym teachers, dudes in track suits who drove us like Egyptian slaves, forcing us to run/ jog/stagger through endless loops on our gravel track in all manner of weather. They'd force us to do indoor activities like climbing straight up thick, bristly hanging ropes, which only Buck could do with the ease of Cheetah. All we wanted to do was swing on them like Tarzan; but we had to do the activity that *wasn't* fun. The gym smelled like dust, floor wax and dirty clothing. The floor always looked shiny clean but never really was—it was covered in a layer of fine, grey dust, which you discovered when you wiped out with a loud squeak of skin.

When it came to organized games in gym class, we'd all be forced to line up along the wall and our asshole gym teacher in a track suit would pick two captains. One was always Buck, because Buck was the biggest and most athletically gifted student in our class. The second captain would usually be the most athletic girl. Then we would begin the gut-wrenching process of selecting teams, a culling of the herd, natural selection at work, leaving only the runts, the malformed and the weakerthans standing alone and embarrassed, our backs against the wall. Some pleaded to be picked, their eyebrows raised expectantly, while I, so used to such routine ridicule, stared at the gym floor waiting for either my name, or pigeon-toed Susie Jenkins' name, to be called dead last. (Susie Jenkins spent much of her time at our elementary school wearing her girl guide uniform, neckerchief and some type of large plastic funnel around her head, attached by a complicated crown of wires and hinges—somewhat resembling Darth Vader with his helmet off.)

Because I believed Buck would do absolutely anything to ridicule me, in as many ways as possible, I knew there was never any way he'd pick me. Sure enough, if it were down to the last two he'd choose Susie Jenkins—head funnel and all. The other captain wouldn't even have to say my name. The gym teacher would bark out with a resigned but somewhat satisfied sigh, "Okay Lawrence, get over there." (I hated being called by my last name only.) Then we squared off at each end of the gym for games such as baton racing, cosom hockey (total chaos), dodge ball (the long-popular elementary school version of a public stoning) and volleyball (almost the same thing as dodge ball, with many of us constantly having to sidestep or dive out of the way of Buck's vicious spikes).

In volleyball we'd rotate in six positions, clockwise after losing a point in each rally. Occasionally I'd be face to face with Buck at the net. He'd snarl through the mesh that I was "DEAD MEAT, WIMP." Buck would then spike the ball straight down over the net so hard that if I didn't dive out of the way it would smack me in the face, sending my glasses flying. During one particular rally when my team actually got the ball back over the net, we somehow managed to land it directly into Susie Jenkins' head funnel, like some sort of bizarre carnival game, causing us all to celebrate joyously. It was ruled a "fault," since Susie Jenkins was said to have "caught" and held onto the ball, which is against the rules in volleyball.

Cosom hockey was the loudest and most chaotic of indoor gym class games. Each kid would get a flimsy plastic hockey stick—real wooden sticks would mark up the floor—and then, like a flock of panicked, squawking seagulls, we'd all collectively chase after the plastic orange puck, our sneakers madly squeaking on the gym floor. Only Buck could pull away from the gaggle, a darting falcon, on breakaway after breakaway, from one end of the gym to the other, easily potting goal after goal past the hapless keeper.

It was in games like these when my knees would dislocate, even while wearing my hinged knee braces. I'd step on a hockey stick, or on someone's foot, and trip. Or I'd get shoved from behind and feel it: a wrenching, bone-on-bone separation, the kneecap violently popping out of its socket. I'd collapse in the familiar heap of excruciating pain and embarrassment, then have to reach down and snap it back into place. As these knee dislocations happened, my body would make an extremely abnormal, racing-emu-like collapsible move that would inevitably get the kids and the asshole gym teacher laughing hysterically as I lay crying on the gym floor in agony. The pain would last for about ten minutes before I could get back to my feet and get moving again, limping at first before eventually regaining full motion.

At home, I wailed to my parents about how frequent my painful knee dislocations were getting. Dad, he of sturdy, muscular knees set firmly in their sockets, would once again sweep me up in his muscular arms and hug me tightly, explaining softly that I just had to be more careful where I placed my feet, and that I always had to wear my knee braces. Then he asked me if I knew who Bobby Orr was. "Yes . . ." I sniffed, wiping tears and snot onto the sleeve of my turtleneck. "When I was a baby I sat on his knee." (I had heard the story around the dinner table hundreds of times by then.) Dad then said, "Bobby Orr was the greatest hockey player who ever laced up skates. He could fly down the ice, score goals, defend, fight and do things no one thought could ever be done. He won two Stanley Cups with the Boston Bruins, he is the only defenceman to ever win the NHL scoring title—twice—and won

33

eight straight Norris Trophies as the best defenceman of the year. And you know what? Bobby Orr had a *terrible* knee."

What Dad didn't mention in his pep talk was that Bobby Orr had to retire early *because* of his knee. Orr's knee problems weren't hereditary, but rather a result of his knee being caved in repeatedly by opposing defencemen as he would fly down the right wing, protecting the puck with his left arm and leg. Many times Orr would be munched and crunched, left in a heap or smashed into the end boards. Many more times he made it past the defence-man's check to score one of his 270 regular season goals or set up 645 others—but the brutal hitting of the 1970s eventually caught up with "That Boston Dandy."

Knees be damned, I still had to take gym. During one gym class in grade four, our gym teacher paired us off for 100-metre indoor "sprints," that were actually races pitting us against each other collectively and one-on-one, yet another attempt to find out who was the very best in our class at something athletic. Even though I was a short, skinny kid with the ugliest of knee braces, the thickest of glasses and the worst haircut, my mom would always find something nice to say about me, sometimes commenting that, despite my bad knees, I had "very long and wonderful legs." I never really thought about her perplexing compliment until this particular gym class.

Our gym teacher whistled us through various sprinting heats, many kids getting eliminated and forced to watch from the benches along the walls like a cross between *Freaks and Geeks* and *Survivor*. Somehow, my wonky knees managed to stay in their sockets long enough to carry me through several heats until we were down to the final four... the semifinals. To my horror, I was paired up to race alongside Buck, who snarled and scoffed, his chestnut-brown bob sitting perfectly just above his eyebrows, Joey Lawrence style.

Our gym teacher lined us both up at the starting line and Buck took his positional crouch, like a rattlesnake ready to strike, whereas I stood stiff and rigid beside him, wanting to be anywhere but there. The whistle blew and we both took off, the hinges in my knee braces audibly squeaking like the rusty springs of a mattress during maximum use. Buck took the first straightaway and was already way ahead of me, but I kept running as fast as my legs could carry me, the toes of my Keds barely touching the dusty gym floor. We rounded the first turn and it appeared through my rapidly fogging lenses that the back of Buck's T-shirt was getting closer and closer. In the next and final straightaway, to the rising, astonished roar of my classmates watching from the sidelines, I shocked myself by actually catching up and passing Buck. Out of the corner of my eye I thought I could detect an unfamiliar look of anguish on his face. I left Buck in my gym-floor dust, rounding the final turn to cross the finish line ahead of him, my skinny little arms raised high in the air, my classmates on their feet to meet me with arms outstretched. They were cheering my victory, our victory, over Buck.

In that instant, my "very long and wonderful legs" that I always felt were so incredibly gimpy and fragile, carried me past my enemy, my tormentor, my Goliath, and made me a hero to my people . . . of grade four. I went on to lose the final race to Donnie Crowe, a new kid who was declared the fastest boy of our grade. But I didn't care. I had beaten Buck, the toughest, meanest, most athletic kid in our class. While my classmates and I celebrated my victory like the cast of *Chariots of Fire*, I looked over at Buck who was still panting and furious. I knew my semifinal glory would be short-lived; I was certain Buck would rain holy hell down on me for the public embarrassment very soon, and for a long time to come, but I had found an edge. I could run *faster* than Buck. I could get *away*. It was my loophole, and I was going to use it every chance I got. Little did I know how long I would have to run.

7

(HE LOOKED A LOT LIKE)
TIGER WILLIAMS

I BEGAN TO TAKE daring liberties with Buck, always making sure there were plenty of witnesses. On a sunny Saturday each spring, there was an annual fishing derby at Dundarave Pier, which jutted out into the ocean a few blocks from our elementary school. All the kids would be handed simple little fishing rods, bait and tackle donated by Monk's Hardware, fishing knots already tied for us by the judges/owners of Monk's. Once we were signed in and handed our nametags, we'd stampede down the gangplank to the dock below to take our places, peering into the bottle-green ocean water with nervous anticipation. Sure enough, Buck was down there with his budding jock buddies, Buck looking more radiant than usual, tanned and glowing from his recent spring break Hawaiian family vacation. His perfect chestnut-brown bob haircut showed streaks of blond, bleached from the saltwater and sunshine. When I arrived he was showing off his souvenir "Hawaii 81" mesh tummy top, yellow Ocean Pacific short-shorts, his requisite clogs, and brand new fishing rod he had bought in Waikiki. Up above on the pier, Mr. Monk bellowed, "Fishermen, are you ready for the Annual Dundarave Fishing Derby to begin?"

"YES!" we all screamed back.

"DROP YOUR HOOKS!"

We fished and fished, waiting for a nibble, some kids sitting, some standing. It was silent at first, and then got progressively louder as various kids started catching shiners and flounders. I wasn't all that interested in the fishing. I was keeping my eye on Buck, who was methodically bobbing his line in the water on the other side of the dock. When I felt the time was right, I softly put my rod down, took a deep breath, pushed my glasses up from the end of my nose and clenched my jaw tight to keep my teeth from chattering. I nervously ambled over to him. "How's the fishing over on this side of the dock?" I asked meekly.

He turned his bob, with a look of surprised anger at my close proximity. "Get away from me, *WIMP!*" he snarled.

I ignored the order and soldiered forward with my plan. "Buck!" I shouted shrilly. "Fish!" I pointed excitedly to the water directly in front of him.

"What? Where?" he replied, scanning the ocean's surface and looking at his line. Other kids heard the excitement in my voice and rushed over.

"Right there! In the water right in front of you!" He leaned over the dock, searching the water, one clog up on the tie bar of the dock, the other positioned slightly underneath it, steadying himself. I made my move, dashing behind him. I shoved as hard as I could. Buck toppled over the side of the dock and into the water head-first, taking his brand new Waikiki fishing rod with him and landing with an inglorious splash. The kids on the dock erupted in shrieks of laughter.

Buck surfaced immediately, his perfect chestnut-brown bob hanging straight down over his eyes like Dumb Donald's toque in *Fat Albert*. The cold spring ocean water had taken Buck's breath away and for once he was speechless. He wiped his hair away from his eyes, revealing a frightened expression. His clogs bobbed in the water beside him as he frantically dog-paddled to the dock, scrambling to hoist himself out as his budding jock buddies knelt to help him. The staff of Monk's Hardware rushed down the gangplank to the dock, one of them grabbing me by the arm and ripping the nametag off my Tintin T-shirt. "You!" Then he quickly read my nametag. "You, *Grant Lawrence*, you are disqualified! Go home *now!*"

I looked over at Buck, dripping wet and whimpering, standing in his waterlogged clogs in a pathetic puddle. When he hit the water, he had let go of his brand new Waikiki fishing rod and it had sunk to the murky bottom, gone. As other adults comforted him, his eyes found me in the crowd and filled with rage. "YOU ARE *SO* DEAD, *WIMP!*" He pulled away from the adults and charged at me like a Brahma bull, head down, feet stomping, sloshing water out of his clogs with every step.

I shook from the grip of the store manager and dashed up the gangplank, barely feeling it under my feet, running full throttle up the pier, knee braces squeaking like a litter of hamsters, praying for my caps to stay in their sockets. Buck was even slower in his wet clogs than in his North Stars and I had no problem outrunning him. He stopped chasing me at the foot of the pier, but I continued running up the hill, along Bellevue Avenue, slowing down only when he was out of sight, laughing to myself all the way home. A kid even smaller than I was, named Nicky Thomas, won the fishing derby that day, and Buck's Waikiki fishing rod was never recovered.

ON MONDAY, BACK at school, Buck threw down the gauntlet once and for all: he challenged me to a fight. Although we didn't have the wherewithal to analyze it as such at the time, being called out for a fight in elementary school was based on essentially the same code-of-honour principles as being challenged to a duel, examples riddled throughout the Old West, Renaissance Europe, Shogun Japan and beyond. Before six-gun repeater pistols came into play, duels with fists, swords, knives and single-shot pistols were waged not so much to kill but rather to restore honour after insult—which is exactly what Buck instinctively had in mind when he challenged me to a scrap.

Enough was enough; we were to settle things once and for all. I had no choice but to accept his terms and meet him by the monkey bars at the very back of the playground after school. Since besting Buck in the gym class foot race and shoving him head over heels into the drink at the fishing derby, I had managed to earn the respect of my peers. I found that I now had a reputation to maintain among my friends and followers, and was forced to put on a brave face. But I knew there was absolutely no way I could ever survive a fight against the towering, muscular, athletic and perfectly bob-cut Buck. I was terrified.

Much like Gary Cooper in the taut western *High Noon*, all day long I watched the clock loudly whirring by with terrifying, unforgiving speed. Every chance he got, Buck would slide by my desk and whisper under his breath, "You're soooo dead, *WIMP*." No news travels faster through a school than the news of an impending fight. At recess and lunch it was all anyone could talk about. Kids I didn't know, kids who had never looked at me before, were now gazing at me with wonder. "*That*'s the kid who's fighting Buck after school?!" they asked while I skulked by. Sometimes the news of an arranged after-school fight became such a hot, fever-pitch topic that it just couldn't stay underground, bubbling to the surface so that the teachers would inevitably find out about it, seek out the would-be combatants and shut it down. I was silently praying that someone, anyone, would leak it to the teachers. I couldn't dare, nor could I proposition anyone to do it for me, for fear of breaking the code and having the leak traced back to me. I couldn't fake sick, I couldn't skip class, I simply had to wait for my *Three O'clock High* public beating, and in the meantime try to come up with some way of surviving it.

I was no stranger to *watching* fights. Dad loved showing me all sorts of movies, old and new, so by the time I was ten I had already seen John Wayne punch out Indians, Charles Bronson punch out rapists, and Indiana Jones punch out Nazis. *Hockey Night in Canada* was a weekly exposé of flying fists, with between-periods "Coach's Corner" commentator Don Cherry being one of the strongest proponents of slugfests. One of his coaching credos for enforcers was, *Always get in the first punch, because if you're lucky, there won't be a need for a second punch.* The Vancouver Canucks had also recently traded for one of the most colourful fighters in the entire NHL: Dave Williams from Weyburn, Saskatchewan, where his peewee coach gave him the nickname of "Tiger" after he refused to wear a mask when playing goal. He didn't last long in that position, switching permanently to winger.

"Tiger" became a huge star in Vancouver. That year, in 1980–81, "Tiger" scored an impressive thirty-five goals in seventy-seven games, the most of any Canuck that season, all while amassing a staggering 343 penalty minutes—the math pointing out that, since you can't score from the penalty box, Tiger used his ice time for maximum bite. He would bring Vancouver fans out of their seats multiple times a night, whether it was for a goal, a scrap or outrageous antics. He was an exceptionally rare, hilariously dangerous character whose goal celebrations knew no bounds. His most famous celebratory move of all was "riding the stick," where he would squat on his stick like a witch on a broom and ride it the length of the ice, pumping his fist to whip the fans into a frenzy. Williams, a bow hunter of big game like grizzly bears and moose in the off-season, would also hunt down the largest and most untouchable beasts in the rink, no matter what size or position, including goalies. Tiger wore #22 on his bright orange and black striped "flying V" jersey, that by happy accident resembled the animal he was named for. He would challenge entire teams to brawls—and if it were the right team, they would accept the challenge.

Benches would be vacated but for the coaches, forcing the generally smaller Canucks to back up Tiger against big teams like the Flyers, the rink organist often accompanying the on-ice rumble

41

with a jaunty tune. In one such brawl, Tiger bared his fangs and actually bit the nose of Flyers' monster enforcer Dave "The Hammer" Schultz. Opposing fans in enemy rinks would pour down boos and debris on Williams, so he chased them into the stands. Putting him in the penalty box was no good; that's where he waged a famously vicious stick-swinging duel with Dave Hutchison from the LA Kings. Once, he even smacked legendary coach Scotty Bowman on the head with his stick when Scotty leaned out and yelled a disparaging remark at Tiger, something Bowman did often to opposing players. According to Williams in his autobiography *Tiger: A Hockey Story*, "Bowman had been behaving like a jerk, and I just thought 'Oh shit, let's give him the lumber.'" Scotty Bowman, the winningest coach in NHL history, collapsed behind the bench, out cold with an open head wound.

The second hand on the big clock above the chalkboard in our grade five classroom raced toward the minute hand, poised to strike three o'clock. When the bell tolled loudly everyone but me gathered their books together eagerly and made for the exits, ignoring whatever sentence our teacher was trying to finish. Slowly I rose to my feet and trudged into the hallway, zombie-like resignation on my face, my arms hanging loosely at my sides, my huge glasses sliding down the end of my nose. Two kids held open the heavy swinging doors leading to the playground. It felt like I was walking through the Gates of Hell. A startlingly large throng of kids waited for me just outside the school, along with Buck, denim arms crossed and smiling, his perfect bob haircut looking ever so evil.

42

Everyone knew there couldn't be a fight that close to the school doors—it would be broken up way too fast by teachers—so we did what we knew we needed to do for a good, prolonged battle royal. En masse, we tromped up the hill, through the playground, to the very back of the school grounds near the monkey bars. Buck and I walked silently, my jaw clenched, while the growing group of students chattered with heightened anticipation like a troop of monkeys. A friend named Timmy Prescott sidled up to me. "I'll hold your glasses for you," he offered. "No way," I haltingly replied. "I need them to see so I can at least get away."

A huge circle of kids from all grades had already formed near the chipped-paint set of heavily used monkey bars, some hanging off and sitting on top of them for a better view. Buck and I stepped into the large open space created by the circle. I felt nauseous and couldn't hold it any longer. My teeth let loose with their telling death rattle. Buck had heard them before other interactions between us and a wide grin crossed his face. Timmy Prescott stood beside me, stoically, like a priest reading last rites, with his hand out waiting to receive my glasses. A chant broke out softly, then gained volume with every collective repetition: *"Fight... fight...fight...fight... FIGHT ... FIGHT ... FIGHT ... FIGHT!"* My head swirled, my glasses fogged, my knees twitched and ached. Buck turned to remove his denim jacket. While he handed the jacket to one of his budding jock buddies, my brain flooded with fist-fight imagery: I thought of Clint Eastwood in *Every Which Way but Loose* and *Any Which Way You Can*, a bare-knuckle brawler taking on the Black Widows biker gang. Suddenly, those nonsensical country song titles meant a lot more to me in that moment of total desperation: "Any Which Way You Can." I thought of Tintin, my favourite comic book hero, a little guy like me who always punched above his weight. I thought of Don Cherry on "Coach's Corner": *Always get in the first punch.* I balled my tiny fist.

As Buck turned back to face me, I made my move, taking two quick steps across the dirt and cocking my arm back just like I'd seen John Wayne/Tiger Williams/Indiana Jones/Clint Eastwood/ Charles Bronson/Tintin do it. A split-second look of bemused surprise crossed Buck's face as he saw me coming at him. The crowd's chant turned into a roar. My right fist rushed through the air and struck Buck straight in the mouth. I expected him to fall over backward, like Rastapopoulos in *Tintin and the Red Sea Sharks.* Instead, Buck's head snapped back from the blow, then immediately rolled back into place, and he remained firmly on his feet. A flash of shock and pain flickered in Buck's slate eyes, quickly to

43

be replaced by blind fury as the locks of his superb bob fell perfectly back into place. The crowd fell silent. My eyes grew wide with panic. A tiny trickle of blood emerged from the side of Buck's mouth. I had gone in for the kill on a grizzly bear and had inflicted a mere flesh wound.

"YOU ARE *SO* DEAD, *WIMP!*" Buck made a lunge for me with both hands outstretched. I ducked, spun and dashed, bursting straight through the wall of students and down the hill onto our gravel playing field with Buck in hot pursuit, our adrenalin pushing us both forward to out-of-control speeds. I could hear him gaining on me, roaring furiously, reaching out for my *Beachcombers* turtleneck. I kicked it into a survivalist gear I didn't know I had, my gimpy, long legs spinning under me like the Roadrunner's, dashing across the gravel field, cutting left and right in circles, Buck desperate to catch me as the huge crowd of kids watched from the top of the hill, screaming in what sounded like Roman Coliseum-esque delight. I kept running, keeping just ahead of him, back up the hill, around the monkey bars, past the swings, under the teeter-totters, until I ran straight into the flowery blouse of our French teacher, Madame D'Eith. Buck caught up, grabbing me with both hands. I let out an anguished scream. Madame D'Eith pulled us both apart, holding us by our necks, and exclaimed, *"Qu'-est ce qui ce passe ici?"*

We both escaped any punishment, the tilt being deemed a "fair fight" by our principal, since Buck admitted under pressure that he had challenged me to the fight in the first place. I had to apologize to Buck in front of our class the next day for punching him, but I had cemented my reputation. I had landed a punch—and drew blood—on the biggest, meanest bully in our class and lived to tell the tale. I had gathered a strong group of friends and followers—misfits, nerds, immigrants and freaks all—but it is true what they say: there is strength in numbers. Unless its name is Williams, a tiger will never attack the thick of the herd, it will only stalk the slowest and smallest gazelle that the herd has left behind. No longer would I be that gazelle. Or so I hoped.

8

OUR GAME

A SUMMER CAME AND went, where I escaped to the wilds of my family cabin in Desolation Sound, not seeing any other kids from school for months. Back at school the following year, things had settled into a comfortable rhythm, a slightly more humbled and mature Buck steering clear of me, and me—not wanting to press my luck any further—trying to steer clear of him. Buck had found a replacement for his denim jacket. He and his budding jock buddies were well entrenched in the local minor hockey league system, and showed it off every day by wearing their blue hockey jackets with white trim, their names proudly sewn onto the sleeves at the bicep level. It confirmed for me that I wanted nothing to do with organized hockey.

Also, slowly but surely the Montreal Canadiens, Philadelphia Flyers and Toronto Maple Leafs jerseys, sweaters, T-shirts and hats were being replaced by the merchandise of another hockey team: our Vancouver Canucks. Thanks to the additions of Tiger Williams and the highly acrobatic goalie "King" Richard Brodeur, and the emergence of young stars like Stan "Steamer" Smyl and Thomas Gradin, the Canucks had finally managed to capture many of our imaginations with a pretty exciting, lunch-bucket, character-filled hockey team, not to mention those outrageous jerseys. In the Canucks' previous season, they had won twenty-eight games, lost just thirty-two and netted twenty ties. That was good enough to make the playoffs, only to be ousted by their expansion cousins, none other than the high-flying Buffalo Sabres, three games to none in a wicked and violent series. Immersed in hockey at home and at school, I finally really started paying attention to the Vancouver Canucks.

Every day at lunch hour, inspired by the Canucks (and the rapid emergence of a phenomenal young superstar in Edmonton wearing #99), Buck and his budding jock buddies sequestered themselves in our elementary school tennis court, which we had never seen used for tennis, to play ball hockey. Just a few of them, at one end, every day. But if you are to truly play a game, you need an opponent; Buck and his buddies were constantly looking for others to play with them.

When a hometown team is exciting, the imaginations of children are engaged; they want to be like their heroes on the ice, to reenact what they hear on the radio and see on TV—scoring goals and making saves. The influence and excitement finally seeped down all the way to my collection of friends: the misfits, nerds, immigrants and freaks. We would collect old hockey sticks from our garages and basements and bring them to school with us, staging our own little game of run-around ball hockey at the opposite end of the tennis court, trying to ignore Buck and his budding jock buddies, but faithfully returning their tennis ball if it was ever shot waywardly into our end—or else we'd get harassed. If our ball was shot down to their end, they'd never send it back, usually either shooting it high over the fence or keeping it. If we put up enough of a stink, they'd return our ball by shooting a high, hard shot at one of our heads.

Finally, unable to ignore the fact that if we merged, we could have a full-court game going all the time, Buck arranged a parley.

46

He and I met at centre court, his bob haircut beginning to show the earliest signs of morphing into an adolescent mullet. Towering over me, he forced out the words, through gritted teeth, "Why . . . don't . . . we . . . all . . . play hockey together?" I looked up at him through my fogging Coke-bottle lenses as he continued, avoiding looking me directly in the eye. "Then we could have a real game, like keeping score and everything."

I paused before answering, watching him fidget with his long, well-worn Koho hockey stick, sitting easily and dangerously in his gloved hands like a warrior's spear. "Sounds cool with us, Buck . . . but if we agree to a game, there will be *no* team captains, *no* picking of teams, *no* kids picked last and *no* kids forced to be on a team they don't want to be on. It will be us over here on this side of the court, versus you over there on that side."

Buck looked down at me with a sly smile. "Choice! Fine with us, *WIMP!*" He turned and bounded back to his budding jock buddies. "We got a game! Us versus the nerd herd!" They all burst into evil jock laughter.

And so we had done it. Buck's parting insult aside, I had pulled off a deal (I was so used to hearing "*WIMP*" end his sentences that I didn't react anymore . . . it was like his version of "eh" that just happened to be a personal and hurtful insult that would stick with me for decades). Buck and I, mortal enemies, had declared a fragile peace in the name of hockey. No mediators, teachers, counsellors or parents: just him in his hockey jacket and me in my knee braces at centre court. We had formed a truce so everyone could play, even Human Alghabi, the new Iranian kid in the David Bowie T-shirt, who was desperate to figure out this bizarre cross between cricket and soccer so he could participate and fit in. Like the British and the Germans in World War I playing soccer on Christmas Day between the trenches, we had laid down our arms and picked up our sticks in the name of sports, competition and fun. When the bell rang to signal the end of lunch hour, my team had lost the first game 24–0.

Lopsided scores aside, we all quickly became addicted to *the game*. And even though I had declared "no captains," it was obvious Buck was in charge of the jocks and I corralled the nerd herd. We'd all scarf down our lunches as quickly as possible and race into the tennis court, whipping the tennis ball around on the blades of our sticks for an hour straight. We much preferred playing with a tennis ball than the hard plastic ball or orange puck that we used for cosom hockey in gym class. The tennis ball hurt less when it hit you, we could lift our shots and, because of its furriness, it seemed to stick to our blades more. Why couldn't our gym teacher figure this out? If shot hard enough, the tennis ball would often pin itself into the chain-link of the tennis-court fence, allowing us to easily decide disputed goals since we didn't have actual hockey nets yet, just jackets piled up about five feet apart from each other at either end.

We quickly figured out that the paved surface of the tennis court ate the bottom edges of our wooden hockey sticks like a hungry beaver. At the end of an hour it was as if our sticks had become sickles. So we sawed the wooden blades off the stick shafts in our garages and basements and jammed on the hard plastic "Superblades" we could buy at Monk's Hardware Store. We kept all our sticks upright in a big box in the corner of our classroom. As soon as the bell rang for lunch, we would make a dash for the box, grab our lumber, and be out the door and onto the court, sun, rain, sleet or hail. It barely snowed in Vancouver, maybe a day or two a year if we were lucky, so we played ball hockey the entire school year. When it rained, the tennis ball let out a plume of water, like a rooster's tail, as it spun down the court, heavier and harder to shoot. Steam would rise off our shoulders as we cheered a goal, or threw our heads back incredulously with an *"Ohhh!"* at a save or a missed shot, while running endlessly back and forth on the court.

At least I tried to run back and forth on the court. Because my knees were most prone for dislocation when there were so many bodies and sticks in every direction, I had many excruciatingly painful accidents. Because I was young, I could usually suffer a kneecap dislocation by writhing around in pain for a few minutes as play continued, and managed to get back on my feet and limp back into the game. I also quickly realized that even though I was the smallest, weakest and geekiest, a deep competitive streak emerged from within, as well as a surprisingly hot-blooded temper. I'd try to do anything to win, to stop Buck.

Buck was predictably, sickeningly amazing at ball hockey. He could zig and zag through the entire court, going fence to fence, while our players lamely tried to slow him down by chasing after him. He would easily laser the ball past our confused and frightened Iranian goalie—the only Iranian boy in our entire school, arriving at the beginning of a large exodus of Iranians to the North Shore of Vancouver. Between games, Human would eagerly tell us about the life he left, how every backyard in Tehran had a swimming pool, how their food tasted so much more flavourful at home than what he'd tasted so far in Canada. He told us the most popular sport in Iran was football, meaning soccer, and the closest thing to hockey he had ever seen or heard of was polo.

Soon, I started pulling little moves on the court like slashing Buck's stick as hard as I could about twelve inches up from his Superblade, a trick Dad had shown me in the driveway at home. Sure enough, the sharp reverberations of the slash went right into the palms of Buck's hands, causing him to yelp in pain and drop his stick. We'd pop on the turnover, dash in and either score or get a good chance at it. Buck would be furious. In retaliation, Buck would catch up to me, cross-check me in the back and knock me to the pavement, my glasses clattering from my face across the asphalt. "Try that again and I'll rip your head off, *WIMP*!"

I eventually figured out that the most painless place for me to play was goalie, a position I would share in rotation with Human, who was still trying to figure out the game and was quickly becoming a close friend of mine. The goalpost piles of jackets were soon replaced by actual nets we were allowed to borrow from the gym.

49

At first, Human and I wore no protection whatsoever, being pelted by the tennis ball on every part of our bodies, mostly launched by Buck, gleefully. It was hard to tell what delighted Buck the most: knocking my glasses off with a high slapshot, nailing the confused Iranian boy in the nuts, or actually scoring a goal. In an attempt to avoid physical confrontation with him on the court, I had unwittingly selected the one vital position that pitted me against Buck one-on-one, over and over again. Most of the time he would score easily and loudly let me know about it. But every once in a while I would get my hand or my shoulder or my foot or my face on his shot, and the satisfaction of thwarting him made the pain worth it. When I got home, I would take off my shirt in the privacy of the locked bathroom. My concave, alabaster chest would be covered in Dalmatian-like round dark welts the shape of a tennis ball.

Soon we expanded the games so we were playing up to ninety minutes before the morning bell, over the fifteen-minute recess, through the hour-long lunch break and for as long as we could after school. Slowly, Human and I pieced together goalie gear from what we could find in the gym equipment room, though most of it was baseball gear. We would shove our toques down our pants to protect the twig and berries. My team usually lost, but if the score was tied and I let one in just before the bell to lose the game, I'd blow my cool like Mount St. Helen's, occasionally bursting into wild, goalie stick–swinging incidents even Buck would steer clear of. But despite various childhood outbursts of temper and emotion on both sides, we were all for the most part having a great time. Occasionally, one of our team members would make a brilliant play and score a goal that we'd talk about for three days. I drew up unsolicited player cards, created team names and assigned player nicknames for both sides.

It was our game and we could do what we wanted when we wanted, which made it so much better than organized phys. ed. My gang of freaks and geeks still couldn't stand gym class, lorded over by a creep of a gym teacher. Eventually, several of us figured out a loophole to get out of gym class altogether. The rules of gym were that everyone had to change into a T-shirt, shorts and running shoes in order to take part. Once, a kid named Ike Patterson showed up wearing long pants and *wasn't allowed to take part in gym*. He was sent to the library. Bingo. Even though we all wore shorts while playing ball hockey morning, noon and night, my anti-gym nerd herd began pulling pants on over our shorts in order to get kicked out of gym and sent to the library. It worked perfectly until too many of us started doing it.

"Lawrence! Didn't I see you playing hockey in your little girlie shorts, just this morning?"

"Uh, not me, I don't think," I offered meekly.

"Are you sure, Lawrence? So you're *not* the worst goalie I've ever seen in my life?" The class burst into laughter. "Get over here." In front of my entire nervously giggling gym class, my gym teacher then shoved his big, hairy hand down the front of my pants. The whole class gasped, then erupted in shocked laughter. Finding what he was supposedly feeling for, he yanked the waistband of my shorts up out of my pants. "These look like shorts to me, Lawrence! Drop your pants and join your gym class for the arm-hang competition. NOW!"

And so began a new ritual in our gym class: our gym teacher's "shorts inspection," lining up the nerds of the resistance along the gym wall. Those who were hiding shorts had to drop their pants and join class immediately. Those who were really just wearing pants and legitimately forgot their shorts were sent to the library a maximum of three times, then to the principal's office. Our gym teacher never quite appreciated that we were getting more exercise and having more fun with our own ball hockey games than we ever were in his dictatorial, boot-camp gym class. For several months he was the focus of our loathing, but then we got happily distracted, during a spring none of us would ever forget.

9

CAMP RADIO

THE VANCOUVER CANUCKS had been through a couple of topsy-turvy seasons to start the 1980s. In the 1980–81 season, they couldn't win out of town. In 1981–82, they couldn't win in their own rink, prompting the Canucks' head coach and quote machine Harry Neale to respond, "Last year we couldn't win at home. This year we can't win on the road. My failure as a coach is, I can't think of any place else to play." But the Canucks were on the verge of climbing to the greatest heights the team had ever experienced since joining the NHL just over a decade earlier. A few key incidents triggered their famous and improbable run for the coveted Stanley Cup.

As the regular season was winding to a close, the Canucks rolled into the highly intimidating Montreal Forum to face the ever-powerful Canadiens, layered with stars like Guy Lafleur, Larry Robinson and Bob Gainey, who were riding an outrageous twenty-seven-game unbeaten streak in their home rink. The Canucks, the team that was hot on the road that year, shocked the Canadiens by beating them 4–2 and halting the home unbeaten streak in its tracks. Two nights later and riding high, the Canucks were in Quebec City to play the Nordiques. A fracas ensued and as usual Dave "Tiger" Williams was in the middle of it. He had thrown the Nordiques' best player and 1981 NHL Rookie of the Year Peter Stastny face-first into the boards near the players' bench. A Nordique rushed to Stastny's defence, driving Tiger's face into the glass. While they tussled, a fan, enraged that Tiger would take such liberties with their young star, ran down the aisle to ice level, reached around the glass and punched Tiger.

Coach Neale saw the whole thing and freaked out. He charged down the players' bench and into the crowd, throwing haymakers at the fan. The Colisée erupted. Seeing fifteen thousand angry Quebecers versus one coach, several of the Canucks, including Tiger, also jumped into the crowd and a melee of pushing, pulling, punching and throwing—both objects and nationalistic insults in both official languages—ensued. Police descended on the madness, trying to pull civilian and hockey combatants apart. Later, Harry Neale was quoted as saying, "I have often wondered why I would be defending Tiger Williams, one of the toughest guys in hockey. But nevertheless I did."

For wading into the crowd and attacking a fan, coach Harry Neale was suspended ten games—the remainder of the season and into the playoffs. Neale was replaced by his assistant coach, a gangly, curly-haired character named Roger Neilson, known mostly for his taste in very loud neckties. He also looked just like Gabe Kaplan from *Welcome Back, Kotter*. The Canucks would not lose again in the regular season, going 4–0–1. With just two games remaining in the season, Canucks captain Kevin McCarthy broke his ankle. Suddenly, with the playoffs looming, the Canucks needed not only a new head coach but also a new captain. Stan "Steamer" Smyl was appointed. Steamer was shaped like a propane tank and was just as explosive. So began the Canucks' miracle run to the Stanley Cup Final.

In the first round, the wins kept coming as the Canucks swept Lanny "The Moustache" McDonald and the Calgary Flames three

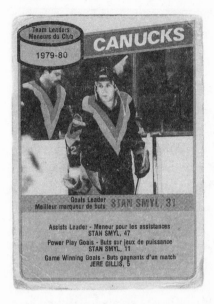

Stan "The Steamer" Smyl, the beloved, hard-nosed Canucks captain who would lead the team to their first Stanley Cup Final appearance in 1982. Smyl would also be the first Canuck to have his number retired. Years later, I proudly wore his #12 on the back of my Vancouver Flying Vees goalie jersey as a tribute to "Steamer."

games to none, in a series that included an incredible overtime goal by Tiger Williams. Meanwhile, the Los Angeles Kings did the Canucks a massive favour by somehow beating the dynasty-bound and Wayne Gretzky–led Edmonton Oilers in a final game that is considered one of the greatest comebacks and upsets in NHL history. The Oilers led 5–0 after two periods, only to lose 6–5 in overtime. By the time the Kings faced the Canucks in the second round, they were spent. The hard-charging Canucks in their intense "flying V" jerseys did what Gretzky (who had broken and set incredible records in the 1981–82 regular season) couldn't do: beat the Kings, which they did handily four games to one. Next up, a semifinal with the Chicago Blackhawks.

Back at school, one of the players we were most thrilled about was Canucks goalie "King" Richard Brodeur. Even when the Canucks didn't seem to be playing well or up for the challenge, King Richard, a little guy by NHL standards at just five foot seven, seemed to stop just about everything shot his way, pucks bouncing off his brown leather pads and matching brown leather glove, his Cooper blocker, his somewhat unconventional Euro-style Jofa goalie helmet with a full-cage mask and his black, straight Louisville goalie stick. He was so slight it didn't even look like he was wearing a chest protector under his "flying V" jersey, but he stopped the puck, and we shrieked with delight when he did. He was a stand-up goalie like all the rest in the early eighties, very acrobatic and often compensating for his lack of size by coming way out of his net to cut off the angle of the shooter. Unlike many modern-day goalies, where less movement is more, King Richard would excite fans by seemingly throwing his entire body into every shot, making every save look incredibly dramatic and exciting, all four limbs always in action and in full extension. If King Richard was making a high glove save, the glove would shoot straight up in the air while his legs would do the splits and his stick hand would shoot out to the side.

During that awesome playoff run in the spring of 1982, there was even a tribute seven-inch single released in honour of King Richard that was given away at grocery stores across the province. On one side was the novelty song "Na Na Hey Hey Kiss Him Goodbye," which Canucks fans would sing mockingly to opposing teams at the Pacific Coliseum if a Canucks win was definitely in the puck bag. On the flipside of the black vinyl single was an original, pounding, simplistic hockey rock song by "King Richard's Army" all about how great Richard Brodeur, #35, was. Mom scooped me a copy at Stong's Market. The record immediately went on the turntable, volume cranked, and the cover was pinned to my bedroom wall—the first piece of Canucks memorabilia that I actually wanted. It would remain there for many years.

The Vancouver Canucks 1982 semifinal series against the Chicago Blackhawks was one mired in controversy and violence, but featured a galvanizing incident that would forever bond Canucks fans in a twisted way. The series would be a memorable record-setter for the Canucks as they notched up an incredible 285 penalty minutes in five games, still unbroken in team records.

Tiger Williams was personally responsible for fifty-one of those minutes. In the middle of Game 2, with the Canucks on the wrong end of four consecutive penalty calls, the usually reserved interim coach Roger Neilson pulled a move that has remained in hockey lore ever since.

When the Blackhawks scored on the power play to make it 4–1 in their favour, Roger Neilson grabbed a white towel from a trainer, draped it over the butt end of a hockey stick and with his right hand, raised it to the rafters, a mock surrender and a silent yet very loud insult toward the referee and on-ice officials. Stan "Steamer" Smyl and several other players quickly followed suit. The furious referee threw Roger Neilson out of the game. When the game ended in a 4–1 loss, the Canucks had amassed 106 penalty minutes in just that single game. NHL head office fined Neilson one thousand dollars and the Vancouver Canucks organization ten thousand dollars with the comment, "The conduct of the Vancouver coach and players disgraced the championship series."

When the Canucks flew back to Vancouver, the sight that met them at the airport astounded them: white towels madly waved by a throng of maniacal fans greeting the team. Neilson had no idea what he had started. At Game 3 in the Pacific Coliseum, Canucks fans frantically waved white towels throughout the stands in solidarity while roaring their upstart Canucks onto the ice in a white blizzard of noise. Waving towels en masse in support of a team is something that would eventually catch on not only throughout the NHL, but other sports leagues as well. It was a Canucks first: a universal symbol of surrender turned into a rallying gesture for victory by a coach with a flair for the dramatic. The Canucks would go on to win the rest of the games against Chicago and for the first time ever, push themselves and their delirious fans into a historic Stanley Cup Final.

In the east, the New York Islanders had laid waste to all challengers, and were confidently adding further bricks in their growing dynasty, having won the past two Stanley Cups. The

57

Islanders had finished first in the NHL that year with 118 points. The Canucks had finished with a mere seventy-seven points, the largest points gap between opponents in the history of the Stanley Cup Final. It was also the first time ever that an Atlantic coast/ Pacific coast matchup for the Cup had occurred.

Our hockey-mad elementary school class was completely swept up by the Canucks, watching every game we could on TV and listening to those we couldn't on the radio, reacting physically and emotionally to every play. I was no different, having made a complete about-face on hockey in just a few years. At school we could think and talk about nothing else, recounting every great goal, save, fight and outrageous occurrence as they unfolded. If the Canucks won we were overjoyed; if they lost we were collectively devastated. After Game 2 in Chicago, white towels from our mothers' linen closets disappeared into our backpacks so we could wave them at school—in the halls, in the playground, in the classroom— our teachers demanding we put them away. Our ball hockey games raged on morning, noon and into the ever-growing lightness of the warm and fragrant West Coast spring nights. Buck would pretend he was Darcy Rota with the puck and I'd pretend I was Richard Brodeur with the (occasional) save. We'd play right up until about thirty minutes to game time, when we'd all stow our sticks, hop on our bikes and race home for the drop of the puck.

Our class let out a horrified gasp when just days before the start of the Final our grade six teacher, reminded us that our entire grade was scheduled to leave on a trip to "outdoor school" at Camp Kawkawa, located in the woods two hours east of Vancouver, on the very weekend the Final was to begin.

"CANCEL THE CAMP!" shouted Buck, jumping to his feet. For once, I was fully on side with him. "The Canucks are in the STANLEY CUP FINAL!" I yelled out. Buck and I made glancing eye contact, surprising each other with our alliance. Our teacher dismissively reminded us that the outdoor school had been planned since the beginning of the year, the camp was booked, and they certainly weren't going to alter the detailed schedule to compensate for some hockey games. We were collectively destroyed, and our subsequent ball hockey games had a bit of a sag in emotion as we dreaded missing even a second of the Canucks' improbable, electrifying march.

The day before the Final was to begin, my class was forced to trudge onto a dirty yellow school bus pointed east. We would be missing games one through four. We begrudgingly took our seats on the stinky bus that would rattle us along the Trans-Canada Highway to the tranquil and remote Camp Kawkawa. As we rolled down the highway, our teacher stood up at the front of the bus: "All right, I know some of you are very upset that you will be missing a few hockey games that are important to you. The bad news is, the rumours are true, there are no TVs at Camp Kawkawa." We let out a chorus of anguished groans. "The good news is, there *is* a radio and we will let you listen to the games each night." We all cheered and broke into "King Richard," which we had already memorized word for word.

Game 1 was on Saturday, May 8, 1982, in Uniondale, Long Island, New York. They served dinner early that evening at Camp Kawkawa. The large log dining hall smelled of linoleum, spaghetti sauce and Pine-Sol. Immediately afterward, we strained to listen to a single-speaker transistor radio set up at a centre table. We were expected to sit politely at tables when listening to the game, but as soon as the anthems started we were all up and surrounding the table that held the radio, leaning in and listening desperately. All the commentators were predicting a long uphill battle for the Canucks, and a defensive strategy to ensue against the Islanders.

The puck was dropped. The play quickly went end to end, and very suddenly, just over a minute into the game, high-flying Canucks forward Thomas Gradin shot the puck on a rebound through the legs of Islanders goaltender Billy Smith for the extremely improbable 1–0 lead! We all flipped out: screaming and running around the dining hall with our hands in the air, jumping up on tables and pounding on the picture windows facing the lake, the cooks running out of the kitchen thinking the building must be on fire.

Nope, just 1–0 Canucks against the star-studded New York Islanders. The Islanders tied it up a short while later on a power play after our huge, helmetless, mustachioed defenceman Harold Snepsts took a penalty. We were roundly offended when we heard the announcer at Nassau Coliseum in New York call our team "the Canooks." Shortly thereafter, Islanders superstar sniper Mike Bossy scored on a top-shelf blast over Brodeur's glove to make it 2–1. The commentators' tone suggested the Islanders were, as predicted, taking over the game already. Then, on a power play of our own, Gradin got his second of the period on a beautiful backdoor play to make it a gripping 2–2 game. The lunch-bucket Canucks were keeping pace with the defending Stanley Cup champs!

Tiger Williams was already getting into it with the Islander spectators. In the penalty box on an offsetting roughing call, Williams hosed down several fans with a water bottle, much to his delight and their soaked disgust. With just a few seconds left in the first period, the Islanders scored again to make it 3–2, ending an emotionally exhausting first stanza and leaving most of us collapsed on the table or laying on the floor of the dining hall, panting, our hands over our faces.

The second period opened the same way the first closed, with the Islanders scoring almost immediately, making it 4–2. Looks of desperation and despair began to creep over our faces as we stared into the radio. But then the Canucks answered with a rallying power-play goal scored by captain Stan "Steamer" Smyl on a backhand shot that slipped through a crowd and the goalie's legs to make it 4–3. A few minutes later, on a beautiful forward pass from Tiger Williams, Ivan "The Bold" Boldirev, the Canucks' occasionally awesome Yugoslavian stickhandler, broke through the Islanders defence to roof an electrifying goal on Billy Smith, making it 4–4 in the middle of the second period! We were jumping up

60

and down, arm in arm, and screaming at the tops of our lungs. We got a scare a few minutes later when King Richard was knocked down with a vicious, non-penalized high stick to the jaw, but the little goaltender was okay and just got better as the game rushed forward.

The third period began with the score knotted at 4–4. But it became clear that the Islanders were dominating. Then, as he had done so many times in so many games, Tiger Williams took to the ice and immediately made an impact, delivering a crushing body-check to an Islander along the boards in their zone. That allowed the recently acquired Canuck Jim "The Thrill" Nill to scoop up the puck and cut across to the Islanders net. He made three deft moves—forehand, backhand, forehand—before putting it under the glove of Smith to make it 5–4 Canucks! Bedlam erupted at Camp Kawkawa, the very pillars holding up the dining hall quivering from our frantic celebrations. As soon as the clock hit five minutes left in the game, we all started singing the "Na Na Hey Hey..." song, letting it bounce joyously off the heavy wooden rafters of the dining hall.

And then, as if on cue to silence us stupid kids, Snepsts got tangled up with Brodeur on a save the little goalie made way out of the net. The puck squirted loose in the slot and Mike Bossy was there to snap it into an open net, tying the game at an unbelievable 5–5. We fell deathly quiet. The game clock wound down. Tiger Williams gave us one more reason to cheer in regulation time when he knocked the Islander goalie flat on his back with a check in the crease at the final buzzer to end the third period. No penalty was called, but Game 1 of the Stanley Cup Final was going to overtime tied 5–5. We couldn't stand it, some of us pacing the length of the dining room, some curled in the fetal position under the table, others dashing to the washroom fearful of missing a second even though the break before overtime was a full fifteen minutes.

Our teachers turned down the radio and turned up *The Corner Grocery Store*, the latest record from Raffi, in an effort to calm our nerves and distract us before overtime. We gathered in a circle and pensively sang along.

It was almost Camp Kawkawa's "lights out" hour of 9 p.m. on the West Coast, midnight on the East Coast, when the puck was dropped for overtime. The radio was cranked up as play immediately rushed back and forth, end to end. On a stoppage in play a few minutes later, they announced "Happy Mother's Day" at Nassau Coliseum, it being officially Sunday morning in New York. Ten minutes into overtime, Gradin had a glorious opportunity to win it, just missing his hat trick. He finessed the puck along the ice past a sprawled Billy Smith who had come way out to challenge, only to have his shot graze past the far post. We all groaned in agony, hands over faces, legs giving out, fearful to even look at the madly squawking radio. And then, with just two seconds left in the first overtime period, all of us wide-eyed and delirious from four hours of high stakes sporting drama, the game ended.

There was a faceoff in the neutral zone, and according to my ears, what I heard was "the puck is shot in . . . the Canucks' Harold Snepsts attacks the net . . . Snepsts . . . will get right in on net . . ." The commentator was briefly drowned out by the roaring crowd, then I heard him shout "SCORES!" I threw my hands up in the air in sheer joy, jumping up and down and screaming. "YEAH! YES! THEY DID IT! CANUCKS WIN! CANUCKS WIN!" All the other kids looked at me, looked at each other, looked at the radio, and then joined me in jubilation, jumping up and down, screaming, hugging and high-fiving. The cooks and dishwashers all came running in, as did our teachers and camp staff, joining in the hoopla, swept up in joyous celebration. Above the din, Buck was standing on a table furiously waving his arms from side to side and stomping his clogs. "NO!!!" he shouted, trying to get everyone's attention. "NO! NO! It was Mike BOSSY!" Slowly we stopped celebrating, calmed down, fell silent and looked up at him. He reached down and grabbed the radio, turning it up and holding it above his head with both hands like Lloyd Dobler in *Say Anything*. "Listen! It was the ISLANDERS who scored, not the Canucks! WE LOST!"

We listened in stony silence as the commentator announced the overtime goal, scored by New York Islander Mike Bossy, unassisted at 19:58 of overtime, the fans in Uniondale going wild. My classmates and friends looked at me with pale, vampire-like faces. Buck slammed the radio down and stepped off the table as my face turned a crimson red. "You stupid, ugly, four-eyed *idiot!*" he barked, leaning into my face so close his breath steamed my glasses before my anxiety could. "You don't know hockey, so you should just SHUT UP, *WIMP!*" And with that he gave me a shove, planting me on my butt on the linoleum floor of the now pin-drop-silent dining hall. Not even the teachers intervened, as apparently Buck was justified in his disgust.

I looked up at the unforgiving faces staring down at me, as if *I* had personally coughed up the puck to Mike Bossy, not Snepsts. In the chaos, I really, really thought I heard "Snepsts attacks the net"... whereas what was said was "Snepsts goes back to the net..." Why I thought Snepsts had any chance of scoring was beyond me, since he had already caused two blatant mishaps on goals against. And so, in the final seconds of overtime, Snepsts had coughed up the puck under pressure, put it right on the blade of the opposition's best, the playoff MVP, who then roof-daddy'd it over King Richard Brodeur.

The magic was over. The Canucks went on to also lose games two, three and four of the 1982 Stanley Cup, handing the heavily favoured Islanders their third straight championship (but not before Tiger Williams ripped the gold chain from the neck of goaltender Billy Smith in Game 3). To add insult to injury, the Cup was presented to the Islanders on the ice of the Pacific Coliseum in Vancouver. The Canucks fans still madly waved their white towels despite the fact the wrong team was parading the Cup around in our barn. Various fans scrambled onto the ice, some managing to touch the Cup as the Islanders briefly skated it around. One headbanger fan even interrupted a live CBC interview with Smith, shouting, "The Canucks will be back next year!" Oh, how deeply mistaken that banger would be.

The next day, the City of Vancouver gave the Canucks a Stanley Cup parade even though they had been swept in four straight games. Over 100,000 proud, thankful, towel-waving fans lined the streets to cheer our gang of pluggers, grinders and characters for the totally unexpected post-season thrill ride. Key figures like Brodeur, Smyl, Williams, Gradin and Neilson would never, ever be forgotten for what they did for our team, our city and our province. "Steamer" would be the Canucks' captain for the next eight seasons, eventually being the first Canuck to have his number retired. Brodeur would backstop the Canucks for most of the 1980s. Tiger Williams punched his way through two more seasons with the Canucks before moving on, eventually retiring in 1988 with the record for the most NHL penalty minutes of all time. In 1982, it would be the closest any of them, as players, would ever get to winning the Stanley Cup.

Back at Camp Kawkawa, I got the cold shoulder from everybody, even teachers, who suggested that next time I "shouldn't be so quick to cry wolf in an attempt to impress other people." The impact of my blown call was magnified worse and worse with each mounting, devastating Canucks loss. Already despondent that the Canucks were losing, the Cup slipping through our fingers, I felt like I had hexed the team. I spent a lot of time alone under the stairs of the dining hall, my teeth chattering, as I hid from the wrath of Buck, who dominated the outdoor school like Survivorman. Hiding from Buck would soon be just one of the many hurdles I was about to face, as high school loomed ahead like the black skies of Mordor. It was a long, lonely bus ride home from Camp Kawkawa.

"There is no position in sport as noble as goaltending."

VLADISLAV TRETIAK, *Soviet Union goalie, 1968–1984*

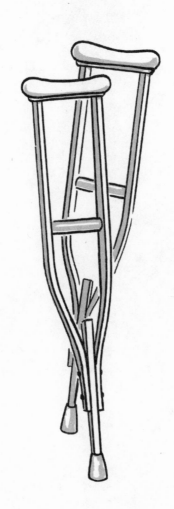

Second PERIOD

★★★

10

HOW DARWINIAN

IT WAS EXTREMELY intimidating to enter into a high school filled with nine hundred kids from grades seven to twelve. Many of them looked like adults: girls so developed they could have been in *Charlie's Angels*, tribes and sects so numerous it felt like we'd been thrown from *Leave It to Beaver* to *The Warriors* in one fell swoop. There were headbangers, mods, punks, preppies, skids/drug dealers, goths, geeks, skaters and jocks. Lots of jocks. Bangers drove muscle cars, hockey jocks had moustaches and cheerleaders had boobs. Sports weren't played leisurely at recess and lunch like we had done so passionately in elementary school. Actual teams existed now, with tryouts and practices and uniforms and schedules and expectations and trophies. At lunch hour in high school, people "hung out" and seemingly tried to exert as little energy as possible while doing so: the hockey jocks in the parking lot, the bangers in the smoke hole, the geeks in the library, the mods in the main foyer, the punks in the stairwell, the preppies by the trophy case, the skids/drug dealers in the breezeway. And each tribe, even the geeks, seemed to have its own designated bully. Suddenly, overnight, Buck went from the alpha dog with the biggest teeth to a rangy lone cub at the back of the pack, having to prove himself all over again from the bottom up. And I was even further down the pecking order.

In the first few days of high school, I stuck closely with my elementary school geek squad, the instinctual survival mechanism of group mentality needed to stay alive. We were like a flock of skittish sheep in a field ringed by wolf-infested woods. We found a quiet, unused, dank corner at the bottom of a stairwell to hide, where we could spend our recesses and lunch hours in relative peace. It was a pathetic existence.

"Why don't we try and get the ball hockey game going again?" I suggested one day, sitting cross-legged at the bottom of the staircase. Timmy Prescott stared at me through the dim light. "Are you completely mental?" he asked incredulously. I didn't honour the question with a response. "*Are you completely mental?*" he demanded again. "We will get *killed* if we go out there. We have to stay here, where it's safe. Ball hockey is over, elementary school is over, our lives as we knew them are over. Get used to it, Lawrence." I hated being called by only my last name. It reminded me of gym teachers.

"Can't we at least go and explore this place a little bit?" a kid named Philip pleaded. A few of the other nerds were in agreement, and after great debate we began to venture beyond the dank stairwell. We quickly found out that Timmy Prescott had been right. The excursions beyond the stairwell did not go well, our curiosity sealing our social fate. If we were so much as caught in a bully's peripheral field of vision, we would be mercilessly hunted down and attacked. It quickly became obvious that because of my diminutive size, hinged knee braces and Coke-bottle glasses, I was the weakest link in the nerd herd. I became the primary target, the attractor of unwanted attention from an array of vicious older bullies from all tribes. In the crowded hallways, there was no open space where we could run away. We were trapped.

Our years of friendship became too heavy a burden to bear for my elementary school chums. It was either shed the runt, or have him drag down the whole flock. I was cast out, a pariah amongst my own kind. It happened one day between classes. I was no longer welcome at the bottom of the dank stairwell. "We can't risk being discovered," Timmy Prescott explained at the top of the stairs, glancing back and forth, blocking the passage downward to safety with crossed arms, avoiding eye contact.

"But I ..."

Timmy cut me off with a hard shove to my shoulder. "Just go!" he yelled. "Leave this place and don't come back!" And so I was set adrift into the predator-infested hallways. I was alone, and I became frightfully easy pickings for anyone who wanted to take a shot—of whom there were many. I was branded with all sorts of new nicknames like "Tiny Tim," "Grunt," "The Littlest Homo," "Webster," "Spazz" and "Dumb Grant." (There was another Grant in my high school who was a mathematical genius. Teachers and students would differentiate us with "Smart Grant" and "Dumb Grant." Smart Grant became a derivatives quantitative analyst for an investment bank in London, England.) I was dropped head-first into garbage cans, pelted with rocks, locked in the reeking lost and found bin, stalked all the way home after school, had lit cigarettes thrown at my hair and was once, infamously and quite painfully, jammed upside down behind the Coke machine for most of the day.

Just like in elementary school at its worst, the library became my sanctuary, but my locker was located at the opposite end of the school, which meant a dangerous traverse through the open social minefields of hallways, stairways and foyers, often ending in a mad dash for the front door of the library with some type of mohawked beast from grade ten or eleven in jackboot-stomping pursuit. I figured out that the library was open one hour before school started and stayed open one hour after the final bell rang, so I would arrive at school early and leave late to avoid the masses.

Buck wasn't too eager to attract any unwanted attention himself. To ease as quickly into high school as he possibly could, he had left his Canadian tuxedo, clogs and perfect chestnut bob behind in elementary school lore. His minor league hockey jacket remained, a few sizes bigger now, with his surname sewn on the bicep. He had traded his clogs for white high-top sneakers with the tongues hanging out and his bob for a full-throttle mullet, long and straight down the back like a chocolate waterfall, flowing from an ugly estuary of aggressive, short, spiky dyed-blond hair on top.

One late afternoon I was making my way out of school at 4 p.m., through the empty, echoing linoleum hallways for the long walk home. I turned a corner and ran straight into Buck, fresh from a workout in the weight room. I cast my eyes to the linoleum-tiled floor. I tried to sidle by but Buck reached out one of his pumped-up arms and grabbed me, slamming me into the lockers, an unmistakable metallic rattle I was getting very used to. He leaned down into my face just like old times, wrapped his big hand around my neck and squeezed. He had grown taller and broader. I felt like I had grown smaller, both in physical size and psychological confidence. Any feelings of power or equality I had worked so hard to achieve had been shredded by the gates of high school. I knew the power had once again shifted, and Buck knew it, too. I was the smallest sheep, caught in the wolf's jaws.

There was no one around in either direction. Buck let out a low and familiar snarl. "*You* are the biggest fucking loser there is at this school, do you know that, *WIMP*?" I was choking, so I couldn't answer, but I didn't want to answer. Pressing me painfully against the lockers, he reached down with his other hand and tore my new red nylon duffle bag out of my grip. Mom had given me the bag so I could start high school with something that wasn't a *Land of the Lost* lunch kit.

"You used to be a real smartass, and loved to run away from me. Didn't you, *WIMP*? Well guess what? Your ugly face gets to run away from me again." I gasped for air as he let go of my neck but held onto my bag. I was willing to forego my math and science homework for my survival any day, so I took Buck up on what I considered a minor price for freedom. I bolted, running full steam, the usual prayers repeating through my head that my knee braces would do their job.

72

BOLAS ARE ARGENTINIAN.

How Darwinian

As Buck watched me dash, he felt the weight of my bag with its three textbooks inside and then he leaned down as if he were throwing a skipping stone over the surface of a lake. He threw my bag in the direction I was running as hard as he could. It came whipping down the hallway, just above the surface of the shiny, slippery floor. It did something Buck himself had not been able to do for years—it caught up to me. It ensnared my legs like an Australian bolas bringing down a kangaroo. One of my Converse sneakers wrapped around a strap while the other got caught up in the weight of the bag. I came crashing down in a heap. My knees held together, but the side of my skull cracked against the thin layer of waxed linoleum covering the hallway's concrete floor like a snooker ball being struck by a baseball bat. The lockers, hall and fluorescent lights spun madly above me like a scene from *Vertigo*. Buck's face leaned over me, hovering at the centre of the spinning vortex. "You tell anyone about this and you're dead, *WIMP*." I knew the code. One could reason this attack was long overdue—that I had it coming. I wouldn't tell. I passed out instead.

I was diagnosed with a concussion by the track and field coach and school nurse, both of whom were still at school when the janitor found me sprawled motionless in the hallway like a scene from *CSI*. I told them the truth: I had tripped on my bag and hit my head. Back then, concussions weren't considered much more than "getting your bell rung." I had a lump the size of a golf ball on the side of my head, diagnosed as a "good old-fashioned goose egg" by Dad when I got home. I also told my parents I had tripped. I complained of a splitting headache. I was allowed to stay home for a few days, but forced back to school much sooner than I would have liked.

With my head throbbing at the temples, my first class back at school was, of course, gym. Buck and I exchanged glances as we all gathered in the change room to slip into our shorts. The change room smelled like B.O., dirty laundry and mildew. Glancing at Buck, I was hoping to see culpability in his face, but received nothing back but an icy, cruel glare and clenched muscular jaw. Pure intimidation. When I thought gym class in elementary school was ridiculous, I had no idea what depths of hell high school gym would toss me into. Our young bodies and minds were all in varying stages of puberty and growth spurts. Some were full grown like Buck, who towered over us all with a fully developed man's body, large and defined muscles exactly where they should be like on superheroes and Greek statues. For others, physical puberty hadn't arrived at all, adversely affecting the mind by keeping us wondering *why us*, and when it would ever come. In my case, puberty arrived in the form of a Chewbacca-like explosion of body hair on my chest, navel, and Jim and the twins, of which I was deeply ashamed.

Even while our male bodies were confusing and confounding us, we were also noticing the opposite sex. For the first time in my life I was interested in a girl . . . head-over-heels, massive-crush interested. I couldn't keep my eyes off an absolutely beautiful blonde, preppy sweetheart named Lizzy who wore tight Gap jeans and cute, brightly coloured Ralph Lauren shirts with the collar flipped up, showcasing her perfectly developing, perky breasts. Up in Desolation Sound where our family's summer cabin sat, Lizzy would have been one of the "Savary People," vacationers from a nearby idyllic island filled with kids who were simply perfect and simply out of my family's league. High school was no different. Lizzy soared above my social station, but I didn't care. I showered her with attention every chance I got, careful that no one would take notice but her and me, and she didn't seem to mind. We actually became friends in a Molly Ringwald–Duckie-type way. I yearned to see her in gym class in revealing short-shorts and loose tank top, but alas, gym class in high school was no longer a co-ed affair.

Our gym teacher was a fire hydrant of a man—all muscle, no brains or neck, and no sympathy for the boys not up to his standard of competition. To his credit, when it came to picking teams for cosom hockey that morning, he simply lined us up and pointed: "Team A, Team B, Team A, Team B." I breathed a premature sigh of relief, thinking that high school phys. ed. would clearly be much more civilized than the barbaric elementary school gym classes. I was happily mixed anonymously in the middle of Team B, and on the same team as Buck, a shocking first. Maybe we could assist on each other's goals and high-five each other, I fantasized. Then the gym teacher shattered my dream by barking out the three most horrendous words I had ever heard in my life—three words that sent my teeth into a chattering cacophony: "SHIRTS AND SKINS!"

"What the hell does that mean?" I frantically muttered to the closest geek I could find. Before he could answer, the gym teacher shouted, "C'mon, let's go, lady boys! Team A shirts, Team B skins!" I panicked, glancing around feverishly, a nightmare unfolding through the lenses of my fogging glasses as the boys of Team B pulled off their T-shirts and threw them in a heap on the gym floor. I *never* took my shirt off in public, ever fearful of revealing my skinny, concave chest and white, near-translucent skin that was now bursting with dark clumps of body hair.

There was nowhere I could run, nowhere to hide, and no switching teams. My goose egg throbbed as I cursed my parents for making me come to school that day. I stalled, trying to make myself invisible along the gym wall. "Lawrence!" the fire hydrant barked. All eyes turned toward me, the geeks once again thankful I was diverting attention away from their own video game screen–toned bodies, their torsos like milk bags. "Take off that goddamn *ET* turtleneck, now!"

"I can't play today!" I blurted out.

"What?" retorted the fire hydrant. "Why?"

"I banged my head the other day and it's hurting really badly . . . feel for yourself," I offered, tilting my head in his direction and pointing to the still-sizeable lump protruding from my skull. Buck shot me a glare. When the fire hydrant's meaty fingers ran over the goose egg it caused a stinging sensation that made me wince, which I made sure he noticed. He stepped back and looked me over, head to toe, while Buck, shirtless, mulleted and muscle-bound like

Harry Hamlin in *Clash of the Titans*, leaned over and listened in, eyes filled with intimidation, making sure I didn't squeal.

"Alright," sighed the fire hydrant. "Can you play goalie? There's a pile of gear over there." I wasn't sure how that was any less of a physical threat to my wounded head, but I took a glance and spotted the chest protector, basically a giant, armoured shirt, and agreed. "Yes!"

I dodged a bullet, but a bomb was next.

With Buck leading the attack, the skins stomped on the shirts like the Spartans laying waste to Arcadia, the feeling of a joint victory between us a rare sensation, though there would be no joint celebration of our cosom hockey triumph. With ten minutes still to go in gym class, the fire hydrant blew his whistle loud and long. "Alright, that's it! Hit the showers!" I was enjoying the game so much, trying to reenact the wild, full body moves of Richard Brodeur, that I forgot about my bruised head. *Winning* was fun . . . I tasted competition again and I loved it.

We all filed down to the locker room, most of the boys hurriedly changing out of their shorts and T-shirts and directly back into jeans and sweaters, assuming the phrase "hit the showers" was simply a euphemism for "end of gym class."

"Whoa!" shouted the fire hydrant, standing with his meaty hands on his hips at the door of the boys' changing room. "When I said hit the showers I meant *hit the goddamn showers!* Your teachers complain that you little rat bastards stink to high heaven, which means each and every one of you needs to shower. NOW!"

It was as if I had been hurtled into a Scream Machine rollercoaster nightmare I couldn't control. Gym class was over. I had survived it, even enjoyed it. I should've been free to go. I had successfully avoided taking my shirt off and now our gym teacher wanted us fully naked and in the showers . . . together? Buck and the other jocks, already well versed in locker room culture and the ritual of showering together after physical exertion from years of minor hockey, were already striding past us, naked and cocksure, lean and mature, seemingly showing off their dark fuzzy growths above their dangling penises. Those who had no dangle couldn't help but steal obvious, astonished glances at those who did. Together the naked jocks stepped into an open, brightly lit and tiled room of a dozen shower nozzles protruding from the wall. "Move it, move it, into the shower, let's go!" shouted the fire hydrant at the rest of us quivering in front of our lockers. I grabbed not one but two of the white towels on the bench in front of me, undressing in slow motion. It was a panicked, out of body experience.

With difficulty I pulled my sweat-soaked and stinky turtleneck over my head and wrapped the first towel around my Gollum-like torso, glancing about feverishly to see if anyone was staring. I faced my gym locker with grim resolution as I hastily wrapped the second towel around my waist and dropped my short-shorts and ginch to the filthy locker room floor. I reluctantly joined the very end of the lineup of other zombified geeks tiptoeing gingerly across the jarringly cold, virus-ridden tiles of the change room. The fire hydrant had relocated himself at the entrance of the shower room on a chair, Popeye arms crossed over his broad chest, legs outstretched and crossed in front of him, keeping one eye on his stallion jock bathers, the other on the shuffling geeks in the change room, making sure none of us made a stinky exit.

A profanity-laced cacophony rose from behind the clouds of billowing steam in the shower room. The hot water had abruptly run out, to be replaced by an icy spray. The fire hydrant spun in the direction of the calamity. It was my only chance. Before he could turn back, I sidestepped silently from the back of the line, both of my towels falling to the ground, slipping barefoot and naked into the warm, yellow puddles of a toilet stall, quickly shutting and bolting the door behind me. I hopped up on the equally wet toilet seat, beaded yellow with some kid's urine. I hunched over and peered nervously through the crack between the door and the stall. The fire hydrant didn't notice my absence.

I stayed crouched naked on the toilet seat as I listened to Buck and the jocks, still naked, rolling up their wet towels post-shower to create "rat tails": instant, wet, whip-like instruments of nerd torture, which the jocks could snap painfully against the alabaster bare skin of the traumatized victims. The din of the change room eventually faded and fell silent. When I was certain everyone was gone, I scrambled down from the toilet and out of the stall, cautiously entering the change room completely naked. I was halfway across the room when the first of several grade twelve boys entered to get ready for their upcoming gym class.

"What the fuck is that?" exclaimed the first one, pointing at the flash of streaking white skin, before they burst out laughing. "It's Casper!" yelled another. I made it to my locker and grabbed clumsily at my clothes, pulling my ET turtleneck over my head. Now shirtcocking, I madly searched for underwear. They were gone, hidden, stolen. I snatched up my beige rugby pants and was forced to go commando. As I pushed open the gym door to make my final escape, one of the grade twelve boys yelled after me, "Try growing a cock for that rat's nest of pubes, kid!" which was followed by more gales of deep laughter. I was horrified. I made it to French class ten minutes late and reeking badly. I floundered through a vocabulary quiz and was called "fatty gay" a few times under the breath of bullies around me. My head pounded with thoughts of how I could avoid gym class for the rest of my life.

11

CRASH YEARS

I WAS LONELY AND desperate. I needed to find new friends, a new tribe, my own community and that ever-important social shield of safety in numbers. I finally aligned myself with the very lowest rung of the high school herding ladder. I found them at the far back corner of the library, seated like Knights at the Nerd Table next to the encyclopedia section (the only acceptable referee when an intellectual battle of words broke out and facts needed to be immediately looked up and proven, bony fingers triumphantly pointing to ridiculous minutiae in tiny print).

They were, sadly, the lowest form of high school pariah: deformed, ugly male creatures, every one of them bespectacled, some with headgear the likes of which I hadn't seen since "Funnel Head" Susie Jenkins. They spoke like wizards, Sherlock Holmes and Yoda. They incessantly quoted Monty Python films. They enjoyed making dioramas. They collected highly stylized and violent comic books way beyond my Tintin and Archie faves. They were in special, streamlined, advanced education classes with fancy French names. Their leader was a know-it-all, beanpole brainiac named Benny. Years later I realized he looked exactly like Jar Jar Binks, *Star Wars'* most hated character.

Benny's second in command was a set of identical twins named Fukartay and Orophel. Benny absolutely abhorred sports, and by extension anything to do with hockey. The game of hockey and its players were never to be spoken of in his presence, because Benny felt it was the kids who enjoyed and played hockey who had forced them into their social exile at the far corner of the library. It was hard for me to disagree. The only game Benny and his acne-encrusted social lepers enjoyed was Dungeons and Dragons, the weird fantasy role-playing, multi-dice casting affair that I couldn't get into or understand no matter how hard I tried... but with no other prospects, I joined their round table.

Much in the same way my social stature had plummeted after enjoying brief notoriety in my final years of elementary school, so too had the on-ice fortunes of the Vancouver Canucks. The Canucks had sadly proven to everyone that the glorious Stanley Cup run of 1982 was but a blip—a rare lucky streak in an ugly uniform. The Canucks were apparently mired in a "Stanley Cup hangover," but with the compounding problem that they woke up in the morning with no Stanley Cup to make the headache go away. In the years following 1982 they either didn't make the playoffs at all, or were repeatedly ousted by the upstart powerhouse teams from Alberta: the Calgary Flames (triumphing over the Canucks in three different first-round playoff series throughout the 1980s) or the dynasty-bound Edmonton Oilers.

As Canucks players came and went, one of the few bright lights during those otherwise-forgettable dark years of futility was a player named Tony Tanti, who racked up stacks of goals playing on a line with Patrik Sundstrom and good ol' Tiger Williams. So proficient was the trio that they earned themselves the nickname "The SWAT Line." Tanti set all sorts of Canucks scoring records in the 1980s, which sadly didn't have the overall effect of pushing the team forward in the win column or playoffs. There was also the addition of a tall, awkward draft pick named "Bam Bam" Cam Neely, from Maple Ridge, BC. After a few developmental seasons with the Canucks, management apparently hadn't liked what they'd seen in the 220 pounds of BC beef, so they traded him to Boston, where Neely's career became rock solid. "Bam Bam," so nicknamed because he hit everything that moved, became the hulking definition of the term "power forward," recording three fifty-goal seasons for the Bruins and becoming one of the biggest hockey heroes of the late twentieth century. The trade would haunt the Canucks for decades.

The Canucks were stuck in the same division as the sickeningly sizzling Edmonton Oilers and their long list of snipers, topped by their captain Wayne Gretzky, who seemed to be setting a new record with every game played, many seemingly set while playing against the Canucks. The Oilers beat the Canucks like a dusty rug almost every time they met and soon began winning their string of Stanley Cups. Consequently, Gretzky and Oilers merchandise began to rival Canucks wear in our school hallways. At home, Dad remained a diehard Canucks fan, whooping from the couch upstairs with every rare goal scored, but my interest began to drift again, mostly in an effort to keep in Benny's good books.

On weekends, my newfound friends enjoyed putting their Dungeons and Dragons fantasies into real live action, often playing a strange spin-off game they had created, which was a bizarre, pagan cross between capture the flag and *The Blair Witch Project*. They would meet in the steep mountain forest above the Trans-Canada Highway to create elaborate and frightening scenarios, the rules constantly changing at Benny's whim. I was trying hard to fit in, so one early spring weekend I brought along one of my most prized possessions in an effort to impress them: my lever-action BB gun rifle complete with leather tassel on a polished wooden stock. The previous Christmas, I was able to convince Dad to convince Mom that it would be okay to have a BB gun. Luckily, Dad had one when he was a boy and he loved it. But Mom hated guns and thought nothing good could ever come from owning one, even a BB gun. She eventually relented, but rules were set in place that I wasn't ever allowed to point it at anyone or any living thing, and that I could only use it to shoot at targets Dad and I set up in the basement, never outside. On a damp, chilly Sunday morning in the spring, while Mom was at church and Dad was sleeping off another Canucks loss, I snuck my BB gun out of the house.

Benny, Fukartay, Orophel and I gathered in a tight circle on the gravel service road that switchbacked through the woods in the rocky terrain. The Trans-Canada Highway roared somewhere below us like a distant waterfall. Benny was dressed in a long black terry cloth housecoat with a saggy hood and rope sash. All three were marvelling at my BB gun, each one wanting to hold it, aim it and take some shots. I was pleased; they were impressed. As they handled the gun, I nervously told them never to point it at anyone and to give it back to me when I asked. I found a couple of empty Lucky beer cans in the roadside bushes, filled them with some water from the ditch, and set them up on a stump on the other side of the road. I showed them, just as Dad had taught me, how to line up the front and rear sights for a bull's-eye shot, the air gun letting off a popping sound as a round, copper BB struck the can with a satisfying THWACK, tearing the aluminum and producing a stream of water. They looked on with astonishment. I ceremoniously handed the rifle over to Fukartay.

"WHOO HOO!" I yelled, as Fukartay knocked one of the cans right off the stump on his first shot. I was reloading the BB gun when we heard the high-pitched whine of a revving engine from somewhere on the hill above us. Already freaked out that I had snuck the BB gun out of the house, I had an odd tingling in my tummy, a gut instinct that we should leave the road and get out of sight, or at the very least hide the gun. I suppressed it, fearing I would lose face. I would regret that very quickly.

The racket drew closer, sounding like a blender on high speed. A dirt bike skidded recklessly around the corner and came into view, rapidly approaching us. I spotted the blue hockey jacket immediately, and then the cocksure, spikes 'n' tails hockey mullet flapping triumphantly in the tailwind. I hid the gun with both hands behind my back, barrel pointing down. I thought for sure it was Buck, living out some dirt bike dream, roaring around the back roads of West Vancouver like he was Fonzie, but it wasn't him. I was halfway through a sigh of relief when I realized who it really was.

It was Barclay "Psycho" Powers, smaller than Buck but twice as dangerous, a certified lunatic. He was a banger through and through and through—such a violent hockey player that he was constantly being suspended and would eventually be kicked out of the league entirely. Barclay was straddling a Honda Red Devil, its thick-tread tires covered in mud, its jacked-up shocks easily absorbing the potholes of the gravel road, its engine revving so high that the bike itself seemed furious at the sight of us. Strapped to the handlebars was a big white number plate speckled in mud, framing the bold black number 22. I could only assume it was a tribute to the jersey number of his role model, Tiger Williams. Barclay skidded to a stop in front of us, his back wheel sliding out sideways, kicking up a spray of gravel. Barclay switched off the engine. The bike sputtered to a momentary silence, followed by a loud backfire, which caused all those not straddling a dirt bike to jerk back in fear. The air was filled with the foreboding mix of blue exhaust fumes and West Coast mountain mist.

Psycho Powers was a brash, solitary figure who had failed multiple grades. No one really knew how old he was. Everybody steered clear of him. He was rarely seen at school because he was always getting suspended for fighting, and when he was at school he skipped all classes to be in the auto shop working on his dirt bike. He seemed perpetually angry and bored, and intent on inflicting harm and chaos on others as often as possible. Wasn't hockey supposed to be an outlet for pent-up rage? If Psycho Powers had any friends on his hockey team—any friends at all—I wasn't aware of them. One of Barclay's mud-splattered, oversized runners with the tongue hanging out flicked the kickstand down and he swung off the bike. He was small but compact: solid muscle.

"What the *fuck* are you losers doing up here?" Barclay demanded of us. I was praying he hadn't spotted the gun.

"Just doing a little target practice," answered Benny, almost boasting.

"Target practice?" Barclay glanced around and spotted the beer cans on the stump. "With what?" Then he bore down on me. "Whattaya got behind your back, *kid*?" I didn't move. "SHOW ME WHAT'S BEHIND YOUR BACK!" he bellowed.

I knew the minute Psycho Powers saw my beloved BB gun there would be trouble. I briefly fantasized about breaking my mom's number one rule and pointing it at him, whipping the rifle out from behind my back like Clint Eastwood in *The Outlaw Josie Wales*, pumping the lever of the rifle and squeezing the trigger, filling Psycho Powers full of BBs. Instead, I slowly revealed my prized BB gun complete with leather tassel on the polished wooden stock.

"*Whoa!* Can I take a look at that?" Without waiting for an answer he took two quick strides and grabbed the gun from my hands. My glasses fogged, I thought of Mom, and I felt myself on the verge of tears. Barclay held the gun up in both hands, examining it with his narrow, beady eyes. He rested the stock of the rifle on his hip, the barrel pointed in the air like he was Lone Wolf McQuade. "Can I shoot it?" he asked eagerly, barely a question.

"Uh... no, it's actually not loaded," I lied.

84 Barclay gave the gun a shake. The BBs I had just loaded into the gun rattled and rolled in the chamber. "Sounds loaded to me. So you were doing some target practice, eh?" With a maniacal laugh, he quickly swung the butt of the gun up to his shoulder and pointed it right at me. "Is it okay if I use your head as my target?"

All four of us instinctively raised our arms and ducked. "Whoa, whoa, what are you doing? Psycho, don't point that at us!" I shouted at him.

"What the fuck did you call me, you fuckin' loser?" he raged. I could sense Benny, Fukartay and Orophel inching away from me. Barclay kept the gun pointed straight at me. Gesturing to Benny and the twins with the long barrel of my BB gun, he snarled, "Why don't you three retards get the fuck out of here?"

Without hesitation, Benny, Fukartay and Orophel disappeared into the woods behind us, leaving me to stare down the barrel of my prized BB gun that wasn't allowed out of the house. So much for my strength-in-numbers theory. I had no idea what Psycho Powers was capable of. I started to whimper, to cry, to back away, my arms raised in surrender. Barclay pumped the lever and took aim.

"Barclay, don't!" I had barely finished my sobbing plea when he squeezed the trigger. The gun let off its familiar popping sound as a round copper BB struck me in the thigh. It didn't pierce the denim of my jeans, but stung like a hornet and shocked me. "OW!!" I screamed, jumping on the spot and rubbing one hand on my thigh. "Barclay, DON'T SHOOT ME!"

Laughing, Psycho pumped the lever again. I turned and dashed away as fast as I could, straight into the woods in the direction the other three had fled. I heard the gun pop again, a BB striking the trunk of a tree beside me—*THWACK*—then Barclay's cackling laughter followed by the thrashing of the bushes behind me. Was this lunatic coming after me, hunting me down with my own gun? I struggled through the soggy spring growth until I burst from the woods, emerging on the edge of a steep cliff. Far below me was the undulating roar of the Trans-Canada Highway, like crashing waves in a storm. I ran along the edge of the cliff until I heard my name.

"Grant! Run this way you must!" It was Benny and the twins, poking their heads out from behind a nurse log. They were on the other side of a little stream that ran along the rocks and spilled out over the cliff to form a small spring-runoff waterfall cascading into a ditch far below. I had learned about the dangers of walking on rocks from the time I spent in Desolation Sound. Dad and others had tried many times to teach me that anything wet, black or green was alive and slippery. All those hard lessons were momentarily forgotten as I tried to get to my friends' hiding place as quickly as possible.

I took a panicked step forward into the water, just a few feet from where the stream spilled out over the cliff. My foot immediately slid out from under me, and then it happened, my worst nightmare: my kneecap violently dislocated from its socket, sending me crashing onto the wet slimy rocks. Face down in the stream, I tried to reach out for something to hold on to. The surface of the rocks was too slippery. I slid right off the edge of the cliff.

I twisted in mid-air, grabbing at nothing. In a split second of frozen time I saw cars rushing by far below me on the Trans-Canada Highway and the cold, bare deciduous tree branches reaching into the grey sky of early spring above me. I descended Alfred Hitchcock-style, forty feet, the height of a four-storey building, hitting the cliff side twice: once whacking the side of my head and knocking off my glasses, the second time crunching my other knee.

I landed in a heap at the edge of the gravel ditch the little waterfall emptied into. Beside me was Canada's most famous ribbon of blacktop that stretched from Victoria, BC, to St. John's, Newfoundland. I turned my head and saw the blurred wheels of cars roaring by just a few feet away. None stopped. The soft, wet gravel felt warm and comfortable under the side of my head. I passed out. Benny and the twins found a way to scramble down the cliff and were beside me when I woke up. I saw my blood on Benny's hands. I grabbed Benny's terry cloth robe as he started to get up to find help. "Don't tell my mom about the BB gun."

86

SCHOOL DAYS
(HAIL, HAIL ROCK 'N' ROLL)

ENNY'S DAD WAS just about as weird as Benny. A tipsy Welsh man, he thought I wasn't that badly hurt after taking what he considered to be a mere tumble. He hoisted me up from the side of the highway and put me into the back seat of his car, where I drifted in and out of consciousness. First he took the time to drop off Fukartay and Orophel, and then he drove me down to my parents' house, finding them both in the driveway when we arrived. Rolling down the window, he cheerily chuckled, "I've got a wee wounded warlock for you in the back seat!" Dad took one look at my crumpled body and saw the blood covering my face. He panicked, dragging me out of the car and into the familiar vinyl back seat of our little green Fiat, where I collapsed. My parents raced me to the hospital, Dad cursing Benny's dad for taking my injuries so casually. I passed out again.

I woke up in the emergency room, lying completely naked on a cool, clean white sheet covering a gurney. The nurse had just finished removing my soggy, torn and blood-soaked clothing. My parents stood on either side looking down on me, worry and panic in their faces. My pain was superseded by self-consciousness about my pubescent appearance; my parents had never seen my explosive, matted, dark patches of body hair. What were they thinking? Who was this Cha-Ka–like child? I was too out of it to cover myself up. I lay there, exposed, wafting in and out of consciousness until the nurse threw another white billowing sheet over my damaged little body a few minutes later.

Dad thought for certain I had fractured my skull, but after I was washed and examined the surface wounds were found to be cuts and scrapes. The more serious damage was internal. The doctor told us I had managed not to break a single bone, but had suffered another concussion, severe this time, and had badly damaged both knees, the tendons and ligaments in the left one pretty much completely torn apart. Nobody paid much attention to the red bull's-eye welt on my thigh. The doctor told us that my knees would require immediate emergency surgery. They would be bringing in the hospital's top orthopaedic surgeon: Dr. McNeill.

"Stu McNeill?" Mom knew the name. The doctor lived in our neighbourhood and was rumoured to have hockey in his past. "The same Stu McNeill . . . who played for the Detroit Red Wings?" Mom asked the ER doctor.

Dr. McNeill indeed had a short-lived career as a professional hockey player in the late 1950s, playing a handful of games with the Red Wings and recording one career NHL goal in 1958. In those days one could make more money fixing body parts than smashing them, so at age twenty-one he left hockey for medical school.

88 Two days after my accident, Dr. McNeill's broad shoulders cast a shadow over my hospital bed. After examining me thoroughly, Dr. McNeill confidently explained to my parents that he would not only operate on my knees, but also fix them so they would no longer violently dislocate. He was going to drill holes through the kneecaps and string a tendon through each one to literally tie them down into their sockets. Then, if I followed a long and strenuous post-surgery exercise routine, my muscles would grow in overtop

and keep my kneecaps firmly in place for the rest of my life. My parents were delighted; I was skeptical.

I was rolled into the operating room on a stretcher, my parents with me until the swinging doors. When I came to hours later I was back in my hospital bed, my parents at my side. It was the agony that woke me. I was in screaming pain. It felt as if Dr. McNeill had left two rusty saw blades sitting deep within both knees. If I moved in the slightest, it felt like the rusty blades were sawing back and forth, cutting deeper into my knees. I wailed in writhing misery for the first few days, the pain alleviated only by pills the nurse would give me every four hours around the clock. With sweat-soaked fervour, I repeatedly described the depths of pain I was feeling to Dad, who told me to write it down, which I did. Mom brought new Tintin books. Benny, Fukartay and Orophel came to visit. The boys confirmed that they were honouring my request to not tell anyone about the BB gun.

I left the hospital after a week's recovery. I was in a wheelchair with straight plaster casts on both legs that stretched from the top of my thighs to my ankles, as if I needed to add more impotence to my high school image. But it wasn't as if I would be going back to school anytime soon. My high school wasn't wheelchair accessible, so I was mercifully allowed to recover at home in bed for weeks. I was supposed to be keeping up with the homework Mom brought me, but I didn't. I was too self-absorbed with the pain of my knees and the even slower recovery of my concussion. I begged my parents to set up a bed for me in the TV room so I could be entertained beyond my exhausted supply of Tintin books. I stayed up later and later at night, discovering a whole other world of television I didn't know existed: *The Tonight Show Starring Johnny Carson*, a late-night old boys' club of Hollywood comedians, movie stars and celebrities, each guest joining the last on the couch, all of them cracking as many ribald jokes as they could between cigarettes and highballs. After Johnny Carson came a darker and stranger spectacle, *Late Night with David Letterman* from New York City, a crazy hour-long show where the host would dip his entire body in various liquids, attach a live camera to the back of a monkey racing around the studio, and have guests who would try to physically attack him. After Letterman I would watch whatever late movie was on, and then sleep through most of the next day. I was very quickly turning into a hobbled teenage deadbeat, painkillers and television as my vices.

Every Thursday night, David Letterman would read "Viewer Mail," flashing an address momentarily on the screen: *30 Rockefeller Plaza, New York, NY, 10112, USA*. I finally managed to scribble it down one night. I wrote David Letterman a letter the next day and had Mom mail it for me. Once I could move around awkwardly on crutches, I was finally forced back to high school. It was an extremely slow and painful process manoeuvring through the halls and stairways on crutches. Bullies didn't make it any easier, tripping me or snatching one of my crutches away to make me topple to the floor in screaming torment, the rusty blades in my knees sawing away with each violent twist and turn.

With the added visual aid of the crutches, the unwanted nickname of "Tiny Tim" rushed back in full force. I was late for every class, often struggling through the door five minutes after the bell and soaked in sweat. I had fallen far behind in most of my subjects, but for the first time in my school career I just didn't care. Up until the accident I had been a fairly good student in every course, Dad always helping me with my homework. But after the accident I couldn't give a shit about any subject. It was extremely disappointing to Dad when he saw me making no effort to catch up. I became rebellious in class, seeking the attention of my peers by mouthing off any chance I got.

I had also returned to find that my first crush had forsaken me for another. Lizzy had a boyfriend. I was enraged. While I was away recovering from a horrific accident my fantasy girlfriend leaves me? I didn't return to the back of the library to Benny and the twins. I was at rock bottom and didn't give a shit. When the bullies came after me, I would make a scene, yelling back at them and swinging my crutches like they were winged appendages. Some of the bullies, embarrassed by a cripple, backed off. For others it was like throwing gasoline on a fire, and they came at me even harder.

Thanks to my bleary-eyed exposure to comedians on *The Tonight Show* like Steven Wright, Louie Anderson, Jerry Seinfeld and Eddie Murphy, I had material to repeat for the kids in the hall. I eventually managed to attract a crowd that wasn't there to beat me up, but rather to laugh at the jokes. Soon I could pull off vocal imitations of any teacher in our high school; my growing circle of new friends would call out a teacher's name and crack up when I could instantaneously deliver. These were nice, cool kids—not jocks, not nerds, not preppies or punks—but somewhere in between: laid-back skateboarders who liked to laugh and have fun. They weren't judgmental and were into all sorts of different music, movies and emerging alternative cultures. They actually welcomed me into their fold—glasses, casts, crutches and all.

On the weekends, I would often go to the movies with one or more of the new gang. We would buy a ticket for the "Rated G" movie but then sneak into the 14+ "Mature" movies that our parents didn't want us seeing on our own. One Saturday afternoon at the Park Royal Theatre, a new friend named Chris Monahan and I had snuck into the new Harrison Ford movie, *Witness.* Chris Monahan was a big, friendly kid who had a dry sense of humour, a strong sense of right and wrong, and a love for Van Halen. The theatre was packed with rowdy, out-of-control teenagers. Before the movie even started, someone threw a half-full cup of Coke at the stage. The pop trickled down the length of the screen and left a stain for the duration of the film.

Witness riveted me to such a degree that I was able to block out most of the teenage chaos around us. At the end of the film, while Ford is fighting it out in a grain silo with Danny Glover, I was violently snapped out of the movie magic. Some older kid in the seat behind me shoved a jumbo-size popcorn box over my head, and held it down with both hands while I struggled madly to free myself. The buttery grease of the popcorn box mashed into my hair and ran down my face, streaking my glasses. I completely missed the climax of the movie while the boys behind me snickered savagely. I stripped the greasy popcorn box off just as the usher's flashlight beam swept across us. The credits of *Witness* rolled up the pop-stained screen in front of me. I whipped my head around to see who had inflicted this latest injustice upon me: three older dudes in hockey jackets, laughing as they made their way up the aisle.

Chris Monahan, who hadn't noticed my popcorn box distress until it was too late, leaned over to me and said in a confident, low voice, "Let's go get those assholes." What did that mean? I struggled to my feet and crutched along behind him up the aisle. The bullies were hanging around guffawing out in front of the theatre. They were jocks, a year or two older than we were, with close-cropped haircuts, blue jeans and white runners. Chris Monahan walked straight up to the popcorn box offender, grabbed him by his hockey jacket with one hand, and slammed him up against the outside brick wall of the theatre. Chris used his other hand to repeatedly punch the popcorn box offender in the face.

My jaw hung open at the sight of it. No one had ever stood up for me before. Chris let go and the jock crumpled to the sidewalk, his hockey jacket stained with blood spurting from his nose. Chris then turned his attention to the other two, who were quickly backing off. This was the scene Dad arrived to as he pulled up in our little green Fiat to pick me up. We gave the valiant Chris Monahan a ride home from the theatre that day, and that's when Dad figured out that Chris's dad was ex-Vancouver Canuck Garry Monahan.

Garry "Mondo" Monahan was a swashbuckling, handsome 1970s-era Canucks forward with bushy sideburns, long brown hair and a Burt Reynolds moustache that made all the puck bunnies swoon. Mondo provided one of the few bright moments in the Canucks' bleak first decade. Backed by the well-travelled, eccentric all-star goalie Gary "Suitcase" Smith, the Vancouver Canucks made the playoffs for the first time in their history in the 1974–75 season. Unfortunately, they had to face the fabulous Montreal Canadiens. The Vegas odds were 50–1 that the Canucks would not win even a single game against the Canadiens. After being routed 6–2 in Game 1, the Canucks held their own in Game 2, a tightly contested 1–1 tie that lasted well into the third period. That's when handsome Garry Monahan streaked down the wing and whipped a high shot toward legendary Montreal goalie Ken "The Thinker" Dryden.

Dryden stopped the shot, juggling the puck in the air with his glove. But then another Montreal player slammed into him, knocking the puck loose. The puck had just enough forward momentum to cross the goal line. Because the referee never blew his whistle when Dryden first stopped the shot, the goal counted. The Canucks won their first-ever playoff game against the best team in hockey thanks to the winning goal by Mondo. The Canucks would return to a heroes' welcome in Vancouver, but lost the next three games to end their first-ever playoff appearance. The goal was special to Garry Monahan for a few reasons, one being that he had originally been selected by the Montreal Canadiens in the very first amateur hockey draft, in 1963, making him the answer to a trivia question forever more: he was the first-ever draft pick in NHL history. Later in his career, Monahan also added the historic bookend of being the last-ever player to fight Bobby Orr, just before Orr retired as a Chicago Black Hawk. A framed picture of the fight hung above the Monahans' living room fireplace for years.

ONE FRIDAY MORNING at school, future MLA Rob Fleming rushed up to me in the hall as I hobbled along on my crutches. "My big brother says Letterman read *your letter* out on his show last night! My brother tapes it every night so I have the VHS copy in my locker!"

I was stunned. I had completely forgotten about the letter Mom mailed to David Letterman. My friends and I gathered at lunch hour in the history classroom that came complete with a top-loader VCR. I leaned forward on my crutches, in gape-mouthed wonderment as David Letterman on NBC Television from 30 Rockefeller Plaza in New York City read out *my letter* on his "Viewer Mail" segment, answering my query about whether or not he had ever been mugged in New York City. His answer came in the form of a ridiculous dream sequence skit with bandleader Paul Shaffer that riffed on the mugging scene from the hit movie of the moment, *Crocodile Dundee*.

After the skit, David Letterman looked into the camera and thanked "Grant Lawrence from West Vancouver, BC, Canada" for the letter. Everyone in the classroom looked at me in shock. We had to give the tape back to Rob's older brother immediately, so that noon-hour history classroom top-loader viewing marked the one and only time I've ever seen my "Viewer Mail" episode of *Late Night with David Letterman*. The news spread quickly through the school that a grade nine kid named Grant Lawrence had his letter read out by David Letterman. My stock was slowly rising.

THANKS TO THE tutelage of a Desolation Sound hermit named Russell Letawsky, I was getting more and more into rock 'n' roll music, an interest shared passionately with my new group of friends. Although I loved Russell's music of the 1950s and '60s best, within our group we listened to anything and everything on our newly purchased portable Sony Walkmans, constantly exchanging homemade tapes of sounds new and old. Together as a group, we attended our first-ever stadium rock concert: ZZ Top at the Pacific Coliseum, the same place where the Canucks played. Chris Monahan defended me against a sea of drunk and stoned bangers who were dangerously fascinated by my casts and crutches. Because my casts were straight-legged, I had to stretch my legs out to the side and crane my head around to watch the outrageously awesome concert. Mom picked us up in the little green Fiat in the middle of the banger aftermath melee. We emerged from billowing clouds of second-hand pot smoke wearing fake ZZ Top beards and wide grins.

I barely saw Buck anymore and ignored him when I did. He was spending less and less time at school for sports-related reasons, but I still saw some of his jock buddies around in various classes. One was woodwork, a "shop" class held in the depths of the school's basement. Buck and his jock buddies were beginning to show an interest in music as well, and had observed me crutching along the halls with my bright yellow, portable Sony Walkman attached to my belt, my headphones constantly bleeding out tinny, up-tempo beats as I struggled by.

I switched off the high-pitch wail of the woodwork shop band saw, removed my safety goggles and turned to find "Gooch," one of Buck's gigantic jock buddies, looming over me. Gooch was a Shrek-shaped hillbilly originally from the small town of Horsefly, BC. Gooch's arms, shoulders and belly were so large that he barely fit into his hockey jacket and had to wear sweatpants because he couldn't fit into jeans. He had a mullet that was extremely short on top and long and greasy down the back. Hockey and pleasing Buck seemed to be all he knew or cared about. Through rotting teeth he uttered under his breath, "Gimme some of those cassette tapes you listen to, *WIMP*." I laughed out loud with surprise, astounded that my taste in music might actually be something a jock would covet.

His huge mottled paw reached out and snatched my Walkman from its clip on my belt. I grabbed at it, but he held it aloft over my head, twisting his massive torso away from me. He rudely ejected my favourite cassette tape, Chuck Berry's brilliant greatest hits compilation called *The Great Twenty-Eight.*

"No! Give it back, now!" I let my crutches fall to my sides as I reached up and grabbed onto his hockey jacket. He dragged me along as he started to walk away from my assigned woodworking station. He turned, and with the quickness of a grizzly, picked me up off my feet, lifted me high in the air, spun me around, and squeezed the air from my lungs with both arms in a tight bear hug.

Then he dropped me like a fencepost, straight down, slamming me onto the soles of my Chuck Taylors. I screamed as I felt the straight leg casts slamming downward with the force, both knees exploding in agony as if the rusty, jagged saw blades had shredded deeply into both joints. I collapsed onto the sawdust-covered floor of the woodshop and convulsed in pain.

Shop class was usually a pretty laid-back hour of the day. The teachers were always relaxed, and our woodwork teacher would often leave us alone for long stretches of time. Hence, shop classes in our high school, be they woodwork, auto repair or metalwork, attracted all sorts of misfits, some actually seeking knowledge on how to work with with their hands, others looking for an easy hour or two where they could shoot the shit and do as little as possible.

One such miscreant in our woodwork class was a sinewy punk rock skinhead known as "Roger the Dodger." He had a shiny, shaved head and wore black wraparound shades, skin-tight black jeans, knee-high, tightly laced combat boots and white undershirts. When "Gooch" bear-hugged me and dropped me on the woodshop floor as if I was a dead salmon, Roger the Dodger saw the whole thing and sprang forward like an uncoiled cobra.

While tinny music blasted from Roger's own headphones, he leapt to my workstation and in one motion reached up and slapped Gooch across his wide, pimpled face. The palm of Roger the Dodger's hand meeting Gooch's formidable cheek sounded like the crack of a pistol. "LEAVE THE KID ALONE, MOTHERFUCKER!" shrieked Roger the Dodger over the volume of his Walkman.

Mr. Pollen, our tiny chipmunk of a woodwork teacher appeared from his rear office. "By Jove! What the devil is going on here?" he chirped, finding me on the ground groaning in pain, and Gooch rubbing his face, advancing on Roger.

"THIS STUPID MOTHERFUCKER JUST PILEDRIVED TINY TIM HERE INTO THE FUCKIN' FLOOR!"

Ignoring Roger the Dodger's profanity, our woodwork teacher went straight up to Gooch. "You did what? Did you harm this boy?"

Gooch looked down guiltily. "I didn't mean to hurt him, we were just messing around."

"BULLSHIT!" Roger the Dodger roared, yanking his headphones from his ears. "THE MEATHEAD ATTACKED THE KID AND STOLE HIS TAPE." I was amazed that Roger the Dodger wasn't hesitating to crack the code, ratting on Gooch in front of the whole woodwork class of mixed grades and cliques. Roger the Dodger, fists balled and seething, was truly fearless. From my perspective, as I struggled to my feet from the sawdust-covered floor, he looked a lot like Tiger Williams.

Mr. Pollen reached up and grabbed Gooch by his hockey jacket. "Give me the cassette this instant," he demanded. When Gooch produced it, the woodwork teacher slammed it down at my workstation, and then pushed Gooch in the direction of the door. "I want you to go up to the principal's office and explain to him why you felt the need to attack a boy a quarter of your size—on crutches no less—and steal his belongings. Now get OUT!"

The rest of our ragtag woodwork class broke into cheers while Roger the Dodger handed me my crutches. He slipped his headphones back on. Grimacing, I straightened myself up. "Thanks," I replied meekly, ". . . what are you listening to?"

"THE RAMONES!" Roger the Dodger shouted, a maniacal grin crossing his face as he raised his hand in a devil-horned salute.

MY NEW FRIENDSHIPS brought on introductions to all sorts of other interesting people throughout the grades: mods, punks, goths, new wavers, geeks, freaks, friendly bangers and one particular high-strung, intensely creative dork who called himself Nardwuar the Human Serviette. Nardwuar was small and wiry, with a shock of black hair and an incredibly friendly smile. He was also extremely hairy for a high school student, his body covered in thick, dark hair like the pelt of an otter. He loved all sorts of insurgent music, never touched booze or drugs, was extremely intelligent, and had an encyclopedic memory that could sponge up any information his brain came in contact with. He was a long-distance track runner who always came in last, and had a high-pitched voice that climbed to glass-shattering heights when he got excited, which was often.

Nardwuar was also the lead singer of the coolest band in our high school: The Evaporators, a hip foursome that specialized in freaked-out garage, surf and punk rock. They were like a cross between the Standells and the Flaming Lips. Nardwuar took a passionate interest in student leadership, and in his final year of grade twelve he earned the student council presidency because no one else bothered to run. Nardwuar turned out to be an unlikely unifying figure to all of us. While Nardwuar was at the helm of student council, he decided to forego the regular canned disco music that was a staple at our dances and instead brought over all the insurgent, live alternative bands, arts and culture that we artistic weirdoes talked about all lunch hour long, from downtown Vancouver straight onto the stage of our gymnasium in very suburban West Vancouver.

Back in elementary school Nardwuar went by his given name of John, but by his early years of high school he and his weird friend Gary created a mash-up of sounds and letters they would yell at people, to scare them away: "NARRRAARRR! NARWARR! NARDWUAR!" In the later years of high school he took keen notice that his rock 'n' roll heroes—Lux Interior from the Cramps, Joey Shithead from D.O.A., Jello Biafra from the Dead Kennedys—all had ultra-cool noms de punk, and so he expanded it to Nardwuar "The Human Fly" (after the Cramps song of the same name). But while eating a bowl of clam chowder in Bellingham, Washington, while on a daytrip across the US border with his mom, chowder fatefully rolled down his chin. He asked the American waitress for a serviette. She had no idea what Nardwuar was talking about. A light bulb of Canadian nationalist linguistic identity went off in Nardwuar's noggin, and Nardwuar the Human Serviette was born. Nardwuar took me under his hairy wing and we became good friends.

Nardwuar the Human Serviette, our high school class president, lead singer of the Evaporators, and a great friend who helped me survive high school. Nardwuar would go on to become a legendary interviewer of epic proportions, pepper-spraying his deeply researched questions at everyone from Canadian prime ministers, including Jean Chrétien and Pierre Elliott Trudeau, to celebrities, rappers, hip hop musicians and rock stars like Kurt Cobain and Marilyn Manson, and even hockey figures like Don Cherry and Felix "the Cat" Potvin.

Nardwuar's cousin was former NHL player Eric "Elbows" Nesterenko, who helped the Blackhawks storm to Stanley Cup victory in 1961. Just as I befriended Nardwuar, Nesterenko had starred as Rob Lowe's dad in the Hollywood hockey movie *Youngblood*. I was impressed. Nardwuar noted how much I was into music, and immediately encouraged me to get involved with the original music going on in our high school. Desperately seeking an artistic outlet and escape, I readily dove in. My friend Nick Thomas shared many of my musical tastes and together we formed our own band to be just like Nardwuar and the Evaporators. After years of stumbling through dark valleys of loneliness, doubt and despair, I had finally found my tribe, *my team*. Music became my life, and from music I found within myself what I had lacked throughout my life

99

thus far: true confidence. Eventually, that confidence would lead to wild egotism, self-centredness and insensitivity, but in high school I needed anything I could get to survive, and rock 'n' roll was the razor's edge.

13

LET'S WRECK
THE PARTY

INALLY, MY KNEES recovered from the surgery. I was able to throw my crutches aside and have the straight leg casts taken off. They were removed at the casting clinic at the hospital by a handheld miniature power saw that cut through the plaster, sending clouds of months-old, sweat-encrusted dust up into my face. When the technician pulled the casts away from my legs, various objects that had fallen into the casts and been wedged between my skin and the gauze wrapping for months were finally liberated, clattering to the clinic's linoleum floor: loose change, bus transfers, dried gum and one of Mom's knitting needles I had used to scratch an itch and stuck too far inside to retrieve.

My legs were heinous twigs covered in matted hair. They were never meaty to begin with, but after months of being trapped within plaster casts with no movement, they now resembled the legs of a newborn fawn. My knees themselves looked terrible, with long, matching, ugly purple scars along the inner edge of each kneecap where the surgical incisions had been made. Once Dr. McNeill pulled out any black stitches that hadn't fallen out or

rubbed their way off, the remaining purple lumps looked like cen-
tipedes trapped just beneath my skin.

Dr. McNeill helped me to my feet. I wobbled immediately,
loose-limbed and weak, grabbing hold of Dr. McNeill's brick of
a shoulder while trying to remember how to walk. Dr. McNeill
explained that in order for his surgery to be effective in the long
term, the hardest part began with me, right then and there, in the
form of a rigorous rehabilitation regime. I nodded affirmatively to
everything he said, barely listening. I promised I'd do all his prescribed exercises, thanked him for his care and told him I would
go straight to the physiotherapist across the street from the hospital. Instead, with lazy, teenaged abandon for my own health
and well-being, I hardly did any of the exercises prescribed by Dr.
McNeill. Exercise was for jocks! I was an artist, and artists didn't
work out, they suffered, and from their suffering, they created art.
I would eventually and very painfully pay dearly, over and over, for
ignoring Dr. McNeill's orders.

While I slowly emerged from many years lost in a fog of failure, so too did the Vancouver Canucks. Losses had been stacked
upon losses, losing seasons upon losing seasons, and little "King"
Richard Brodeur was in the net for much of it. The team had not
won a single playoff series since the 1982 playoff run and changes
needed to be made. The first to go was the ridiculous "flying V"
jersey, still the laughingstock of the league. It was replaced by
another strange logo that had first appeared as a shoulder patch
on the "flying V" jersey: a futuristic, orange and black circular
design that featured the word *Canucks* embedded into a skate that
was rushing very quickly . . . downhill. As soon as I started seeing
the design on TV when Dad watched the games at home, I asked,
"Isn't . . . going downhill considered a bad thing?"

"Um . . . yes," Dad answered with a sigh of resignation all too
familiar to Canucks fans. Like all Canucks jerseys, its unveil-
ing received a widely mixed reaction from the fashion-fickle
West Coast fans. The new logo immediately earned unflattering

nicknames like "plate of spaghetti," "waffle iron" and "dog's breakfast." Thankfully, although the jersey depicted the skate rapidly doing otherwise, the Canucks were slowly headed uphill.

A new threesome would soon emerge to lead the Canucks to their greatest achievements yet. The first player of the power trifecta to arrive was a stand-up goalie named "Captain" Kirk McLean (he was never team captain; the nickname was just a shout out to *Star Trek*). In 1987, new general manager Pat Quinn made a trade with the New Jersey Devils that brought the calm, young goaltender to town. McLean immediately impressed by playing a strong style that was consistent, steady and reliable, something the team had sorely lacked as the much-adored King Richard got older and older. At the end of the season in which he arrived, Captain Kirk took over between the pipes as Vancouver's new number one goaltender; King Richard was finally dethroned, unceremoniously shipped to the Hartford Whalers, where the King played just six more games before he retired. The trade was bittersweet for Canucks fans. Although they loved the King and everything he did for the team, fans loved one thing more: winning.

The next member of the good-news trio was a tall, lanky, always-smiling eighteen-year-old draft pick from Medicine Hat, Alberta, named Trevor Linden, who wore #16. Trevor Linden would go on to become arguably the most important and popular player in the history of the Canucks. His impact was immediate, scoring thirty goals in his rookie season. At age twenty-one he was made captain of the team shortly after Steamer retired, making him one of the youngest captains in league history. Unlike the rough-and-tumble, lunch-bucket Canucks of the early 1980s, Linden represented a wholesome and positive change. He was an instantly trustworthy, born leader with a squeaky clean, almost-nerdy boy-next-door demeanour. He managed to complement his Richie Cunningham image with a tireless, farm-boy work ethic on the ice that fans adored. Though lean, he could pack a heavy bodycheck and occasionally, if unsuccessfully, fought when he had to. Linden continued to rack up the goals while his new best friend, Captain Kirk, stacked the pads and the wins. In his first season, 1988–89, the team made it back into the playoffs for the first time in years, losing a gruelling, blood-soaked seven-game series to Trevor Linden's bad boy rookie counterpart: Theo Fleury and his Calgary Flames, who would go on to win the Stanley Cup that year.

Although I felt my life had been saved by rock 'n' roll, I had an awareness of what was going on with the Canucks through Dad's passionate ravings at our family dinner table and by the steady rise of #16 Canucks T-shirts streaming down our school's hallways. Trevor also upped the sex appeal of the Canucks for the first time in a long time. It is rumoured that so many older women started prowling after the Canucks in bars and clubs, that the players came up with the term "cougar" one day after practice, meaning an older woman sexually preying on a younger man. "Cougar" would eventually become common slang throughout North America.

In the meantime, Nick and I had formed a band called the Smugglers. Nardwuar and his Evaporators had graduated and the Smugglers had inherited the mantle as coolest band in the school. We played all the dances and live music events, dressed up in our coastal mythology costumes of dock-worker pea jackets, rubber boots, toques and black sunglasses—what we thought was the image of West Coast rock 'n' roll cool. Many of our fellow students were big fans. We were the cocks of the walk, finally attracting bona fide attention from girls.

I was still very much in love with Lizzy, who over the years had gone through a few alpha-male boyfriends, but she still had zero romantic interest in me. My very first girlfriend was Sheena, a rocker chick a year older than I was who sometimes wore an old Tiger Williams jersey under her red-and-black checkered Mackinaw jacket. She had long blonde hair with dyed purple streaks, and wore her torn jeans tucked into motorcycle boots. Sheena hung

One of the first promotional photos of my band, the Smugglers, oddly enough taken at the West Vancouver Ice Arena, a place we would otherwise rarely set foot in. For this photo shoot, we snuck in late at night after the hockey games were over and bribed the Zamboni driver with a six-pack of Black Label to let us out on the ice with our dinghy. L–R: Paul Preminger, Nick Thomas, David Carswell, Grant Lawrence, Adam Woodall.

out in the smoke hole every day with the skids and bangers, chain-smoking Export "A" Lights.

If I wasn't the lead singer in the most popular band in high school I doubt she would have even exhaled smoke in my direction, but she loved rock 'n' roll. I had never come close to having a girlfriend in six years of high school, so I was pretty excited to cement our relationship. Our status was decidedly one-sided. While I considered her my first girlfriend, I was definitely not Sheena's first boyfriend—nor, I deeply feared, was our relationship even remotely monogamous. This was proven time and time again when I would arrive to meet her at a raging West Vancouver teen party to find her passionately making out—or worse—with myriad manimals from my high school. She told me it came down to the fact that she disagreed with the word "boyfriend." I wasn't quite sure how a relationship was supposed to work, but Sheena always came back to me, often in the form of tapping on my bedroom window very late at night. I lost my virginity to Sheena. As I would eventually find out, most of my other friends did too.

On a wet and miserable winter night, I was limping along a dark lane on my way to another teenage house party to meet Sheena, praying I wouldn't arrive to find her tongue implanted deeply in some random banger's mouth. I was dressed as cool as I could be, mostly in my Smugglers wardrobe of tight black jeans, skinny black tie and pointy black Beatle boots, with the added twist of a ridiculously large Clint Eastwood–style woollen poncho and Davy Crockett–style coonskin cap. The rain poured down in sheets. Water bounced off the shiny wet pavement, slowly soaking my Beatle boots with each soggy step. Rain dripped off my failed attempt at a long, garage rock–style mushroom haircut and formed beads on the lenses of my John Lennon granny glasses. Head down, I trudged on, trying to get to the party as quickly as I could.

From behind me I heard the rumble of a muffler with holes punched in it for that very intentional and intimidating sound effect. The cascading rain in front of me became illuminated like a curtain of liquid silver in the high beams of a car approaching quickly from behind. I stepped off to the side of the road to let the car pass. A dark 1970s-era Chevy Nova rumbled past and jerked to a stop ten feet in front of me. I was hoping it was someone from school, maybe even Sheena with some friends, offering me a lift to the party. The doors on either side of the muscle car swung open. D.O.A.'s "Fucked Up Ronnie" blasted forth momentarily until the ignition was turned off. Two bulky figures emerged. "Where are you headed, *hippie*?"

Two muscular skinheads approached me in the pouring rain. Both wore tightly laced Doc Martens boots, rolled-up blue jeans and puffy black bomber jackets; one had a shaved head, the other a close-cropped mohawk. Both had graduated from our school a couple years earlier. The one with the mohawk was Angus "The Anvil" McFadden, a notorious troublemaker who was well over six feet tall with shoulders like cinder blocks and the chest of a wine barrel. The anvil was his fist. He was an extremely rare specimen: a counter-culturist who actually stuck with playing hockey through his teens, a punk among jocks, mostly because he was really good at it. He would make a formidable name for himself as a powerful centre in junior hockey before his shoulders gave out.

"Hey, guys." I tried to sound as friendly, welcoming and confident as I could, as though seeing two skinheads get out of their car on a desolate, dark lane in the pouring rain was a good thing. My teeth began to chatter as Angus the Anvil shoved me toward his chum.

"I'm friends with Roger the Dodger," I blurted out, hoping the punk rock skinhead allegiance stretched as far as these two.

Angus belched. His breath reeked of hard liquor. "Roger the Dodger is *a fucking idiot*. Got any booze on you?"

"N-n-n-o," I lied through my chattering teeth. Before I left home for the party, I had raided our fridge, borrowing three of Mom's Coors Light Silver Bullets and slipping them into the inside pockets of my poncho.

"Oh really?" Angus spat back. Angus yanked me toward him and roughly patted me down. He instantly found the beer, pulling back my poncho and yanking out the cans.

"No booze, eh?" Without my even being able to see him do it, he punched me straight and hard in the stomach. I doubled over and gasped for air, unable to breathe, wondering if I ever would again, my eyes bulging behind my glasses. His skinhead friend put his Doc Martens boot up to my hip and kicked me to the ground. I lay in the fetal position in the pelting rain, hands on my tummy, choking for oxygen. Angus the Anvil and his buddy each cracked a Coors Silver Bullet as they climbed back into their car. D.O.A. blasted forth again while they burned rubber with a loud screech on the wet asphalt as they peeled away.

After lying on the ground for what seemed like a pathetically long time, I realized my breath had returned to normal. I struggled to my feet, my stomach aching, poncho soaking wet, confidence shattered. Standing in the gushing November rain, I

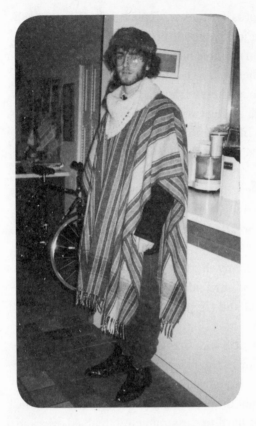

I desperately tried to look cool in my Clint Eastwood–inspired poncho, John Lennon–inspired glasses, John Wayne–inspired coonskin cap, and Gruesomes-inspired tight black jeans and Beatle boots. This look did not go over well with a couple of skinheads on the prowl on a dark and rainy night.

started to cry. In mere seconds my long built-up coolness had been stripped down to the quivering nerdiness I had tried so hard to leave behind. I was immediately reduced from a rock 'n' roll king-pin back to a stuttering, teeth-chattering invalid. Buck had been right all along; I was a *WIMP*. My instincts told me to turn and go home, to retreat, to surrender to the already-miserable night that the skinheads had turned into a hideous reminder of past failures. And then I thought of Sheena, who I hoped and imagined would be waiting for me to show up, worried about me, so I kept walking in the direction of the party, still twenty minutes away.

The rain stopped as I eventually approached the caterwauling teen party. Cars lined either side of the street, the wet pavement littered with beer cans and debris. Kids clustered in groups against cars and fences, smoking, as I made my way up the driveway to the house. The Chevy Nova was parked at an entitled and obnoxious angle at the top of the driveway, the surrounding teenagers knowing not to dare lean on *that* car. Inside, the party was raging at full tilt, the Doors' honkin' harmonica rocker "Roadhouse Blues" blaring out of the living room stereo, kids drinking everywhere. Nick spotted me from the living room and rushed up to me, handing me a warm can of Black Label beer. "What happened to you?" he asked, looking me up and down as I stood dripping in the entrance foyer of the house.

"Have you seen Sheena?"

"Um yeah, I think she's down in the basement... but I don't think you want to go down there." I pushed by Nick and other random partiers to the basement door. Opening it, "Roadhouse Blues" cacophonously bled into the Cro-Mags' "Don't Tread on Me," which blasted up from the darkened basement rec room.

"Wait!" warned Nick. At the top of the basement stairs hung a veil of beads just like the entrance to Greg Brady's bedroom on *The Brady Bunch*. I descended into the darkness with Nick behind me, both of us coming to a stop on a landing halfway down the stairs. Only the soft light of an O'Keefe's Extra Old Stock wall lamp and a bubble hockey game left on in the middle of the room illuminated the basement rec room. It took a moment for my eyes to adjust to the light.

On the shag carpet floor, in a shaft of bubble-hockey light, was the hulking frame of Angus "The Anvil" McFadden. His jeans were around his ankles, but he was still wearing his nylon bomber jacket. Wrapped around his waist were Sheena's bare legs, her ankles locked together. I heard her familiar moans of pleasure as her fingers were clawing passionately at Angus's broad shoulders. Sheena looked like she was wearing her Tiger Williams jersey and nothing else. Nick and I stared down from the staircase landing in shock, our presence shielded by darkness and the Cro-Mags.

109

Angus's white bare bum pumped up and down with blunt, brute force, like a jackhammer trying to bust concrete.

We stared for a few exceptionally depressing moments, not being able to take our eyes off the raw sexual spectacle, and then slowly retreated back up the stairs. Neither Sheena nor Angus the Anvil ever knew we were there. I stood in a state of dejection in the middle of the throbbing teen party. The punk who mugged and assaulted me was now having sex with my girlfriend, and I couldn't do anything about it. As soon as I was able to rid my life of one bully, another seemed to step right in, as if coming off an assembly line of hockey thugs.

Sheena eventually left the party with me that night, but as we walked back down the lane in the fall mist, I told her that I finally agreed with her, that I too was having a hard time wrapping my head around the concept of the word "boyfriend." Sheena never admitted to her rec room rendezvous with Angus the Anvil, and I couldn't summon the courage to bring it up. I suggested that maybe we should break up. Sheena laughed, lit up a cigarette and looked at me with her devilishly sexy eyes. She exhaled in my face. "Break up from what?"

14

TOTAL
GOOMBAH!

GRADE TWELVE FINALLY came to a close. I was able to leave high school behind me forever. I truly hoped that would also include never seeing the likes of people like Buck, Gooch, Psycho and Angus the Anvil ever again in my entire life. I had managed to successfully avoid gym class for years due to perpetual notes from Dr. McNeill, and spent way more time working on the simmering career of the Smugglers than I ever spent on any of my subjects. But I had survived. I had endured the social rite of passage known as secondary school. I had limped into it a weak, four-eyed lamb, and had emerged six years later still limping but alive and stronger for it. And I was the lead singer of a successful band that was already touring and making records.

As the Smugglers' reputation grew for being an over-the-top party band, we became regular, sought-after entertainment at university and college campus pubs, bars, halls, student union buildings and fields across North America. Dad wasn't impressed with my post-secondary plan when I'd explain it to him over terse family dinners. Sometimes he'd change the subject to hockey.

A favourite hockey topic Dad loved to both rant and marvel at was the rapidly escalating player salaries in the NHL. That season, Dad explained excitedly that Trevor Linden would earn $700,000.00 for captaining the Canucks. Dad emphasized every syllable of the huge number with a jab of his index finger across the table toward me. I couldn't tell if he was impressed or outraged at Linden's paycheque. It was a far cry greater than anything I could ever expect to make in the Smugglers. I was playing university bars for $1,000 a night that was split between five guys after paying for gas and a litany of other expenses. But the university gigs paid off in other ways.

Our guitarist Nick had sandy brown hair and blue eyes, and was stocky and muscular, an unusual body type in rock 'n' roll. The common indie-rock physical stereotype was sickly, skinny, pale and hunched over, like a coughing question mark, a look I was working to perfection with glasses and a ridiculous afro. (In an attempt to grow my hair long like Bobby Beaton of the Gruesomes, it grew outward instead, causing me to look like a cross between Woody Allen and Jimi Hendrix for most of my late teens and early twenties.) Nick was also charming and flirtatious, and was already the band's designated sex symbol amongst our fans. When he began to receive favourable physical comparisons to a brand new rookie phenomenon on the Vancouver Canucks, his resident Smugglers heartthrob status went top shelf. Hot university girls fawned over Nick, comparing him to Pavel Bure, a red-hot new Canuck who would quickly become known as the "Russian Rocket" because of his explosive speed.

Pavel "The Russian Rocket" Bure was the last piece of the trifecta to join Trevor Linden and Kirk McLean, replacing my previous favourites of Brodeur, Smyl and Williams. Wearing #10, no player in a Canucks jersey before or since has brought the crowd out of their seats, as if they had all collectively sat on tacks, like the Russian Rocket. Bure had explosive, blinding, reckless speed, which allowed him to streak away easily from any opposing player in the NHL. He could split a defence pairing like Moses on skates. He could weave through entire teams like a rabbit in a minefield He could score goals like Alex P. Keaton aced exams. Kirk McLean commented that he never saw another player happier to score goals than Bure, known not only for his non-stop scoring but also his celebrations, throwing his arms up wildly in the air, fully extended, still skating at speed, sometimes dropping to his knees and pumping his fists, always with a huge smile. Pavel Bure was the Vancouver Canucks' first genuine superstar.

Nick scored on many a five-hole with his trusty Sherwood as a result of the flurry of complimentary comparisons he received regarding his physical resemblance to the Russian Rocket. Though Nick may have looked the most like a Canuck, it was our other guitarist David Carswell who was the resident hockey fanatic in our band. While I was focused entirely on running the band and by knee-jerk habit still fended off anything to do with what I perceived as jock culture, Dave always made sure the very moment we arrived at the club we were playing that night, no matter where it happened to be, that the ponytailed soundman flip on a fuzzy television screen at the bar to try to find the Canucks game. There was typically nothing to do but sit around for hours in these stinky beer-soaked taverns waiting for sound checks and cardboard pizza dinners, so Dave would fill the void cheering for the Canucks. We'd often be paired up on tour with American bands, and Dave would be constantly trying to convert new fans to the game of hockey and the fledgling Canucks army. He did a pretty good job, too. Tacoma grunge-punk band Seaweed became big fans, as did country singer Neko Case, who dated Dave for years before she became a Grammy-nominated star. (Neko cheers for the Canucks to this day.)

Our bassist, Beez, was a conflicted case. He was from the hockey heartland of rural Ontario, but was forbidden to play the game at an early age by his mother. She thought of Beez as a fragile, special child. Instead of hockey, she enrolled Beez in figure skating. Even we anti-jock rock 'n' rollers scoffed at hearing this story in the van.

But shield him though she tried, Beez's mom couldn't completely fend off hockey's influence. Beez's real name was Kevin Beesley, but like every other kid in his entire hometown of Kleinburg, Ontario, his nickname became a shortened form of his last name, something derived directly from the omnipresent hockey culture in Ontario. Beez and his friends were art-house, rockabilly punks, but they still called each other "Ush," "Shy," "Trugs" and "Beez." The popular nicknaming style of shortening surnames wasn't as prevalent in BC, but as soon as I met Beez, shortly after he moved to Vancouver, he started calling me "G," my first-ever nickname that wasn't an insult thrown down from on high by a bully.

The Smugglers' first shuddering bodycheck of hockey and rock 'n' roll was the year we did an entire Canadian tour with the Hanson Brothers, a band based purely in violent, tongue-in-cheek, lowbrow hockey lore. They were a "puck rock" side project of Victoria, BC's successful hardcore punk band NoMeansNo, but instead of the mind-blowingly complicated eleven-minute jazz-punk-politico-hardcore opuses NoMeansNo was famous for, the Hanson Brothers played fast, catchy, simple, loud Ramones-style pop-punk tunes about hockey. They named themselves after the fictitious goon line, known for their taped glasses and tinfoil-wrapped fists, in *Slapshot*, the be-all-and-end-all greatest hockey movie of all time starring Paul Newman.

This puck rock version of the Hanson Brothers copped the role perfectly, trading hockey sticks for guitars. They wore Ramones-style leather jackets, often over obscure, defunct minor league hockey team jerseys they found at Value Village. "Johnny Hanson," the lead singer, wore a backward Canucks baseball cap, black-framed glasses with white tape holding them together at the nose bridge, and a Victoria Cougars jersey, while bassist "Robbie Hanson" wore an old-school goalie mask with the word DUMB painted in black across the forehead. "Tommy Hanson," the guitarist, also wore glasses, counted in the songs with a quick Ramones-style "one-two-three-four!" and would often have gobs of drool hanging

The Hanson Brothers were the catchy, simple, loud and fast Ramones-style "puck rock" alter-egos of NoMeansNo. When the Smugglers toured across Canada with the Hanson Brothers during the Stanley Cup playoffs, it was the first time I had ever seen hockey fans and alternative music fans happily coexist (most of the time), something I previously thought impossible. L–R: Lead singer Johnny Hanson rocking out with brother and bassist, Robbie Hanson. PAUL CLARKE PHOTO

from his lower lip as they played. They told audiences they were from Cold Lake, Alberta.

The Hanson Brothers had a rapid-fire repertoire of their own hockey songs that included "Danielle (She Don't Care About Hockey)," "Rink Rat" and "(He Looked a Lot Like) Tiger Williams." The Hanson Brothers loved Tiger Williams so much that they even started a petition to get #22 into the Hockey Hall of Fame. They felt that since fighting was an accepted part of the game, and Tiger Williams was the all-time leader for penalty minutes in the NHL, he should be honoured like the rest of the all-time goals and assists leaders found in the Hall. The petition accumulated more and more signatures each night at the bands' merchandise table. Eventually, the petition containing thousands of scrawled signatures was mailed to Don Cherry of *Hockey Night in Canada* and to

115

the Hockey Hall of Fame. Needless to say, the petition didn't have the desired effect.

Strategically, it was often the kiss of death for a Canadian band to tour across Canada during the spring, when musicians were forced to face off against playoff hockey. If one's team was in the Stanley Cup playoffs between April and June, even the most staunchly devoted rock 'n' roll fan would skip a gig without a second thought so as to not miss a second of the game. The Hanson Brothers stared that basic logic down like Tiger Williams on a lightweight winger, and had planned their cross-country tour exactly for that time of year on purpose. They would provide the hockey party at the bar *after* the big game, and the Smugglers would ride their black leather coattails and not have to play to empty rooms. Unless games went deep into overtime, our concerts with them were usually planned to begin immediately following the games, as amped-up fans spilled onto the streets of Canadian cities looking for somewhere to celebrate a delirious victory, or distract themselves from a devastating loss.

It all seemed like a win-win situation, but I was fearful of what kind of fans would show up. Music was my escape, the very bastion of culture I had chosen to take me as far away as I could from the jocks and the meatheads and the violence. But with the ironclad credibility of the "featuring members of NoMeansNo" branding association following the Hanson Brothers everywhere they went, the fans followed. We quickly figured out that it was an opportunity to play in front of a lot of people, no matter what portion of the crowd might be meatheads.

The gigs were packed from coast to coast with a surprising mixture of punk rockers and hockey fans: two tremendously different sects I had hardly seen get along with the *rare* exception of Angus "The Anvil" McFadden. I was particularly amazed at how much social harmony existed at the gigs each night. The Hanson Brothers in their sweat-stained leather jackets, old hockey jerseys and method acting rock 'n' roll goonery made it acceptable for punk rockers to celebrate a sport and a culture many loved deeply in their Canadian core, but were repelled from for the same reasons I was: bullying, forced competition and machismo. On a few occasions the frothing pit in front of the stage at the gigs got ugly, resembling more of a bench-clearing brawl than a dance floor, but more often than not it was the punks who were the provocateurs, not the jocks. We noticed that the jocks were more often cautious in the foreign surroundings: the black cinder-block-walled punk rock bar was a long way from the safety of the white cinder-block-walled rink. But for the most part, everyone got along, enjoying the fist-pumping rock 'n' roll—Ramones and Angry Samoans T-shirts side by side with Oilers and Jets jerseys along the front of the stage.

Sitting at the bar waiting for sound check to begin, I'd have conversations about sports and hockey with Johnny Hanson. I told him I hadn't really been able to enjoy hockey since I was a child. I told him I had chosen rock 'n' roll as the *alternative*, and that what I had seen on the tour was a huge surprise to me. That's when Johnny turned into part bar-stool philosopher and part rock 'n' roll Don Cherry. He told me that there really wasn't much difference between a great hockey team and a great band. For both to perform well, the members have to be completely in sync with each other. If one member of the band is playing out of time, it doesn't work; same thing as a hockey team skating up ice and a player going offside—the play is dead.

Johnny said even the way players line up on the ice is like a rock band on stage. The goalie is like the drummer, using all four limbs to keep everything humming along. The defenceman is just like the bassist holding down the back end, locked in with the goalie/drummer. The centre is the lead singer, the most powerful member of the team and the band, the focal point. "Wayne Gretzky, Mario Lemieux, Doug Gilmour, Mark Messier. Those guys are the rock stars, the lead singers of hockey. They're Iggy Pop, David Bowie, Jerry Lee Lewis, Mick Jagger... Doug Gilmour and Jerry

Lee Lewis even share the same nickname!" ("Killer.") The wingers, Johnny explained, were the lead guitarists. They could do whatever they wanted without reproach and pretty much get away with it.

"And don't think what we do day in, day out on a rock 'n' roll tour is much different from hockey, either," said Johnny. "The backstage, that's our locker room. The matching outfits we wear on stage, those are our uniforms. Up on the stage, that's our sheet of ice! And our stinky tour vans? That's the team bus, right? Our groupies are their puck bunnies. And just like we nitpick over our shows, everything that went wrong and everything that went right, in the van, driving away from the gig? Hockey teams do the exact same thing on the bus. It's really not that different. It's entertainment, we're both putting on a show. Great musicians *and* hockey players get that. And just like in hockey, we have the occasional fight to deal with, eh?"

15

GRAB ME
BY THE LAPEL

*O*UR CROSS-CANADA TOUR with the Hanson Brothers eventually crossed the Northumberland Strait to the rolling green hills and red dirt of Prince Edward Island, where we played the University of PEI Student Union Barn in Charlottetown. At this particular show we were joined by a couple of other out-of-town bands not part of our tour, including one that definitely didn't fit the high-energy punk rock bill. It was a band from New Brunswick called Fecal Impact, a Pink Floyd-meets-*The Lord of the Rings* pagan rock nightmare, complete with members heavily cloaked in hooded druid costumes. They started their show by holding aloft candle boxes that illuminated the barn as they shuffled in from the back door, through the crowd, chanting some unintelligible elfin verse. Climbing onto the stage, they put their candle boxes at their bare feet, picked up their angular guitars and began to perform deafening Wiccan prog rock.

Their roadie looked nothing like them—he was a massive, mulleted cretin standing in the middle of the dance floor with his arms crossed and a cigarette in his mouth, watching Fecal

Impact with a smirk across his face, surrounded in smoke. He wore a hockey jacket that bore the logo of the Moncton Hawks, a minor league team that was the farm club for the Winnipeg Jets and known for a history of violence. Since he didn't have to schlep equipment during Fecal Impact's bizarre, medieval rock set, the roadie thought it would be a fine time to pick up chicks, cruising the dance floor, leaning into young university girls, dropping lines into their ears between exhales of his Export "A" Mediums. I stood at the back of the dance floor observing the roadie's antics, his bulky frame and ugly mullet launching my mind back to high school and all the crap I had to take from guys in jackets like that.

The first two girls the roadie approached ignored him completely. The third turned and yelled something that was inaudible over the druid drone of Fecal Impact. After turning the roadie down flat, she took a few steps forward on the dance floor to distance herself. Furious and likely embarrassed at the public putdown, the roadie took the lit cigarette from his mouth and flicked it at the girl, hitting her squarely in the back of her hoodie. The cigarette sparked upon impact and fell to the floor. She didn't even notice the roadie goon had assaulted her, but I did.

It was one thing if hockey thugs picked on their own gender. It was another when they targeted women. I crossed the dance floor, reached up and grabbed the roadie's shoulder. He spun around and glared down at me, filling my entire field of vision. It was like looking up at one of the monsters from *Where the Wild Things Are*. I yelled out over the music the first thing I could think of: "Don't throw cigarettes at girls!" He chose to avoid using words in his response. Instead, he answered my protest by taking one hand and grabbing the lapel of my jacket. With the other, he coiled back his ham-sized fist and slammed it directly into my face. I flew backward on impact, the back of my head smacking the barn floor. I lay there, flat on my back with a bloody nose, completely stunned. The goon was closing in for more, but luckily the rest of the Smugglers rushed to my defence, holding the goon back. The incident happened so quickly and efficiently, and was so shrouded because of the volume of the band, that the girl whose honour I had defended never even noticed her rock Prince Valiant had been flattened by one punch.

By the time Fecal Impact finally finished their séance-esque set, my nostrils had been stuffed with paper towel to stop the bleeding, just in time for us to play. I had the power of the microphone in my hand and the raised stage under my feet, so I made sure to ridicule the hockey goon roadie at every opportunity between songs, angrily shouting into the mic that if we came to blows again, he would most certainly have to blow me first.

After the show was over, we were informed that all the out-of-town bands were to be housed in some empty rooms of a nearby student dormitory. Sure enough, Fecal Impact and their now dangerously drunken goon roadie were in a dorm room directly across the hall from ours on the second floor, and all the bands were to use a shared washroom at the end of the hall. The rest of the Smugglers went to the washroom and came back with the news that the roadie goon was "hanging around" near the entrance. My bandmates were angry with me that I had inflamed the situation even further with the verbal jabs on stage. I opened our dorm-room door a crack and peeked through. The roadie goon was leaning one of his shoulders against the wall outside of the washroom, glaring at me. He unfolded his gorilla-sized arms and crooked his index finger at me, beckoning me toward him. I slammed our door shut and bolted the safety lock. Fifteen minutes later I was pacing the room, desperately needing to pee. I peeked out the door again. "Just suck it up and go to the washroom!" Nick barked at me from his bunk bed. The thug was nowhere to be seen, but still I couldn't leave the dorm room. I was too afraid, all of my high school trauma rushing back at once.

I glanced around the room for a bottle, a sink, some type of receptacle to urinate into. Then I turned to the window. It had a lower portion that opened up a few inches like a Canada Post mailbox, just enough to let in some air, and perfect for peeing out of. Hopping up and down on the spot, I unzipped my pants and let out a sigh as an arcing stream of steaming urine cascaded down two storeys to the ground below. A few seconds later I heard the screaming. Looking down at the parking lot, I realized to my horror that my urine stream was spraying directly onto the wind-shield of a van with FECAL IMPACT painted in Tolkienian lettering across the hood.

The doors of the van slid open, pot smoke billowing out, as the enraged members of Fecal Impact scrambled out of their hotbox. With them was their goon roadie in his Moncton Hawks jacket, who clearly spotted me in the lit-up dorm-room window as I uncontrollably added urine to insult, unable to stop my pro-pulsive golden shower all over their van. Within two minutes they had bounded up the stairs and were furiously pounding on our door. The rest of the band was woken up as I filled them in on what had just happened. We double-checked the safety lock and shoved a chair under the doorknob for good measure. After many loud and angry threats of beatings, torture and human sacrifice, they finally gave up and retired to their room across the hall. We very quietly snuck out of the dormitory at 6 a.m., and got the hell off of Prince Edward Island thanks to the newly opened Confederation Bridge.

BY THE TIME the tour ended, we had become fast friends with the Hanson Brothers, and the night-in, night-out touring experi-ence with them had done a lot to convince me that art and sports could actually coexist together. To prove that point, shortly after returning from the tour we received a phone call from Johnny Hanson telling us he was putting together the first-ever "puck rock" compilation album featuring Canadian rock 'n' roll and punk rock bands singing about hockey. Johnny invited the Smug-glers to contribute a song. I still didn't think I could bring myself to write a song about hockey, so I handed the project over to Dave, our resident diehard hockey fan. Within hours he had written a song called "Our Stanley Cup," all about the day the Vancouver Canucks would finally win it all:

OUR STANLEY CUP

by DAVE CARSWELL/THE SMUGGLERS

This is the season that we've waited for
(Kill the Calgary Flames)
Can't you hear our hearts singing?
Soon buzzers will be ringing
This is the season
My sweet Canucks
They'll destroy all that comes before them
Slashing spearing penalties ignore them
Ooo sweet Jesus, blood spurts to the bleachers
We will love you until the final faceoff
Remember beating Calgary 10–1?
Buenas noches, strangulate *los hombres*
After all the killing has stopped
We'll rejoice with the Stanley Cup
And now that we have won
Our sticks will cross the sun
Blue skies on Vancouver will shine
On this our Stanley Cup
Blue skies on Vancouver will shine
On this our Stanley Cup
Blue skies on Vancouver will shine
On this our Stanley Cup . . .

The track was released on *Johnny Hanson Presents: Puck Rock, Vol. 1* in the spring of 1994. It was so, so close to becoming a very prophetic song.

16

HEROES OF
THE SIDEWALK

TO EARN SOME scratch between Smugglers tours, I had taken a job at Carlisle's Chicken Café, an outrageous little restaurant in a low-rent strip mall in New Westminster, BC. The chicken shack smelled of grease, deep fryers, beer and raw chicken. Often I would be the only employee on shift at the chicken shack, serving as host, waiter, cashier, bartender, cook, dishwasher and janitor. The little chicken shack attracted an array of characters—blue-collar railroad workers, First Nations fishermen, unemployed bangers, mod scooter enthusiasts, hip-hop gangsters, hookers, thugs and schizophrenics, all of whom had two things in common: they loved our chicken and they loved hockey. This motley crew would gather noisily under the glow of *Hockey Night in Canada* on the wall-mounted TV while munching away on hot wings, wedge fries and coleslaw, washed down by cheap beer, as I madly tried to keep up with their shouted orders.

That spring, even though the Vancouver Canucks had some fantastic players, the team just managed to squeak into the play-offs, earning them a first-round Stanley Cup playoff matchup with their archrival Calgary Flames, just as the lyrics of Dave's song had predicted. Much to the chagrin of the sloshed patrons of Carlisle's Chicken and Canucks fans everywhere, the Calgary Flames, led by the extremely effective pest Theo Fleury, had already gone up on the Canucks a rarely surmountable three games to one in the best-of-seven series.

Many of the chicken shack regulars thought it was all over and few were interested in Game 5, but when the game was tied 1–1 late in the third, I had a hard time kicking them out at closing time, many of them scrambling to the nearest bar to catch the overtime. Alone in the chicken shack, wearing my heavily grease-stained apron while mopping the filthy, sticky linoleum floor, I looked up at the TV as overtime began. The teams went end to end with reckless speed, both goalies making repeated spectacular, acrobatic saves. It was a long time since I had seen playoff hockey and it was electrifying. I glanced at the clock above the cash register and realized I couldn't stay—it took two buses to make it all the way home and I had to leave immediately if I was to make my transfer and catch the last bus of the night back to West Vancouver. I pointed the remote at the TV and the high-pitched chaos of overtime faded to black.

When my first bus arrived at my transfer stop, I had completely forgotten about the game. I stowed my Tintin book *Flight 714 to Sydney* into my backpack and climbed off the bus, walking the few feet to my next stop outside of the Hudson's Bay department store in downtown Vancouver where I had bought my Buffalo Sabres hockey sweater so many years earlier with Dad. An old panhandler was sitting up against the granite slabs of the Bay's outer wall. "Spare some change?" he asked with a friendly creak in his voice. I looked down at him, grizzled and grey, his tassled buckskin jacket worn and tattered. His weathered face reminded me of Russell Letawsky, Hermit of Desolation Sound, whom I hadn't seen for many years. I dug into my pockets and dropped a couple of loonies into his outstretched claw of a hand, gave him a slight smile and kept walking. "Thanks," he responded. "The Canucks won tonight, eh?"

I turned back to him. "What?"

"The Canucks won tonight! In overtime. Geoff Courtnall scored the goal on a slapshot down the left wing. There's going to be a Game 6!" The old panhandler smiled at me with a toothless grin and a sparkle in his eye, blissful that the Canucks had won, even though he was destitute and begging for change. When he shared the news of the overtime win, a win the entire motley crew of customers at the chicken shack had deemed impossible, it rocketed me back to my childhood of cheering for the Canucks, reminding me that sports and its surprise victories could be an awesome thing, of why cheering for a team can be unifying and invigorating. Unlike a *Little House on the Prairie* episode that you knew had to hit its climax by forty-five minutes after the hour to wrap up the storyline by 9 p.m., you never knew what could happen in sports, and how it was going to end. As I stood looking down at the smiling, grizzled man, right then, right there, at that exact moment, I became a hockey fan again.

The next day I asked Dad for more details of the game, which he had of course watched every second of. He was surprised I was interested, and hesitantly asked if I wanted to watch Game 6 with him the following night. I wasn't working at the chicken shack, so I accepted the invitation. Game 6 also went to overtime, and again the Canucks won, this time on a goal from Linden, jamming it past the fallen Calgary goaltender with the assist from Bure. Dad and I cheered the victory together. That meant the deciding Game 7 was next, and for an unbelievable third-straight game of pure nerves and adrenalin, the game went into overtime. It was in that Game 7 overtime that the two most famous sequences in Canucks history occurred: "The Save" and "The Goal." I saw them both with my own bespectacled eyes.

First to make history was Captain Kirk. On a hard-charging three-on-one rush in overtime, a Flames player named Robert Reichel raced down the left wing. Theo Fleury passed the puck perfectly across to him, which allowed Reichel to wrist the puck into a wide-open net to win the game and the series, but . . . NO!? It was

127

at that very moment that Captain Kirk made the most famous save in Canucks history. He slid across his goal crease, stacking his goalie pads into a wall of black leather amidst a flurry of airborne ice shavings, SLAMMING SHUT THE DOOR. From the goal line, he kicked the puck out of the crease in one fluid motion, and was back on his feet in a split second. The game continued. The crowd was in a frenzy. When I had the opportunity to meet him years later, Theo Fleury told me that many times he had woken up in the middle of the night thinking of that very play, wishing he had taken the shot instead of making the pass.

Next to make history was Pavel Bure. In the second overtime period, Canucks defenceman "Downtown" Jeff Brown spotted the Russian Rocket loose in the middle of the ice behind the Flames defence. Downtown Brown shot a perfect forward pass straight uptown onto the blade of the Rocket who took off toward the Calgary goal with both jets blazing. With blinding ferocity, the Rocket deked Flames goalie Mike Vernon to the stick side, sliding the puck into the back of the net for a gorgeous, oil-painting goal, the Canucks' most famous goal of all time. A province-wide joyful pandemonium erupted, including me and Dad jumping up and down in our TV room screaming "CANUCKS WIN!" Mom and my sister, Heather, came running in, finding us hugging and high-fiving.

Dad warned me that Vancouver's desperate, lucky, rope-a-dope wins against the Flames had likely emptied the Canucks' tank. They would be very hard-pressed to beat the Dallas Stars, their next opponent in the playoffs. That team featured another great goalie in Andy "The Organ" Moog, young star player Mike "Mo" Modano and Geoff Courtnall's speedy brother Russ. Dallas had swept the St. Louis Blues in four games and had been resting ever since, whereas the Canucks would have to play in Dallas with only two days' rest after the highly emotional and physically pounding seven games against the Flames. Even still, I was surprised at how decades of losing made so many lifelong Canucks fans brace themselves for pessimistic outcomes. Clearly remembering the magic of 1982 when I was eleven years old, I gripped my white towel with optimism and suddenly couldn't wait for the next series to begin.

To the shock of many, the Canucks made short work of the reportedly mighty Stars, beating them four games to one. The most memorable moment of the series was when the Russian Rocket showed he could do more than skate like a cheetah and score like Brad Pitt at Lilith Fair. He could also throw an elbow like Gordie Howe. Harassed, hounded and bullied by several Dallas players, including the intimidating Shane "The Hurler" Churla, the Russian Rocket finally had enough. After Churla had repeatedly shoved around several Canucks in sequence, the Rocket came out of nowhere with his elbow cocked like he was doing the chicken dance at a Russian wedding, connecting directly with the Hurler's jaw. Bure dropped the muscle-bound winger to the ice like a sack of pucks. Churla lay completely motionless. The officials missed the whole thing. Most Canucks fans including Dad were certain the Russian Rocket would be suspended for at least one game for the vicious blindside head shot, but amazingly the only punishment Bure received was a $500 fine. It was one more galvanizing moment for the Canucks—they rose to the challenge, beat the Stars and won the series, which set the stage for one of the most exciting semifinals in *Hockey Night in Canada* history: the storied Toronto Maple Leafs versus the Vancouver Canucks, the first and only time the two teams had met in the playoffs. And the Leafs had their own three pillars: Doug "Killer" Gilmour, Felix "The Cat" Potvin and Wendel Clark.

On May 24, 1994, a lanky, bent-nosed Canucks forward named Greg "Gus" Adams scored immediately after the opening faceoff of the second overtime of Game 5, sliding the winning puck past the Leafs' hugely dejected goalie Felix Potvin, who liked to play so deep within his net that his stick often sat on the goal line. The Canucks poured onto the ice as confetti and fireworks rained down on the white towel-waving, delirious fans in the Pacific Coliseum. The players pinned Gus in the corner, his arms aloft, his eyes shut, his smile wide, as he drank in the moment. The Vancouver Canucks were going back to the Stanley Cup Final for the first time since 1982, and once again they would face a Goliath team from New York . . . the heavily favoured New York Rangers. The team was stocked with no less than seven players who had won the Cup with the Edmonton Oilers in 1990, including the captain, five-time Stanley Cup winner Mark "Moose" Messier. Many Canucks fans immediately suffered flashbacks to the last time our team was in the Stanley Cup Final and were swept by a team from New York. "Shit . . . here we go again," said the railway workers at the chicken shack.

Johnny Hanson's puck rock compilation came out during the playoffs. Almost immediately, radio stations and various media outlets gravitated toward our seemingly prophetic song "Our Stanley Cup." We heard it on all types of local radio stations. CBC, sports, news, college and commercial radio were all spinning it, crediting us, tongue-in-cheek, for predicting the run in song. We were asked repeatedly to perform it live, though it was thrown together so hastily we weren't sure how to play it anymore. We ran with all the attention anyway, and suddenly I was doing interviews about the song and the Canucks' Stanley Cup run.

Dave's hockey song seemed to be the few notes of optimism in a rising chorus of doubt. Just like the Islanders back in 1982, the Rangers had finished first overall in the regular season. Once again, there was a massive point spread between the teams, the Rangers finishing with 112 and the Canucks 85, making it the largest gap in regular season points in the Final since . . . the Canucks played the Islanders in 1982. That and many other depressing stats caused hockey pundits everywhere to predict another New York sweep of the lowly underdog Canucks.

Game 1 was on a hot May night in New York City, and lo and behold the plucky Canucks could indeed skate with the mighty

Rangers, tying the score in astonishing fashion in the last minute of the third period to send the game to overtime at 2–2. The Rangers stormed the Canucks' zone for most of overtime but Captain Kirk put on a goalie show for the ages, stopping fifty-two shots in all manners possible, pushing the sell-out crowd at Madison Square Garden to the edge of panic. In the last New York minute of overtime, Captain Kirk felt the puck whiz by his shoulder, which was followed immediately by a loud CLANK. The puck had hit the crossbar and bounced back out, and was scooped by the Russian Rocket for an odd-man rush the other way. Ahead of him was Adams and their centre, a tiny player named Cliff Ronning. The Rocket fired the puck up to Ronning, who feathered a pass to a wide-open Adams. The lanky hockey player with the crooked nose and the big smile did it again, one-timing a rubber bullet past Rangers goalie Mike Richter for the glorious overtime win. The Canucks won their first-ever Stanley Cup Final game 3–2, taking Game 1. The party was on.

The party was short. The powerful New York Rangers quickly rallied to beat the Canucks in the next three straight games, crushing the swelling Canucks Nation that now stared up at a 3–1 lead that looked as insurmountable as scaling the Empire State Building. The Canucks had to fly back to New York for Game 5, which everyone expected to be the Stanley Cup–winning game for the New York Rangers and their evil coach "Iron" Mike Keenan. But it wasn't to be, as the mighty Canucks picked themselves off the ice for a stunning 6–4 victory, sending the series all the way back to the west coast, three time zones away, much to the Rangers' extreme frustration.

Vancouver was not used to hosting NHL games in June, and the atmosphere in the warmth of late spring was hedonistic and finally overflowing with optimism. The orange and black Canucks logo was everywhere: on buses, cranes, office towers, bridges, cafés, cars, schools, homes, trains, freighters and tugboats. The Canucks returned home for Game 6 to a massive welcome, and played possibly the greatest home game in the history of the team. Nick came over to watch the game with Dad and me. Surrounded by total chaos and pandemonium in the rink and throughout the city, the Canucks won a vicious game 4–1, but not before the sore loser Rangers tried to permanently rub out valiant Canucks captain Trevor Linden.

In the last minute of the game with no hope of victory, Rangers forward Adam Graves tried to send a message for the inevitable Game 7 by viciously butt-ending Linden in the temple with his stick, felling the lanky captain to his hands and knees in the neutral zone. As Linden tried to crawl to the bench with blood pouring from the cut while the crowd screamed in indignation, Mark "Moose" Messier got in his own cheap shot, cross-checking Linden and flattening him to the ice. The ref saw neither infraction. But Game 7 was a go . . . all the way back in New York City.

Nick, Dad and I were totally ecstatic, having never experienced our team ever getting this far, the Cup just one win away and all the momentum on the Canucks' side. After the game, the local CBC News showed footage of downtown Vancouver, still basking in the warm evening sunshine of early June. It was Saturday night and the streets were packed with joyous revellers. Nick and I knew we had to be a part of it. We hopped into the Smugglers tour van and rushed across Lions Gate Bridge, headed for downtown. We turned onto Robson Street and were instantly in a parade of honking cars with people hanging out of car windows. They triumphantly waved white towels and Canucks flags, sitting on car tops and hoods, as their Canuck-mobiles inched along, everyone smiling, laughing, hugging and celebrating.

The citizens of Vancouver had never seen anything like it. The players had never seen anything like it while they tried to drive home from the rink. The mood was festive, friendly and safe, even though the impromptu city-wide party had caught the police by surprise and booze was being openly guzzled everywhere. Never ones to pass up an opportunity to join a party, Nick and I popped open the cooler in the van, grabbed a few cans of Black Label and joined right in on the parade, inching for hours down Robson, up Burrard, over to Granville and down Georgia as a warm darkness fell on the festive city.

The hockey pundits were with us: with the Canucks having improbably tied the series at 3–3, it was universally agreed that the young, strong and fast Canucks had the aging Rangers stars on the run. The New York Rangers, used to the cushy East Coast travel schedule of the regular season, were being run ragged not only by the hard-hitting games but also by the harsh travel and time changes endured in the series, five-hour flights back and forth across North America, something the Canucks were already well acclimatized to throughout the regular season.

Madison Square Garden crackled with a nervous energy as the puck dropped for Game 7. A massive number of Canadians from across the country tuned in for the David and Goliath battle in the Big Apple. Harry Neale, now a commentator for *Hockey Night in Canada*, called Madison Square Garden a "snake pit." The Canucks got the first great chance but were denied in close on a goalmouth scramble. By the ten-minute mark of the first period the hitting started with heavy, hard and high checks along the boards being dished out by both teams.

Then, at the eleven-minute mark of the first period, the Rangers' killer defenceman Brian Leetch struck for the first goal on a perfect passing play started by Messier, firing the puck into an open net as McLean had come too far out of his crease. The Big Apple went bananas, but back at home, Dad and I slumped into our couch, crestfallen at the early setback. A few minutes later, with the Rangers on a heavy forecheck, the Canucks' limber Finnish defenceman Jyrki Lumme took a penalty for cross-checking. A few seconds into the power play, the Canucks penalty killers got caught chasing the puck, leaving baby-faced Adam Graves alone in the slot. He took the pass from the left wing and rifled the puck past the blocker of Captain Kirk for a 2–0 New York Rangers lead.

I slumped further down into the couch but the goal amped Dad up more. He turned to me and said, "The Canucks have been down

133

this entire playoffs, they'll come back, it's early yet, they'll come back!" I felt a distant, urgent need to zen out to Raffi's *The Corner Grocery Store* and calm myself down, but instead I shuffled forward to the edge of the couch, leaning toward the TV, and followed the scattered, nasty play filled with outrageous hooking, holding, slew-footing and tripping infractions from both sides that went uncalled by the refs. Players flew in all directions. Plays that easily would have been a parade of penalties in any other game were never called. Both Dad and I thought the Rangers were getting off easy.

The second period began with the Canucks still down 2–0. Within the first thirty seconds, the puck was coughed up to Messier directly in front of McLean, but Captain Kirk was able to kick the puck out. A few minutes later, Messier was knocked flat by the Canucks' Downtown Jeff Brown as he tried to chase down the puck and a penalty was called against the Canucks. On the ensuing penalty kill, Trevor Linden, both eyes blackened from the two times he had broken his nose in the playoffs, jumped onto the ice, snatched the puck up at centre and broke in on a partial short-handed breakaway with the Rangers' best defenceman, Brian Leetch, in hot pursuit. Linden swooped in with the puck on his backhand, and while fighting off Leetch and leaning at an almost forty-five-degree angle, shovelled the puck from his backhand to his forehand and flipped it over the falling New York Rangers goalie for a beautiful goal.

It was an inspired individual effort that sent all of Vancouver into delirium. Dad and I could hear screaming coming from the open windows of neighbouring houses, and when CBC TV cut to the Pacific Coliseum, which had opened its doors to Canucks fans to watch the game on the Jumbotron, it was nothing but a sea of towels frantically waving in celebration. Trevor himself barely celebrated, knowing that even though they were within a goal, they were still deep within the canyons of New York. The goal had come completely against the flow of play that up until that point was all Rangers. With their red, white and blue uniforms, Mike Richter's

Statue of Liberty mask and countless American flags and banners of red, white and blue stripes in the stands, I saw the Rangers as petulant and self-righteous brats who, like their fans, felt they deserved the Cup because they were *New York*. At the moment, much to our rampant fear, Dad and I had to admit the Rangers were playing like they deserved to win, and even with Linden's heroic goal, it looked like our riders on the storm were losing their gale force.

Just over halfway through the second period with the Rangers out-shooting the Canucks by a wide margin, the Canucks' big veteran defenceman Dave "Scrub Brush" Babych, he of the incredible moustache, took a tripping penalty in front of the Vancouver net. On the ensuing Rangers power play, during a mad scramble in front of the net, an unmolested Messier was parked by the right post and squeaked a pinballing puck through the pads of Captain Kirk to make it 3–1. Dad and I sank back into our couch, each letting out a groan and simultaneously slapping our hands over our faces, not even able to look at the agonizing slow-motion replays.

The third period began with the score still 3–1 for the Rangers, but hope remained. As Bob Cole, the announcer for *Hockey Night in Canada*, stated so clearly, "The Canucks are now going to have to open it up and go for it!" Unfortunately the Rangers did anything but sit on their lead, storming the Canucks zone with shot after shot that Kirk McLean continually kicked away. Then, with four minutes already gone in the third period, the Russian Rocket ignited with a burst of speed into the Rangers zone and was hauled down by yapping Finnish forward Esa "The Tick" Tikkanen. The Rangers were called for a hooking penalty. After getting just one shot away on their earlier power play, finally the Canucks snipers began to click. On a beautiful zigzag passing play, Ronning passed the puck across the ice to Geoff Courtnall, who passed it back across to Linden waiting by the far-side post. With Richter thinking shot, he was surprised by the backdoor pass and acrobatically did the splits but his elastic move was too late; Linden had already dropped to one knee and slammed Courtnall's pass into the back of the net at the edge of the goal crease to narrow the Rangers' lead to 3–2. The first thing Trevor Linden did after scoring was look up at the clock to see how much time remained, again barely celebrating. Some of the Canucks who were on the bench didn't even get up. Meanwhile, Dad and I were jumping up and down, screaming, hugging, clapping, cheering. Win or lose, Trevor Linden was further etching his legend into the hearts of Canucks fans forever. The Canucks had fifteen minutes to make history.

The Rangers seemed nervous, the game opening up in the Canucks' favour, going end to end with the Canucks getting more and more scoring opportunities. As the game clock ticked down to ten minutes left, the referee put away his whistle and fans on both coasts, both countries, both rinks, could barely keep themselves from hyperventilating. Both teams came very close to scoring but neither could get the puck in the net despite the frantic, wide-open action.

And then, at just under six minutes left in the third period, it happened. On a rush by Trevor Linden and Geoff Courtnall into the Rangers zone, the puck got deflected into the corner, where Geoff instinctively passed it out into the slot in front of the Rangers net. Sure enough, the puck found the blade of the third member of the line, a rookie named Nathan LaFayette, who looked like Spike Lee in skates. LaFayette did the right thing and one-timed the puck 'at the net. He caught Rangers goalie Mike Richter out of position, diving across his crease with his glove outstretched. Time stopped. My eyes widened. I flew off the couch, arms in the air in wild celebration, screaming, running back and forth across the carpet of our TV room. "YES! YES! YES! CANUCKS SCORE! CANUCKS SCORE!" My mom and sister came running in.

I turned to look at Dad. He too was standing, but the look on his face was one of agony. He was pointing at the TV. In slow motion he mouthed the word "*no.*" I looked back at the TV screen in despair. Play had continued and was rushing back up the ice in the direction of the Canucks net. Even the legendary Bob Cole seemed momentarily flummoxed, making a different but equally wrong call: "*WHAT . . . A SAVE . . . BY RICHTER!* Oh my goodness! That puck was going in *for sure!*" I was stunned, crestfallen and slack-jawed, arms hanging loosely at my sides. Twelve years after Camp Kawkawa, I had managed to blow the call again. I collapsed to the floor in shock and curled into the fetal position in the corner. Dad ignored me as the action continued. A few minutes later, when we finally got to see the replay, it was revealed in excruciatingly slow motion over and over again that the young rookie had indeed beat Richter, but hadn't beat the bright red right goalpost, the puck knuckle-balling and clapping the post on its wide, flat surface, which is why no one heard the signature *PING* of ricocheting hard rubber. The Madison Square Garden crowd erupted when they saw the replay, but for the rest of us, it was for whom the post tolled . . . that pass, that shot, that goalpost, cemented into the memories of the Canucks players and fans forever.

With just under two minutes left in the third period, the game became drawn out with stall tactics and time outs as the Canucks coaching staff tried everything to stretch time and give the team a chance to score. One of the *Hockey Night in Canada* cameras slowly panned down the Canucks bench, revealing grizzled, sweaty men, bloodied but unbowed. The players were all leaning tentatively on their sticks, a look of nervous anticipation on most of their scarred faces. The fierce Tim "The Puncher" Hunter at first looked like he was crying, until we realized it was blood running out of his eye.

At the end of hockey games, the clock becomes either a friend or an enemy, depending on the score. On this sticky June night, the clock ticked down like an elevator to hell. When the last whistle blew, there were 1.6 seconds left. It seemed like a cruel fate, but it ain't over 'til it's over, and you just never know what might happen as long as time remains, so they dropped the puck again. The final faceoff was between Bure, hoping for an immediate shot off the draw, and Craig "Mac-T" MacTavish, the last player in the

NHL to not wear a helmet. The puck was dropped, Bure took a wild stab at it, and the curly-haired MacTavish slammed the puck to the boards. The buzzer sounded. The Vancouver Canucks lost the Stanley Cup.

Messier won his sixth and final Stanley Cup ring, and became the first and only player in the NHL to captain two different franchises to Stanley Cup victory. Game 7 on *Hockey Night in Canada* attracted an audience of just under five million viewers, at that time the most ever for a televised CBC sporting event. The Canucks were hunched over on the bench and along the boards at their end of the rink, like bodies on a battlefield, having to endure the Rangers celebrating on home ice under streamers and fireworks before they would line up for the traditional handshake at centre ice. The Canucks laboured off the ice before the Stanley Cup was handed to Messier, who famously hopped up and down like a schoolgirl upon receiving it. After the game, it was revealed that Trevor Linden had played Game 7 with a broken nose, four cracked ribs, torn rib cartilage and his heart on his sleeve. Cutting away from the Rangers' champagne-soaked celebrations in their dressing room, Linden appeared on the screen, slumped in silence in his dressing room stall, in his undershirt, hockey pants and skates. His eyes were black and yellow, he had a deep cut across the bridge of his bent nose, his shoulder and ribs were wrapped in bandages. He was crying. Back home in Vancouver, a large number of fans chose to mourn the loss with decidedly different emotions.

DRUNK
TEENAGERS

*T*HE PHONE RANG. I stared at it while Dad answered. Who would dare call at this time of mourning? It was Nick, who had watched Game 7 with his father. Dad chatted briefly with Nick in a sombre tone about the game and passed the phone over to me. Then he got up and left the room to see what Mom and my sister were up to, and in turn, to rejoin the normal stream of life he had vacated since April. Nick and I commiserated over the game, then he suggested that we drive over to our bandmate Dave's house, where a group had gathered to watch the game. Nick figured that since misery indeed loves company, we might as well drown our sorrows amongst friends. I agreed.

When we arrived at Dave's and descended into his basement TV den, the mood was as dark as the dimly lit, subterranean room. Empty beer cans, plastic two-litre bottles of pop, various mickeys and half-eaten bags of chips were strewn about the deep, red shag-carpeted room. Slumped on the couch were Dave, his girlfriend Neko Case, and our pals Nardwuar and Roger the Dodger. Roger was drunk, shirtless and seething in his black wraparound shades.

139

Dave flipped on the local news for a recap of the game to torture us even further. Expecting the replays of the Canucks' carnage on ice, we were startled to instead be met with footage of what appeared to be a full-scale riot unfolding in the streets of downtown Vancouver, the exact opposite mood of the festive city-wide party Nick and I had enjoyed just a few nights earlier. According to the news, police estimated an unruly crowd of somewhere between fifty thousand and seventy thousand people had descended onto the downtown core. Booze was flowing steadily like the Fraser River, fights were erupting, and looting of various shops along the high-end fashion strip of Robson Street had begun.

Upon seeing the shameful footage of First World sporting unrest, Roger the Dodger immediately sprang to his feet. "We gotta get in on *that* action!" he shrieked, pointing to the violence on TV. A city-wide riot was right up Roger the Dodger's alley. None of us moved, and none of us looked at Roger. We were too transfixed, staring at the chaotic events unfolding on TV. Most of the rioters were white males wearing Canucks paraphernalia.

"I'm not going anywhere near that," Dave grunted, speaking for the rest of us. "It looks insane down there."

"Exactly!" shouted Roger. "That's why the fuck I'm going down there right now. Who's with me?" Again none of us moved or even looked up at Roger. I certainly wasn't going to join him. I was still licking the wounds of a riot in my backyard when a household party had spiralled out of control a few years earlier. Correctly interpreting the silence, Roger blurted out "WELL FUCK YOU GUYS!" He grabbed his Tiger Williams jersey from the floor and snatched up his last six-pack of Iron Horse malt liquor from the fridge. He stomped out of the basement, hopped into his Mercury Montego and loudly peeled out of Dave's parents' driveway, headed for the melee downtown.

By the time Roger the Dodger was able to bust his way into the heat of the action, the downtown core was in complete chaos. The epicentre of the action was at the corner of Robson and Thurlow streets. Amongst hundreds of injuries, one fan crawled up onto a street lamp, then onto a telephone wire, attempting a high-wire tightrope walk above the throbbing, screaming crowd. He inevitably lost his balance and fell to the pavement below, seriously injuring himself. When the paramedics tried to wade into the crowd escorted by police on bicycles, hooligans like Roger tried to steal the police officers' bikes, which made the cops and paramedics retreat to the sidelines. An ambulance was eventually able to remove the man from the throng. Roger joined the frenzied crowd as they chanted "Riot! Riot! Riot!" and "Rangers suck, Canucks rule!" and various other mindless phrases.

Much to Roger's delight, a huge mosh pit broke out, sans music, in the middle of the street, bodies slamming together in a circular motion, fights splintered out of it on all sides. Street signs were wrenched from their posts; neon signs were kicked in; bricks, beer bottles and newspaper boxes were thrown through store windows; and stolen merchandise was passed out into the outstretched hands of rioters. City police attempted to maintain order but were attacked with flying objects, their hats stolen, before they were forced back out of the crowd. Before long, over the din of the crowd, Roger the Dodger heard drumming—a rhythmic, tribal beat. This being a West Coast riot, he assumed hippie hand drummers were pounding on their tablas while others danced frenetically around them holding aloft their stolen booty of free jeans and CD Walkmans. Roger pushed through the mayhem toward the sound. When he broke through the crowd he realized the loud beat was anything but festive drumming. A heavily armoured riot squad marched toward him. They wore black helmets, bulletproof vests and gas masks, slamming their batons in unison against their clear plastic body shields.

Roger whipped off his Tiger Williams jersey and tied it around his face as the first volley of tear gas bombs clattered to the pavement around him. Roger reached down to grab the nearest tear gas canister that was spinning in circles and spraying out an opaque smoke. It was burning hot to the touch as Roger hurled it as hard as he could back at the marching procession of police. He squinted, blinked and choked on the gas, tears gushing out from under his black wraparound shades, but was able to see other rioters do as he did, returning fire with the cops' own ammunition.

The police appeared to fall back and the crowd celebrated their short-lived victory. The fans swelled forward. The police countered, moving toward the mob again in a rush of force, billy clubs swinging and tear gas spraying, sending the crowd retreating in panic. Several revellers got knocked down and trampled. A fleeing banger beside Roger the Dodger was shot in the back with a tear gas canister and knocked flat to the pavement. Over and over, like waves crashing on a beach in a storm, the two opposing forces ebbed and flowed, while the rioters behind the front lines continued to break more and more storefront windows. Each shattering of glass was met with a cheer from the crowd.

Soon, the loud *POP* of the tear gas cannons was accompanied by an explosive *WHOOMP*. The police were strategically shooting rubber bullets at riot ringleaders who refused to back down. When Roger the Dodger heard a rubber slug scream by his ear like the climax of a horror movie, he thought better of his shirtless, masked position on the front line and retreated to the safety of the thick of the mob. One supposed ringleader wasn't so lucky, collapsing after being shot in the head with a rubber bullet.

The rioters managed to swell around behind the wall of police, outflanking them, overturning police cars that were left behind the lines. Police dogs attacked, launching gleaming white fangs into many a Canucks jersey, as the police dragged more and more rioters from the fray into waiting paddy wagons. In an effort to halt the flow of people into the downtown core, transit was stopped, unfortunately preventing those who were already downtown from leaving. Security was set up at the downtown hospital and the injured weren't permitted entry. Huge clouds of tear gas wafted through the warm June night air into thousands of open

windows of the surrounding apartment buildings, affecting inno-
cent residents.

The police ran out of tear gas around 11 p.m., but were soon
restocked by the RCMP from North Vancouver. When the riot eventually died out in the wee hours of the night, over two hundred
people were injured, over fifty had been arrested, and damage to
the downtown core was estimated at over one million dollars. The
man shot in the head with the rubber bullet was in critical con-
dition with suspected brain damage. Roger the Dodger's combat
boots crunched through the broken glass covering the deserted
streets as he made his way back to his Mercury Montego. His eyes
were swollen from the tear gas and his head was bleeding from a
thrown bottle that smacked his bare skull. A block from his car,
he passed a long-haired, bearded organist busking on a downtown
corner, wearing a top hat with a Canucks logo pasted onto it. Sur-
really, the organist played a jaunty version of the theme to *Hockey
Night in Canada* while casualties of the melee lay on the sidewalk
and street around him, outstretched and bleeding, nursing various wounds. The Stanley Cup riot of 1994 cast an international
dark cloud of shame over both the city of Vancouver and the team—
authorities, citizens, fans, Canucks management and players alike
vowing nothing like that would ever happen in Vancouver again.

THE CANUCKS LOSING the Stanley Cup to the New York Rangers
brought on not only a dark period of time for the team, but also
for all of Canadian hockey. The Canucks would have a long time to
stew over Nathan LaFayette's third period Game 7 post clanking,
since, for the first time in NHL history, the owners would lock out
the players in a labour dispute, leading to the start of the 1994–95
season being postponed several months, shortening the season by
half. Idle minds and bored hockey fans, analysts and players created rumours that Pavel Bure had been negotiating his contract
throughout the Stanley Cup run and had threatened to withhold
his services in Game 7 if the team didn't promise him six million

dollars for the following season. Management repeatedly denied this ever happened, but it was the beginning of the end for the most exciting player the fans of Vancouver had ever seen.

In the following seasons, the Canucks fell into complete disarray as several coaches were hired and fired, and the dream team of the 1994 Stanley Cup run was slowly dismantled. Rumours abounded of an intra-team marital affair. Gossip swirled that Bure had ties to the Russian mafia. A new coach tried to ban post-game beer, which was pretty much met by a full-on team mutiny. During those dark ages, all three members of the Canucks power trifecta of Pavel Bure, Trevor Linden and Kirk McLean were injured for significant periods of time while the team lost game after game. The Canucks' history with jersey designs was notoriously suspect at best, but they soon outdid themselves, introducing salmon-coloured tie-dyed jerseys with the rapidly descending skate logo sewn over top to reflect that laid-back West Coast hippie lifestyle. The jerseys were disgusting and the players reportedly couldn't stand them.

Soon the Canucks and their fans would see the unthinkable happen . . . Mark Messier would join the team as a massive free-agent signing. Adding insult to injury, he would unceremoniously strip the captain's "C" from the beloved Trevor Linden. And to pour acid on injury, the delusional Canucks management then hired Mike Keenan to be both coach and general manager of the Canucks. Iron Mike immediately accused the Canucks of having a country club-like atmosphere, saying the team was still riding on their Stanley Cup Final high of years earlier. He called out stalwart goalie Kirk McLean in front of the media for being out of shape. He bullied the mild-mannered Linden, yet fawned over the aging Mark Messier. The dressing room was divided and the atmosphere was ugly.

In an unprecedented blitzkrieg that Canucks fans could only watch with horror from the sidelines, Keenan traded away almost every player associated with the Stanley Cup run. In January of

1998, Captain Kirk was traded to the Carolina Hurricanes. Linden was traded in February to the New York Islanders for hulking power-forward-in-waiting Todd Bertuzzi and a young defenceman. Two-thirds of the trifecta were gone; only Pavel Bure remained and he wanted out, too. Eventually he demanded a trade and refused to play until he got it.

Meanwhile, across Canada, an equally depressing pall had fallen over Canadian hockey. It was as if the Canucks losing the Stanley Cup in 1994 was a defeat for the Canadian game itself. The Quebec Nordiques became the Colorado Avalanche (and promptly won the Stanley Cup in their first season in Denver, causing anguish for the Quebec City fans left behind), the Winnipeg Jets relocated to Phoenix and threats abounded that the legendary Edmonton Oilers would be next to be deported to the United States. The Canadian teams couldn't afford the skyrocketing salaries of the league's best players, and the Canadian loonie was in the tank. The on-ice product suffered, which added up to a lot of losing games. Teams that couldn't make money were relocated. Canadians didn't know what we had lost until it was gone.

I still tried to catch as many Canucks games as possible as I toured with the Smugglers. We'd receive depressing updates and game scores via fax from our record company in Vancouver to whatever European youth hostel or Australian outback lodge we were staying at that night. As I read those reports so far away from the action, little did I know that the Smugglers would shortly wind down like an old dog, and I would need a new outlet for my passion and energy. Soon I would find myself partaking in something I never would have guessed in a million years: actually playing hockey.

"Because the demands on the goalie
are mostly mental, it means that for a
goalie, the biggest enemy is himself."

KEN DRYDEN, *NHL goalie, 1970–1979*

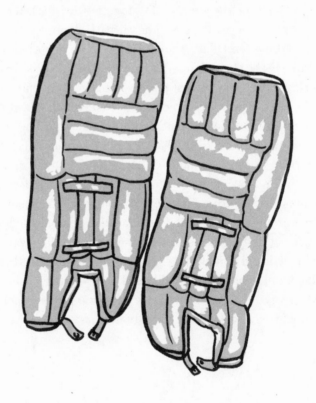

Third
PERIOD
★★★

18

HOCKEY
SOCK ROCK

Y EARS AFTER THE release of our dinky, terribly sung, loose, one-minute-and-twenty-three-second hockey song "Our Stanley Cup," which received so much play during the 1994 Stanley Cup run, I was shocked to see the song had garnered a mention in the pop culture/music section of the huge tome *Total Hockey: The Official Encyclopedia of the NHL*. Over the years, fans and other musicians began to send us recordings of other hockey songs and hockey bands. To my constant amazement, "puck rock" was practically an entire genre unto itself, and had roots beyond just the loud punk rock of bands like the Hanson Brothers and others found on Johnny Hanson's *Puck Rock* compilation series.

It turned out that oodles of bands have dabbled in singing about our nation's favourite frozen game for years. The Etobicoke art-rock band the Rheostatics (featuring future hockey and music–fuelled author Dave Bidini) were the first non-punk rock band I ever heard singing about hockey, on their song "The Ballad of Wendel Clark Parts 1 and 2," all about #17, their beloved mustachioed captain and heart and soul of the Toronto Maple Leafs. Alternative favourites the Pursuit of Happiness had a cool cowpunk song called "Gretzky Rocks," and the Toronto jazz-bop saxophone band the Shuffle Demons did a really cool version of the *Hockey Night in Canada* theme.

When I started working at CBC Radio, "Hockey Rock" was one of the first on-air specials I got the approval to do. I played many of these songs on Saturday night on CBC Radio 2's national service. The special became a tradition for several years, introducing me to pop culture hockey historians from across the country. After the first year, listeners sent me all sorts of rare and bizarre novelty hockey rock records to play in future specials: Alan Thicke's 1967 single called "Wondrous Bobby Orr"; a single by members of the New York Rangers and the LA Kings circa the late seventies called "The Hockey Sock Rock," backed with "Please Forgive My Misconduct (Last Night)" (both songs written by Thicke); as well as novelty giveaway singles from the Buffalo Sabres ("The French Connection"), the Toronto Maple Leafs ("Clear the Track, Here Comes Shack"), the Chicago Blackhawks ("The Golden Jet") and the Boston Bruins ("Derek the Turk"). Their release dates ranged from the 1950s to the 1980s. There were a few weird LPs, too: an instructional disco record from Guy Lafleur of the Montreal Canadiens, and an oddball collection of piano ballads from rugged Buffalo Sabres defenceman Jim Schoenfeld called *Shoney!* The turntables of the CBC also crackled to life that old Vancouver Canucks' "King Richard" single that I had kept ever since my mom brought it home from Stong's Market so many years earlier.

There were other modern-day musicians, aside from the Hanson Brothers, who dedicated their entire bands to hockey, specifically a hilarious indie-rock group from Connecticut called the Zambonis. They performed their tunes such as "Hockey Monkey" and "Breakaway" in full equipment, including helmets and skates, between periods at their local Bridgeport Sound Tigers games. A pop-punk band called the Riverdales, featuring infamous American underground punk rock singer Ben Weasel, became briefly obsessed with their local minor league team the Chicago Wolves.

They wrote a blistering tribute to the violence they witnessed at the game, called "Blood on the Ice." Before I knew it, I had been sent so many hockey-related recordings that I had a huge collection. My connections with the weird, unlikely musical side of hockey led to many further interviews and meetings related to the culture and folklore of hockey, including my first-ever interview for the CBC with someone who would become a great friend, mentor, and ambassador of a kind of hockey I didn't know existed.

19

MAIN OFFENDER

THE CANUCKS WERE slowly pulling themselves out of the
Messier/Keenan era like citizens who had lived through an
oppressive dictatorship and lived to see it crumble—but on
a millionaire athlete level. Sporting new jersey colours of white
and navy blue and a new team logo that featured what looked like
a deeply constipated killer whale bursting out of a stylized letter
"C," the roster was almost completely rebuilt. In net was Dan "The
Man" Cloutier, a hot-headed French-Canadian goalie who loved
to toss his blocker and glove and fight. An even more frequent
brawler was monstrous enforcer Donald "The Basher" Brashear
who was vicious and ambidextrous, changing from left to right at
any time to the surprise and pain of many opponents. Strangely
enough, he was also a classical pianist and would often tickle the
ivories at pianos in fancy hotel lobbies when the team was waiting
around for their bus. I had a chance to interview "The Basher" for
one of the CBC "Hockey Rock" specials about his piano playing. He
was very soft-spoken and seemed like a gentle giant off the ice.

A new trifecta of puck power was also taking shape on the
Canucks, in the form of the roster's top line: speedy centre

Brendan "Mo" Morrison, massive power forward Todd "The Uzi" Bertuzzi, and the slender new Swedish captain Markus "Nazzy" Naslund, who possessed one of the best wrist shots in the NHL. The trio would eventually become one of the very best lines the Canucks ever had, earning themselves the nickname "The West Coast Express." A couple rungs down on the roster were two of the most buzzed-about draft picks in recent NHL history, a set of dorky, identical, ginger twins from Sweden named Daniel and Henrik Sedin. The chatter was mostly curious negativity: fans, commentators, and other players around the league publicly chastised and bullied "Dank and Hank" relentlessly in newspapers, on television and on sports-talk radio. They were accused of being "soft." They were nicknamed the "Sedin Sisters," "Thelma and Louise" and "Pinky and the Brain," among worse insults, for apparently not being tough enough for the NHL.

Nonetheless, whomever the Sedin twins played with suddenly became a scoring star, and the twins slowly racked up better and better offensive statistics with each passing season. Vancouver's love affair with the Canucks was officially thrown back into high gear when exiled former captain Trevor Linden was brought back home to Vancouver after years of tumultuous, losing crusades in Long Island, Montreal and Washington. Linden returned a little older, a little greyer and a little leaner, but the city was overjoyed at his homecoming. Linden immediately noticed not only the bullying the twins were receiving from media and fans alike, but also inappropriate behaviour directed toward them right in their own dressing room. He took the Sedins under his wing for the duration of his career with the Canucks and became like a father figure to the rising identical hockey stars.

WITH THE SMUGGLERS touring less and less, we were in Vancouver far more on weekends than we had been in years. Nick must have been feeling restless, because he joined a regular Sunday morning outdoor ball hockey game that would occur at a local court in all manner of West Coast weather throughout the fall, winter and spring. Several of our friends were taking part, including Beez and other local musicians from various bands. Roger the Dodger also played. Eventually, Nick asked me if I wanted to come out and play. Even though I adored the Canucks, and had fallen for the excitement, tradition and pop culture that surrounded hockey, my knee-jerk reaction to the prospect of actually participating in sports was still to recoil. Besides, my wonky knees were shot after years upon years of dislocations at the most inopportune times. My teenage surgery to fix the problem was a distant memory brought back every time they dislocated, and by the faded scars that ran along the insides of my kneecaps.

I hadn't played ball hockey since I was in elementary school, getting pelted and welted in net by the wet tennis ball on a daily basis by Buck and his budding jock buddies. If I agreed to play ball hockey—and I totally sucked—would someone like Buck be waiting to lean down in my face and call me *WIMP*?

"Ah, c'mon. We're adults now. You should try it! Play in net. We're always looking for a goalie and we have some equipment."

I hummed and hawed. I peppered Nick with cautious questions. "What is the play like? Is there much attitude? Does it get rough? Do jocks play?" He assured me that it was a clean, fun game, with only Roger the Dodger or our other friend Rory occasionally losing their tempers, mostly at each other. While one hand clutched the telephone receiver, I reached down to my right knee brace and gave it a wiggle. My kneecap felt like a hardboiled egg in a saggy paper bag. I took a deep breath. "Okay."

A few days later, I arrived at a concrete hockey court in deepest East Vancouver for the game. Stepping onto the court, flashbacks to my daily elementary school games came flooding back. I was so much older but so much was the same: the plastic Superblades on the sticks so they wouldn't wear down as quickly on the pavement, the guys wearing shorts, T-shirts and hockey gloves, the pile of smelly goalie gear that seemed about as old as I was: small, stiff

155

leather pads stuffed with horsehair, a baseball mitt for catching and a flimsy waffle blocker. The goalie stick was plastic and awful. Roger the Dodger tossed me a white plastic goalie mask, like the kind Jason wore in *Friday the 13th*. I didn't want to know what Roger the Dodger used it for, but I doubt it was for hockey. I took off my Buddy Holly glasses and put in contact lenses. There was no chest protector or groin cup, so I shoved my Canucks toque down the front of my jeans like I did when I was a kid, zipped up my beloved black punk rock leather jacket I had worn on Smugglers tours for the past decade, bent my knees, leaned forward and hoped for the best.

When I got home that night and took off my shirt to look in the mirror, I saw that my torso was covered in purple welts just like when I was a kid. The bruises hurt in a good way. I was just as lousy a goalie as I was as a kid, but I found it invigorating to play. The pace was quick and dramatic. We had played a series of games; whichever team made it to five goals first won. My team lost all three, but . . . I loved feeling the ball smack up against my chest again, hearing the *WHUMP* of a shot hitting my pads or diving to poke the ball into the corner with my stick. I slowly started patching together slightly better goalie gear from various used sporting goods stores.

The games were "pickup," meaning anyone with a stick who wanted to play could. Eventually, we developed a strong group of regulars. So many hopeful players started showing up that we could take shifts and play regular positions. There would be no picking teams or team captains. Instead, sides were determined by something Rory called the "Prince George Shuffle": all the sticks were thrown into a pile at centre so Rory could randomly and evenly separate the sticks into two piles to form the teams.

Our team eventually found out about a court on the west side designed specifically for ball hockey, with regulation nets, boards and benches, so we relocated our weekly Sunday morning tilts to there, meeting every week at 11 a.m. More players joined in the

Twenty years after my ball hockey wars with Buck, I could barely believe I was back on a concrete court letting my body get covered with those purple welts all over again. The games were fast, furious and out of control, often leading to a lot of road rash, dislocations, temper tantrums and great times. Back row: Steve Turner, John Silver, Hugh Baker. Front row: Beez, Grant Lawrence, Mike Ledwidge, Darwin Green, Nick Thomas.

pickup games and became regulars, some who were friends, others who just wandered by and loved the competitiveness and speed of the games. Over the years, players included "The Deker," "Stinkfinger," "The Greek," "The Purple Pirate," "Cotton Ginny," "Peaches," "The Stoned Mason," "Jamaal the Wall," "Hard Rick," "Soft Rick," "Fair Weather Winter" (a guy who only showed when it was sunny), "Jailhouse Tats," "Galapagos," "Not Welcome," "Not Welcome 2," "Not Welcome 3" and on it went.

"Hard Rick" and "Jailhouse Tats" looked just like their nicknames suggested. They were a pair of streetwise dudes who appeared as if they just swaggered off the set of *The Wire*, with shaved heads and dozens of tattoos all over their bodies. Hard Rick was big and rugged with a shaved head, over six feet, whereas Jailhouse Tats was small and greasy like a sewer rat. Both were mean and tough and always wore loose-fitting basketball jerseys and baggy shorts, showing off their heavily inked pipes and calves. They'd share a flask of something that smelled like nail polish remover before taking to the court. During the games they'd smoke cigarettes, puckered between their lips while squinting and dashing up and down court. After the game they'd wind down with a couple of joints. Despite their ferocious exteriors, both played a pretty honest, hard-nosed game, and loved it so much they started showing up every Sunday.

THE SMUGGLERS STILL played the occasional concert in Vancouver, usually on a Saturday night when friends in another band were touring through town. Whichever band it was, we often convinced them to come down to the ball hockey court on Sunday morning to play hockey with us. Over the years, bands like Chixdiggit, Sloan, the Hives and various others took part in the game. We were always on the hunt for other local ball hockey teams to play instead of playing each other every week in pickup, and were excited to hear of another game across town run by a gang of downtown bike couriers. They agreed to play us on their court, many of them showing up on their customized street bikes made for darting in and out of traffic, hockey sticks strapped to the frames. The couriers were a wily, ragtag bunch of punks, a cross between the casts of *Breaking Away* and *The Road Warrior*.

Word to the wise: never challenge a team who ride bicycles all year long to a ball hockey game. The couriers' stamina and lung capacity was nothing short of Olympic. Between shifts on the court, most of them would sit like a bedraggled murder of crows along the boards, watching the play while lighting up cigarettes and joints, not even needing to catch their breaths before racing back for more. On the court they were devil-may-care cheetahs with bad coughs.

The games were rough and breakneck, with players often slamming into each other, wiping out on the pavement or face-first into the boards. My knees managed to just barely stay in their sockets as I breached like a humpback to stop corkscrewing one-timers or did the splits to stop backdoor dekes. I would be fine unless one of the couriers ran into me at full steam and took me out at the shins. When that happened, I also realized that my long-suppressed competitive streak and hot temper that first emerged when I played ball hockey as a kid had been lying dormant for decades like the dragon Smaug, just waiting to emerge and explode.

My nightly goaltending influence was the Canucks' Dan "The Man" Cloutier. He ferociously defended his net at all costs, taking on all comers who tried to crease-crash, whether it meant giving them the lumber with his goalie stick, slamming them in the face with his blocker or throwing down his mitts and going bare knuckles. I had never seen a Canucks goalie behave like that. He didn't take shit from anyone. Once, I saw him skate halfway down the ice and explode into a line brawl at centre, stripping off his chest protector and jersey, taking on Islanders goalie Tommy Salo, whom he proceeded to beat into the ice with a series of flailing, vicious haymakers. Even well after Salo had curled up into an armadillo-like protective ball, Cloutier stood over him and kept pounding his fist into his kidneys and spleen. It was a whole new type of goaltending. I figured I could be just like Dan the Man on the ball hockey court.

My plan predictably backfired, leading to a lot of unnecessary and regrettable roughing, slashing and stick-swinging against cagey bike couriers who were just trying to score goals. Some games I even managed to make Roger the Dodger look gentlemanly. If by chance I made a save, I'd squeeze the hard orange ball somewhere in my equipment, but a couple of the couriers just couldn't or wouldn't let up, barrelling into me. The collisions would literally rattle my cage and often knock the hockey ball loose for a whack-in rebound goal. This would cause me no end of grief, not to mention the pain of the piledriving bodychecks. The combined factors would send me into a rage, especially if the ball

159

went in. My protests would often get little or no reaction from the couriers or even my own teammates, and there were no referees to do anything about it, so I thought of what Dan The Man would do. I would try to take matters into my own hands. I'd toss off my face-mask and my glove and blocker while charging after the assailant. Nick or another teammate would thankfully intercept me before I could ever actually do anything, many times wrestling me to the pavement in a blur of flailing limbs and obscenities. My goalie equipment would be scattered all over the court, which my team-mates would refer to as the "angry yard sale."

I always immediately regretted losing my temper, but Nick let me know that I was so hypersensitive about getting pushed around that my reactionary rage was turning me into the very jerk I was so desperately trying to avoid. But I hated to get scored on, and I hated to lose. Unfortunately, I let in *a lot* of goals from every angle imaginable. I truly wanted to learn how to be a better goalie this second time around, so I started fervently studying goalie books on loan from the library from the likes of Oilers party animal Grant Fuhr, doomed Red Wings legend Terry Sawchuk and Devils mainstay Martin Brodeur. Those books were so much more than just instructional to me, leading me to soon devour hockey liter-ature of all kinds and become further immersed in the stories of the game.

NORTHERN WISH

HE FIRST INTERVIEW I ever conducted at CBC Radio was
with Dave Bidini, one of the founders of the long-running
and much-loved Canadian art-rock band the Rheostatics,
who performed that song about Wendel Clark. The interview with
Dave wasn't about his band, however, it was about his first book,
On a Cold Road: Tales of Adventure in Canadian Rock. I loved it,
so impressed that a musician could so aptly capture, with moving prose and hilarious stories, what it was really like touring our
massive, mostly empty country. I was also stunned to read within
the book's pages that Dave himself played ice hockey, that his
band had sung the Canadian national anthem at Maple Leaf Gardens, that members of the Tragically Hip also played hockey and
that Tragically Hip lead singer Gord Downie was a goalie.

After a few questions about the book, I began asking Dave
specific questions about hockey. I was fascinated at how non-
aggressive art-rock bands like his could ever be directly connected
to actually playing organized ice hockey. His answers echoed my
own experiences. He drifted away from hockey in high school
because it seemed to be the domain of jocks, meatheads and

MORNINGSTARS
EXCLAIM! SUMMIT 2004

Dave Bidini blew my mind when he told me all about his anti-jock Good Times Hockey League of the Arts, a frozen nirvana based on the principles of sportsmanship, fun, inclusion and empathy, among other attributes I had never associated with sports. Dave's team was the Morningstars, which included league and tournament founder Tom Goodwin, and other musicians, actors and music industry insiders. Tom is in the front row, second from left. Dave is in the back, on the right.

bullies. He was drawn to the arts and music instead, where he found his tribe. But he explained that when he finally got back into the game in his late twenties and early thirties, he found other artistically minded hockey outcasts who loved the game and wanted to play, but weren't into the raging, muscle-bound testosterone.

162

Dave's hockey team was called the Morningstars, its roster filled with artists, musicians, authors, actors, music industry insiders and the occasional pot dealer. I couldn't believe that such a dream hockey team actually existed. And there were more, explained Dave to my wide-eyed amazement, a whole league of them, with team names like the Gas Station Islanders, the Jokers, the London Fog and the Dufferin Groove. They were all a part of something called the Good Times Hockey League of the Arts, conceived by a man named Tom Goodwin. Tom worked at *Exclaim!* magazine, a free, national rock 'n' roll publication.

As Dave explained the hockey association to me, it sounded like some sort of make-believe Shangri-La of sport, complete with a list of values I had rarely if ever associated with hockey: *sportsmanship, fun, safety, creative expression, inclusion* and *empathy*, just to name a few. I felt like Tom Joad in *The Grapes of Wrath* as he and his family finally discovered the safe, socialist camp at the end of the road in California after so many wrong turns. I just couldn't believe that something like the Good Times Hockey League of the Arts existed.

Dave let me know that Tom Goodwin was planning a large national tournament of sorts, a "Hockey Summit of the Arts," on Easter weekend in Toronto. Tom would invite and include like-minded, arts-based teams from across the country. I knew I had to be there, to see it with my own eyes, so that Easter weekend I did my first of many live broadcasts of my annual "Hockey Rock" special rink-side in Toronto at the Hockey Summit of the Arts.

I hadn't entered a community hockey rink in years. The smell hadn't changed: a chilly blast of nostalgia to the nostrils . . . bleach and chemicals I couldn't name, human sweat, wet rubber floor mats, instant hot chocolate, cheap hot dogs, wet leather, rotting equipment and the ice. The scents rocketed me back to the situations I had so feared as a child in frozen barns like this, but I put one Converse sneaker in front of the other in the shallow puddles on the thick black flooring. I could hear the urgent play on the ice reverberating off the steel rafters high above the rink before I saw it. Skate blades carved and sliced into the frozen playing sheet like knives against sharpening stones. The CLACK of stick blades whacked the ice, demanding the puck, which boomed loudly against the end boards like distant cannon shots.

I climbed three or four wet stairs and squinted at the bright ice surface. To my delight I saw two teams adorned in cool,

163

customized jerseys battling for the puck: the Peterborough Pneu-
monia versus the Winnipeg Wheatfield Souldiers. The Wheatfield
Souldiers had not only named themselves after a classic album
by Winnipeg band The Guess Who, but also had the mustachioed
mug of lead singer Burton Cummings emblazoned on the front
of their jerseys. The stands were filled with people: bundled up
men, women, teenagers and kids leaning forward, cupping their
hands around coffees and hot chocolates, their breath billowing
from their mouths as they cheered on the teams. It looked more
like an audience for an all ages indie-rock concert than a hockey
game. Live bands played between whistles and periods, and some
of the teams sold merchandise adorned with their customized
team logos.

Broadcasting rink-side from the Hockey Summit of the Arts
was a thrilling if freezing experience. Between blasting out the
weird hockey-rock songs from my collection, I did live, shivering
colour commentary of the play on the ice while teams like the Halifax–Dartmouth Ferries, the Ottawa Songbird Millionaires, the
Parkdale Hockey Lads and the Edmonton Green Pepper All-Stars
took to the ice for friendly battles. Whether they skated to glory or
defeat, both were accepted humbly.

Between games, I interviewed the Canadian rock royalty that
played on the teams: members of Barenaked Ladies, Sloan, the
Constantines, Rheostatics, the Sadies, the Sam Roberts Band and
many others. I was in pure hockey-rock heaven. Off the ice, there
were organized "Hootenannys" at a designated downtown bar,
where many of the musicians on the teams would perform sets. It
was more of a hockey convention than it was a tournament, with
entire teams dressing in thematic outfits both on and off the ice.
Parties would rage deep into the night, everyone somehow bouncing back the next morning to lace up the skates and play more
hockey.

I ended up spending most of my time that weekend with
the Ottawa Songbird Millionaires, by far the wildest and most

Blake, the tiny, exceptional goalie for the Ottawa Songbird Million-aires, who played an old-school Ken Dryden stand-up style while wearing very heavy, ancient brown leather equipment. Blake pledged to spend this particular Exclaim! Cup Hockey Summit shirtless, which is why he isn't wearing a shirt under his two-piece camel-hair suit.

colourful team of the tournament. Their roster was filled with wily characters from the Ottawa music scene. Three members of the team stuck out the most. A wild drunk and top goal scorer named Squirrel Boy would often celebrate his goals by returning to the bench to violently puke up the party from the night before. Their tiny goalie, Blake, who played in a band called Hot Piss, par-tied just as hard or harder than Squirrel Boy. Blake was barely five feet tall and as skinny as his goalie stick. He wore ancient brown leather goalie gear and sported a long, bushy, matted brown beard that at first glance gave me the impression that the Ottawa Song-bird Millionaires had recruited a homeless dwarf to play in net for them. Blake played goal the old-school stand-up style and made dramatic kick-saves on the ice just like a miniature Ken Dryden, if Dryden ever played really drunk or really hungover. Off the ice, Blake the tiny goalie had pledged to spend that particular entire tournament shirtless and was successfully doing so, exemplifying his destitute hockey wino look.

165

Another remarkable member of this team was an elephantine forward named Josh, who wore a helmet that lit up with various flashing lights when he skated. Josh was a stand-up comedian off the ice with an alter-ego named "The Unknown Wrestler," who would perform in a Mexican wrestling mask and one-piece red leisure suit between sets at the hootenannys, usually firing off a string of offensive jokes directed at the bands taking part in the tournament. ("What's the difference between a stage coach driver and the manager of Sloan? A stage coach driver only has to stare at two assholes all day.") Occasionally, Blake would inexplicably appear on stage during Josh's set dressed in what appeared to be a thoroughly soiled Hamburglar costume to help out with the act. (Josh's other impressive claim to fame was that he had once won an entire "Showcase Showdown" on an episode of *The Price Is Right* when it was still hosted by Bob Barker.)

The Ottawa Songbird Millionaires had played well throughout the tournament, making it to the final, which was being played on Easter Sunday morning at 9 a.m. On Easter Sunday morning at 5 a.m., I was still partying with most of the team in one of the Morningstars' tool shed. I had to ask goalie Blake where his band name Hot Piss came from. He called big Josh over, and like a drunken Rocky and Bullwinkle, they eagerly explained the origin.

Their group of friends had long played a party game called "Hot Piss," which was essentially an elaborate and disgusting take on Hot Potato. Hot Piss involved everyone at a house party (usually Josh and Blake's derelict house that they rented together in downtown Ottawa) peeing into a large pot. When it was filled to the brim with urine, Blake and Josh would hoist the pot up onto their stove and turn the heat to maximum. When the urine was extremely hot and nearing a boil, filling the house with an unfathomable stench, they would gather all who dared to play Hot Piss to stand in a circle in the kitchen. Blake or Josh would then grab the red-hot handles of the scorching piss pot and very quickly pass it to whomever was next in the circle. That person would pass it

SONGBIRD MILLIONAIRES '06

The Ottawa Songbird Millionaires were arguably the most colourful team to ever play in the Exclaim! Cup Hockey Summit. The team featured a who's who of the Ottawa music scene, and while they didn't emerge victorious as Cup winners the year I met them, they did eventually win it all a few years later, and my face was pressed up against the glass cheering for them when they did.

to the next person, and on it went until inevitably some drunk couldn't handle the searing metal of the handles or the weight of the sloshing pot.

All would try to stagger out of the way while the contents of an entire pot of near-boiling urine poured out all over the kitchen floor, into the heating grates and down the basement stairs. In theory, the loser of this hot piss game was the person who finally dropped the pot. The penalty was to clean up the piss, but apparently that rarely ever happened and they all just kept partying into the night. I stared at Blake and Josh, waiting for them to tell me they were joking. We partied for a couple more hours, watching the sun rise on a freezing Easter Sunday morning over the rooftops of Parkdale. A few hours later, the Ottawa Songbird Millionaires lost the final.

I said my goodbyes late Easter Sunday afternoon, and I promised Dave Bidini and Tom Goodwin that I would be back to broadcast live from the rink the following year. Tom reminded me that there wasn't a team in the tournament from Vancouver, and suggested I should return with an entire ice hockey team in tow, one that I should play on to really and truly experience the living, breathing, feel-good hockey experiment they had created. I agreed that I should, that I would, but as overjoyed as I was to find this rarified, non-jockular sporting community, I secretly thought forming my own team would be impossible. For one thing, I hadn't been on skates since I was a kid.

I spent my five-hour flight home thinking of the amazing camaraderie I saw within and among the arts-based teams at the Hockey Summit in Toronto. I thought of how much of a thrill it was watching those teams play, how inspiring I found it. Then I thought of the ball hockey marathons, my love of the Canucks, and then it hit me.

My mind raced back to my conversation with Johnny Hanson from the Hanson Brothers, waxing poetic on a bar stool in Thunder Bay about the similarities between hockey teams and rock 'n' roll bands. I *could* form a hockey team made up of Vancouver musicians and friends, a bully-free zone just like the teams I had seen skate with flash and dash in Toronto and it would be *okay* if we sucked. By the time my flight landed on the West Coast, I had the team name in my head: the Vancouver Flying Vees.

THE VANCOUVER
FLYING VEES

*"I play a position where you make mistakes. The only people
that don't make them at a hockey game are the people watching."*
PATRICK ROY, Montreal Canadiens

THE FIRST PERSON I called when I returned to Vancouver
was my old pal Nick, telling him all about the tournament in
Toronto and how we had to take our ball hockey antics to the
ice. Nick was all for it, having already dabbled on ice along with a
few other friends on a men's beer-league team. Next I called John
"The Silver Screen" Silver, an Ontario transplant who played both
ball hockey and ice hockey regularly and was always trying to convince us to take our ball hockey game to the ice. Since he was the
most experienced player we knew, I asked him to be the captain of
a team that didn't exist yet. He accepted.

From the rest of our regular West Coast ball hockey gang, only
a few guys were willing to make the financial, mental and physical leap to the ice. So we spread the word among our Vancouver
music community to be on the lookout for hockey players. Slowly
but surely, a guitarist would tell a drummer who would tell a

bassist who used to play hockey as a kid before turning to music, and they'd somehow find a way to get in touch with me. Like a cross between *The Commitments* and *Slapshot*, I would bump into musicians I barely knew on the street corner in downtown Vancouver, like Scott Walker, lead singer of the Salteens, who approached me saying, "I heard you're forming a musicians-based hockey team. I play centre." I stuck out my hand and said. "Welcome to the Flying Vees!" Soon we had enough for a roster.

Since the dream was to form a team made up of mostly musicians, we were named partly after the iconic Gibson Flying V guitar and partly in tribute to the Vancouver Canucks' short-lived but infamous "flying V" jersey the team wore in the 1982 Stanley Cup Final. That all-encompassing intense, unwieldy design and fall-harvest colours were too much even for our Vancouver Flying Vees hockey club, so we adopted the more aesthetically pleasing classic original Canucks colours of green, blue and white. For our chest crest, we lovingly paid tribute to the Canucks' equally maligned yet artistically perfect original logo, the "stick-in-rink," which formed an almost invisible-at-a-glance conceptual "C" for Canucks. To tie it all together, we turned that hockey stick into a Gibson Flying V guitar, now a melding of what we thought were two of the coolest symbols in rock 'n' roll and hockey.

THE SAME SPRING we were forming the Vancouver Flying Vees, in 2002, the rebounding Vancouver Canucks were back in the Stanley Cup playoffs, sneaking into the eighth and final spot. They were facing the powerhouse Detroit Red Wings, stacked with stars like captain Steve "Stevie Wonder" Yzerman, defenceman Niklas "The Perfect Human" Lidstrom and goalie Dominik "The Dominator" Hasek. Because the Red Wings were at the top of the standings, the first two games of the potential seven-game series were in Detroit. To the shock of the entire hockey world, the rebuilt Canucks won both games in the Joe Louis Arena, Detroit's fabled "Hockeytown" barn.

Games 3 and 4 shifted back to Vancouver, in front of an arena full of deliriously happy fans who were allowing themselves to hope. Everything was going fairly well for the Canucks in Game 3. With just under thirty seconds left in the second stanza, the game was tied 1–1, and the Red Wings were barely getting a sniff. That's when Lidstrom skated to the centre red line and fired a seemingly harmless one-hundred-foot slapshot into the Canucks zone. Dan "The Man" Cloutier, that feisty Canucks netminder, dropped down to scoop up the routine floater with his glove at the top of his crease. Nightmare. Somehow, the puck managed to elude his outstretched glove, his leg pad and his stick to skim right by him, unmolested, slamming into the bottom metal rung of the net. It rang out like an ominous bell, and that bell was tolling for Dan Cloutier and the Canucks.

There was a momentary stunned silence in the arena followed by an audible gasp of shock rising from the crowd, a cloud of panic, as palms slapped foreheads and arms were thrown in the air in disgust and despair. The goal came against the flow of the game and against the play of the series, both of which were going the Canucks' way until the titanic goalie gaffe. It gave Detroit the wind beneath their Wings and they never looked back. The Red Wings won that game 3–1, won the next three straight to take the series, then soared through the rest of the playoffs to win the Stanley Cup. Dan Cloutier found himself at the lonely end of the rink on that shot, and subsequently for the rest of his tenuous tenure with the Canucks.

171

OUR VANCOUVER FLYING Vees had the concept, the players, the team name and the logo (designed by bassist, defenceman and young entertainment lawyer Kyle "Foggy Town" Fogden) and sparkling new polyester jerseys. Now all we had to do was actually get on the ice. I hadn't been on skates in decades. Would I still remember what to do? How to move, how to stop, how to skate backward? There was an acid-reflux anticipation in our dressing room at the community centre rink we rented as we slowly strapped on enormous amounts of equipment, many of us pretending we knew in what order and how everything was supposed to be arranged on our bodies. I laced up a pair of used goalie skates that immediately felt like vices on my feet and forced my mind back to the community rinks of my youth.

Our first practice with the Flying Vees looked like a cross between *Disney on Ice* and the basketball scene from *One Flew Over the Cuckoo's Nest*. Wedged into the net in my odds and sods combination of ball hockey and ice hockey equipment, I was happy to see that a couple of the musicians actually knew how to skate and handle the puck. It was painfully obvious that others had no clue. If the puck came anywhere near them, they would fall down in a violent contortion of limbs and skates, body parts twisting in ways the human body was not meant to twist. But somehow they would get up again, skating like they were dragging an anvil. Not that I was any better. Every time I tried to skate backward I collapsed into a snow angel. Standing in the crease when play was at the other end, it felt like there were rusty nails being driven up through the used goalie skates into the soles of my feet, and then I realized there probably were, as I hadn't inspected the skates very carefully before slapping down twenty dollars for them. But each time I took a tumble, nothing hurt. I was also able to get up a lot faster than I could on the ball hockey court.

On the off-chance I made a save, I felt the heavy WHUMP of the puck against the thick, horse hair–stuffed leather pads that protected my legs. It was such a satisfying feeling. I was a wall! Then the next five or six shots would beat me, and I felt the angry beast that had burst out of my chest protector so many times on the ball hockey court quelling up inside. On ice, I was determined to keep the beast chained. Or so I hoped.

Within a couple of practices, positions, lines and nicknames were created. The few guys who crossed over from ball hockey were John "The Silver Screen" Silver, Nick "Lock-Eye" Thomas,

Paul "The Deker" Needham and Darwin "Galapagos" Green. New players included "Flowin'" Kevin Rowan, John "The Hammer" Stiver, Jeremy "Bomber" Bidnall, Jordy "Killer" Kenna, Kristian "Oly" Olsen, Brian "Lattatude" Latta, Anthony "Hempy" Hempell, Scotty "The Talker" Walker, "Weavin'" Steven Craig and Scott "Cabo Wabo" Cabianca. I was dubbed Grant "Kingpin" Lawrence because I managed the team. After four or five practices, we deemed ourselves ready for action. Off the ice, several members of the team and I also formed the Flying Vees band, learning to play all those weird novelty puck rock songs I had broadcasted for years on my CBC "Hockey Rock" specials. Naturally, our guitarists played Gibson Flying V guitars in our matching Flying Vees jerseys. So we had a hockey team and a band, which meant we were set to become the first official team entry west of the Rocky Mountains to join the Exclaim! Hockey Summit of the Arts the following spring. The Flying Vees were Toronto bound.

22

THE BUZZ
IN MY FLESH

IT WAS ON Easter weekend inside a dripping, smelly, cinder-block building called the McCormick Arena, located in the West Toronto neighbourhood of Parkdale, when I gingerly stepped out onto the ice for my first-ever official ice hockey game. I was thirty-one years old and in full goalie gear, already soaked in sweat, trying to tell myself I was ready to backstop the Vancouver Flying Vees in a *real game* with whistles and everything. We were in the Zed Division, the lowest possible playing level of the Exclaim! Hockey Summit of the Arts. After a brief warm-up to the deafening strains of a live, rink-side band featuring members of Sloan and the Sadies, the ref blew the whistle and then straddled the centre red line like he was Lee Van Cleef on an Appaloosa. He held the puck aloft with one hand, waiting for the players to align. The puck was dropped. The game was on. We were slaughtered 8–0.

The Exclaim! tournament guaranteed each team three games in the round robin portion of the tournament. We lost all three games badly, and had flown across most of the continent to do so. Our last game, against a team called the Calgary Corndogs,

After seeing me play goal on ice for the first time, Blake from the Ottawa Songbird Million-aires belched in my face, then slurred out his review of my performance, which included various disparaging goalie nick-names like "The Guesser," "The Wounded Moth," "Sunburn" and "Guy Who Just Fell Out of His Wheelchair."

turned surprisingly sour near the end of the drubbing. Other than that brief skirmish, we had a fabulous time despite the on-ice out-comes. Blake and Josh from the Ottawa Songbird Millionaires watched our final game and were eager to give me their review of my goaltending performance. When I saw them in the parking lot, Blake belched, then pointed at me and loudly yelled out, "Hey, it's the Guesser!" When I asked Blake what he meant, he explained. "It's amaaaaaaazing!" he drunkenly drawled, jabbing his little index finger into my chest. "You don't waaiiiiit for the shooter to fire the puck! You collapse *before* the shot, guessing on where the puck *might* be going!"

Josh chimed in, slapping his heavy hand on my shoulder. "And it *never* worked! And hey, Grant, we've all heard of butterfly-style goaltending, but *you* seemed to have mastered a whole new style: 'the wounded moth.'"

176   Blake picked it up from there: "When you went down to make a save you looked like a guy who had fallen out of his wheelchair."

Josh jumped back in. "Hey, Sunburn! Do you need some aloe rubbed on the back of your neck from that red goal light burning so intensely behind you all game long?"

After each jibe the two of them doubled over laughing. Had these heinous reviews been coming from some Buck- or Gooch-like jock, spitting out the words with venom, I would have emotionally

Exclaim! Hockey Summit and Good Times Hockey League commissioner Tom Goodwin (centre), the man with hockey idealism that was as pure as freshly fallen snow. Here he is surrounded by an assortment of adoring and appreciative rock 'n' roll freaks and geeks from across Canada who gathered each Easter weekend in Toronto to lace 'em up for the Shangri-La of hockey tournaments.

turtled. But hearing the critique come from a stand-up comedian and his tiny, bearded buddy, both lovably drunk and never taking the game seriously, I laughed right along with them. They were friends, none of it mattered, as long as we were having fun. I was playing hockey! On ice! Wounded moth!

Once the champions of the tournament were crowned, the attention turned to a local bar where an awards ceremony was held. Commissioner Tom Goodwin handed out all sorts of trophies for best forward, defenceman and goalie, as well as an award called the Roger Neilson Tie, named after the famously flamboyant coach who led the Canucks to their first Stanley Cup Final appearance in 1982. This award, a loud and ugly necktie, went to the player that showed the most "colour," the most team spirit. One of the Ottawa Songbird Millionaires almost always won it, and this year proved no different.

177

The Vancouver Flying Vees may not have won a single game at our first trip to the Exclaim! Cup Hockey Summit, but we did start a notorious back alley after-party tradition known as "Live at the Durango." The outdoor, shivering vaudeville extravaganza attracted the most hilarious characters the tournament had to offer, while we entertained ourselves with comedy acts, singalongs and illegal bonfires late into the night.

The Flying Vees didn't have much to celebrate at the awards ceremony, but even after our losses, our Good Times hockey adrenalin was pumping and we didn't want the party to end. We had rented a Dodge Durango, a gigantic, gold SUV to get us around to the different rinks and events in Toronto. It was parked out back and filled with beer. Once the awards show wrapped up, we invited everyone to come around to the back alley and keep the party going at our Durango. We popped open the hatch, cranked up the tunes and handed out beer after beer into an alley full of artsy, co-ed hockey players partying deep into the Easter Sunday night.

Doo-wop songs were sung, dance moves were busted out, a bonfire of broken hockey sticks was started, and by the glow of those totally illegal urban flames, our back-alley booze party turned into an impromptu talent show. First, the Unknown Wrestler did a set of stand-up. Comedian Sean Cullen, a member of a team called the Jokers, followed him up with a song-and-dance vaudeville routine. Chris Murphy from Sloan sang the Canadian anthem accompanied by Nick on ukulele. There was crowd-surfing. Anyone with any sort of "act" was getting up on "stage" (the curb) and letting it fly. The late-night, contraband event became known as "Live at the Durango," and would become a yearly tradition at the Hockey Summit of the Arts until it was eventually and infamously busted up by the cops . . . but it was great while it lasted. We woke up on Easter Monday morning sore, hungover, winless and extremely happy. The Flying Vees had bonded and vowed to return. We had indeed found what we thought was a hockey nirvana.

23

TOOK ME
BY SURPRISE

ACK HOME IN Vancouver, we made the collective decision to
keep the Flying Vees going on a regular basis. One of our
players, Brian "Lattatude" Latta, signed us up to division
eight of a ten-division local beer league called Duffers Hockey for
an entire thirty-game winter season. Division one was considered
the best: guys who were very skilled, some even having played pro
or junior, whereas division ten was considered absolutely base-
ment-level novice (that's where I thought the Flying Vees should
have started). Even though it was a huge league, other like-minded,
arts-based teams were also signed up, like the Ultra Maroons, East
Van Halen and the Bombers, a team that featured members of
bands like the Odds, Skinny Puppy and SNFU. New players joined
the Flying Vees' ranks for the full season like Saleem "The Dream"
Dar, Greg "The Guarantee" Anderson, Chris "Clutch" James and
Jay "Snakebite" Johnston. Beez from the Smugglers would play
with us too, as a substitute player when we needed him.

The Flying Vees' first official league game was on a warm night
in early September. The quality of the rink in the North Vancouver

ice complex was so much nicer than the community rinks we had competed in during the Hockey Summit in Toronto. The ice felt hard and fast. Almost three periods later, in the dying seconds of our first game, I was crouched in the crease as the play rattled around at the other end of the ice. I stayed still, tightly gripping my goalie stick on the verge of panic, sweat dripping through my goalie mask. There were only thirty seconds left and we were up by a score of 5–3. Sure, it was a beer-league hockey game with a bunch of musicians on skates, but as the final buzzer sounded it hit me: the Flying Vees had won! All my teammates skated over to my goal crease and tapped my helmet or whacked my pads. Our first win... *my first win*—of any kind in organized amateur team sports... ever... in my entire life. I loved it!

We clamoured into our cinder-block dressing room, pumped with adrenalin and bursting with conversation and laughter. Cans of cold Black Label were passed around and cracked open, the sound of success. Wet, reeking equipment was peeled off and tossed into the puddles on the rubber floor mats. Helmets were removed, revealing matted, sweaty hair. Smiles abounded while boisterous chatter clattered off the cinder blocks. Many of us hung around just to drink and talk long after the game had ended. Only when the next team showed up to get ready for their game did we vacate the dressing room, and did so begrudgingly.

It was the beginning of a long-standing Flying Vees tradition. That cacophonic dressing room became our own private men's club. If our game was the last of the night, we'd hang out in the dressing room until the janitor would kick us out. One night, the arena staff didn't realize we were still in there several hours after our game had ended, so they shut off all the lights and locked us inside the rink. Johnny Hanson was right: there were many similarities between the emerging Flying Vees hockey rituals and the Smugglers' nightly life in rock 'n' roll that greatly helped ease the pain of having my beloved band coming to an end.

TO THE SHOCK and awe of everyone on the Vancouver Flying Vees, we not only won our first game, we won our first *five* games. We were ecstatic, until we realized that Duffers was a socialist hockey league. If your team was successful, the league taxed your success by moving you up a division so the games would be harder to win. If your team lost most of its games, they'd give you a break by moving you down a division to make it easier for you to win. I was perfectly happy winning every game every night in division eight, but after the quick-start winning streak, we were moved up to lofty division seven. I thought it was all over.

We lost a couple games here and there, but somehow, even in the higher division, the Flying Vees kept winning. I even notched a couple of shutouts, one of them with my parents in the stands. They were just as stunned as I was that their arty weirdo kid was actually, unimaginably, playing an organized sport, and that I still maintained vague muscle memory of their skating lessons of yore. I'd been trying my best to keep my competitive temper iced, only holding one or two angry yard sales during the season. And there was the one time when I challenged the other team's entire bench to fight, Tiger Williams style, while at centre ice. There was also the time when I mistakenly fought a "little person" with my parents looking on. Another time, a clumsy big guy barrelled into me on a two-on-one. I was knocked flat on my back and he landed directly on top of me, face mask to face mask. I was just about to clock him with my blocker when he whispered, "I really love your CBC Radio 3 podcast!" The comment instantly diffused the heat of moment. "Oh!" I whispered back, lowering my blocker. "Thanks for listening!"

When that first regular season finally wrapped up, we had won a very surprising seventeen games, lost only seven and tied four. It was time for the playoffs. The first team to garner four victories won the championship. We won the first two games by scores of 5–2 and 3–2. The third game, our semifinal, went into overtime. Greg "The Guarantee" Anderson lived up to his nickname by netting a gorgeous top-shelf wrist shot for the Flying Vees' first-ever overtime win. And so, at the end of the Flying Vees' first year of beer-league hockey we found ourselves in the championship final. I was stunned.

Unfortunately, during our semifinal, my wonky knees acted up for the first time all season, one of them slipping out of its brace and dislocating ever so slightly but oh so painfully. I was able to finish the game, but as soon as I had stripped off my mountain of wet, soiled goalie equipment, my still-scarred knee swelled to the size of a hairy cantaloupe. I tried limping around the dressing room, and felt that lifelong, familiar jolt of pain when I put weight on my heel. When I was a kid, I could be back on my feet after a dislocation within minutes. By the time I was in my thirties, it sometimes took weeks for me to be mobile again. The championship final was in seven days. I hoped it would be just enough time to ice the knee, blast it with Advil and make a quick recovery.

Six nights later, I lay awake in the darkness of my bedroom with an icepack on my still-swollen knee. It was the night before our championship final against the number one team in our division, a high-scoring club called the Snow Cats, featuring Doug "the Blizzard" Snow, the team's namesake and best goal scorer in our entire ten-division league. In our games against them during the regular season, Snow had scored on me constantly. He could snap in goals from any position to any corner of the net, showing off razzle-dazzle skills that gave me post-traumatic Buck stress flashes.

I called our captain at 1 a.m. the morning of the game and rasped my concerns into the phone. John thought about it for a while and then suggested the unorthodox beer-league hockey move of bringing a backup goalie to the game in case I couldn't play. We checked: there was no rule against dressing two goalies for one team.

I tossed and turned for the rest of the night, unable to sleep, darkly obsessing over the game. Every time I tried to force my eyes shut, I saw the face of "The Blizzard" charging down the ice on a clear-cut breakaway. Every time he would easily score, doing whatever he wanted like a tiger swatting at a lamb. I called our captain the next day to execute the backup goalie plan. We arranged for a local rink-rat goalie named "Save-On" John to back me up on the bench.

Sure enough, Doug Snow scored three minutes into the first period. Pulling myself up from the ice as the Snow Cats celebrated, I could feel my knee throbbing. We got out of the first period down by just one, but in the second the Snow Cats scored another, and then a third goal with just one minute left in the stanza. It was a killer goal. The score was now 3–0. When the buzzer sounded to end the second period, I lay slumped in the crease like a discarded puppet. My end of the rink had never felt so lonely. Captain Silver skated over and leaned down. "How's the knee?"

"Not great," I grunted. "Should we go with Plan Backup?"

"Maybe," our captain answered. "For a little while."

The Snow Cats were shocked and amused to see us replacing goalies for the third period, yelling catcalls down the ice at me and the rest of the team. I sat slumped and embarrassed at the end of the bench while Save-On John skated into our net. Three minutes into the third period, our defenceman Saleem "The Dream" Dar scored on a blistering slapshot to get us into the game. With just over five minutes remaining, The Guarantee scored a power play goal to claw us within one of the Snow Cats' lead. As the final thirty seconds ticked down, we were throwing everything we could at their net. One of their defencemen gathered it up and fired it from their end all the way down to ours, icing the puck with just twenty-one seconds left in the game.

Captain Silver pulled Save-On John for an extra attacker with the final faceoff deep in the Snow Cats' zone. Both Flying Vees goalies stood side by side at the bench, our masks off, staring down the ice. The puck was dropped. There was an intense scramble as the seconds raced toward the final buzzer. Players from both teams madly swung their sticks at the puck like kids at a piñata party. Somehow, our big power forward Kristian "Oly" Olsen shovelled the puck into the high slot where it sat for a split second before Captain Silver rushed onto it and swung at it like a Scottish barbarian inventing golf. The puck torched through a thicket of players toward the net. The goalie desperately reached for it but it sizzled past his outstretched glove with millimetres to spare. The Flying Vees . . . had tied the championship game . . . with *four seconds* left in regulation time. Total bedlam broke loose on our bench as the Snow Cats looked on in catatonic shock, Cheshire grins wiped clean.

A five-minute, pressure-cooker overtime followed. Oly Olsen almost went from hero to zero when he took a too-many-men-on-the-ice penalty, but Save-On John made some brilliant stops to keep us alive. The buzzer sounded to end the overtime with no scoring; the championship would be decided by a shootout. We were totally unprepared for the game stretching that far and weren't sure who our three shooters would be. Captain Silver and I quickly discussed it. The Guarantee was an easy choice. Second would be Scott "Cabo Wabo" Cabianca, the Dean Martin of beer-league hockey and a great goal scorer. Third would be a skilled player named "Weavin'" Steven Craig who could hammer the puck, but when we called his name, he held his ungloved hand up from the bench, showing his pinky bent, twisted, broken. We had to pick someone else.

One of the ball hockey players who had crossed over to the cold side was Paul "The Deker" Needham. On pavement, he loved pulling off all sorts of snazzy, highly annoying in-tight stick manouevres that always fooled and frustrated me. He didn't have much opportunity to do that on the ice because he couldn't skate fast enough to get loose. But maybe he could if he was alone and unmolested on a goalie in a shootout. Could those ball hockey sleight-of-hand tricks translate to the ice? Captain Silver scribbled his name down on the score sheet.

The Flying Vees would shoot first and the Snow Cats second in a best-of-three. Cabo Wabo was up. He skated in fast, backed the goalie up into his crease, stopped hard and roofed a forehand top-shelf goal, much to our excited cheers from the bench. The Snow Cats shot next. We were all certain it would be "The Blizzard," by far their best goal scorer, the best goal scorer in our entire league, but it was one of their other lesser Cats. Save-On John stood tall and made a fabulous shoulder save. Up next for the Flying Vees was the Guàrantee, who had won it for us in overtime of the last game. He skated in and took a low shot between the goalie's legs, but the goalie collapsed and snuffed the puck before it could squeak through.

The next Snow Cats shooter lined up at centre and again we were shocked to see it wasn't Doug Snow. Again, Save-On John came through with the save. It was Paul "The Deker" Needham's turn for the Flying Vees. It all came down to this shot: if the Deker could score, we'd win the best-of-three shootout and the championship.

Our captain was so nervous he couldn't even watch, burying his head between his legs at the bench. Charlene the Ref blew the whistle. With his dad looking on from the stands, the Deker gathered up the puck and streaked in, finally one-on-one with a goalie. He was within three feet of the net when he began his dance, whipping the puck forehand, backhand, forehand, backhand with lightning succession. He successfully opened up the goalie like a cheap can of tuna. The Deker deftly slid the puck into the net.

We won. We had completed the incredible, improbable comeback from being down 3–0 in the third period to win the first-ever championship for the Flying Vees. It was the first and only sporting championship most of us had ever won in our lifetimes. We poured onto the ice in joyous celebration, looking at each other with shock and jubilation in our faces. We mobbed The Deker in the Snow Cats zone as his dad leapt up and down in the stands. Doug "The Blizzard" Snow would have been their last shooter, but

187

he never got the chance. The dejected Snow Cats goalie skated by us, shoulders slouched, helmeted head hung low. In our mass celebration, I still couldn't help but glance over at him with empathy.

THE FLYING VEES

2004/2005 CHAMPIONS

DIVISION SEVEN

DUFFERS HOCKEY LEAGUE

That's what was permanently engraved onto a shiny gold plate on the trophy's wooden base, and put on display in the glass trophy case in the main foyer of our rink. Upon entering our rink over the years since, many times I have paused to peer through the glass at our engraved team name, and thought back to the trophies encased in my high school's main foyer—trophies that seemed so impossible for someone like me to ever win, it was like they were untouchable museum pieces.

A lingering regret that I couldn't help but admit to myself (and only myself) was that the only part of our championship game that I could take credit for was us being down 3–0. It was elephant-in-the-dressing-room obvious that the game's TSN Turning Point was the moment I got pulled and Save-On John went in. Save-On John didn't allow a single goal, including overtime and the shootout, while we beat the other goalie five times in the comeback to end all beer-league comebacks.

My teammates never said a disparaging word. I was part of the team and I had won the championship along with everybody else. But I couldn't shake the regret, and the sinister, phantom whispers of jocks past, wrestling inside my head after that game. *They had to take you out so the team could win,* WIMP. I wondered if I would ever get the chance to prove myself in a championship hockey game again. As luck would have it, I would—much, much sooner than I ever would have anticipated.

The Vancouver Flying Vees' valiant captain, John "The Silver Screen" Silver, an Ontario transplant who knew the game of hockey better than anyone on our team. As tough as nails, as honest as a judge, as hard-working as a mule, he scored the tying goal in our championship final with four seconds left in the game. PHOTO BY GEOFF KEHRIG

EVERYTHING YOU'VE DONE WRONG

O NLY A COUPLE of weeks after our beer-league championship, the Flying Vees were on a plane making our return trip to the Hockey Summit of the Arts for Easter weekend. My knee was still feeling a little wonky but I was determined to play, despite the demons I had wrestled with after our victory. The Vees touched down in Toronto, brimming with confidence, determined as a group to at least win one game this time. We picked up our rented Durango and headed into the city for our first game at De La Salle Arena.

The win that totally eluded us the year previous came quickly. Our first game was against a team called the Parkdale Hockey Lads, filled with a bunch of great guys who had a cool Who–style target as their logo. "I Can't Explain" exactly what happened, but we smoked the Lads 8–2. Our game the next day was against the Niagara Crystal Beach Comets, one of the greatest hockey team names I had ever heard. We beat them 3–0, my first-ever shutout at the Hockey Summit of the Arts. I made a particularly satisfying blocker save off a rush down the left wing with just ten seconds remaining. When the puck hit my blocker it sounded

Besides all the action on and off the ice, and the great friends we made at our appearances at the Exclaim! Cup Hockey Summit tournament, surely one of the biggest surprises for many of us was to be presented with our very own team hockey cards to bring home from the experience. Back row L-R: Scott "Cabo Wabo" Cabianca, Beez, Scotty "The Talker" Walker. Middle row L-R: Kyle "Foggy Town" Fogden, Brian "Lattatude" Latta, Anthony "Hempy" Hempell, John "The Silver Screen" Silver, Kristian "Oly" Olsen. Front row L-R: Nick "Lock-Eye" Thomas, John "The Hammer" Stiver, Grant "Kingpin" Lawrence, "Flowin'" Kevin Rowan, Jeremy "Bomber" Bidnall.

like a shotgun blast and the crowd in the bleachers let out a loud "*oooooo*." I loved it.

The third game of the round robin was against the Montreal Ninja Tune Wicked Deadly Karate Chops, a team run by the man behind the amazing Ninja Tune Records, which also featured amongst its players Patti Schmidt, long-time host of CBC Radio's *Brave New Waves* and a personal broadcasting hero of mine. We were honoured to play a hockey team from Montreal, and even more flattered to tie them for a final score of 4–4. That meant we were unbeaten in the round robin portion of the tournament, and in just our second year we were bound for the playoffs, something many teams who had played for years in the tournament had never experienced.

The semifinal was against the London Fog. The game was tied 2–2 late in the third period when their best player tripped me as he was skating through my goal crease. Whether it was a mistake or not, the ref caught it and gave him a two-minute goalie interference penalty. Kristian "Oly" Olsen scored a wicked power play goal to win the game 3–2 and send us to our second championship final in a month. We celebrated deliriously at centre ice. We couldn't believe our fortune . . . until Tom Goodwin informed us we would be facing the Calgary Corndogs in the final.

The Calgary Corndogs was the team that creamed us the year before, during our last game of the tournament when things got rough. I didn't want to play them again. They had an agitator named Corky "Cracker Jack" McCracken who seemed to like to get under my skin every time I bumped into him at the tournament, on or off the ice. He was about my height and was built like a New York City garbage can: short, round and always overflowing with trash. He was one of those guys who was always looking for the upper hand, the advantage in any situation; he didn't have an off switch. He was an absolute master of the backhanded compliment.

Maybe Cracker Jack could smell my insecurity when he was around me—he somehow just knew I was a phony goalie, nervous of every shot directed my way, sleeplessly analyzing every goal I let in for days, desperate for most games to be over when we were in the lead and hugely relieved when the buzzer sounded. Whenever I ran into Cracker Jack at the tournament, before we even knew we'd be playing each other, he'd block my path: "Congrats on your tournament so far, Lawrence! Hey, I saw your win against the Hockey Lads . . . Did they even get five shots against you? And you still let in a couple of goals, eh?" Or, "Sorry to hear you guys blew your one-goal lead against Montreal . . . I heard the tying goal on you was pretty fuckin' weak."

I answered his questions outwardly with a smile, but inside he drove me nuts. I thought that was exactly the kind of stuff that wasn't supposed to happen at that tournament, that the players were above crap like that. I wanted to scream in his face, but I kept repeating Tom Goodwin's Hockey Summit guiding principles in my head: *sportsmanship, fun, safety, creative expression, inclusion* and *empathy*. Smiling through gritted teeth, I admitted to Cracker Jack that yeah, I had let in a couple of lousy goals in the tournament so far. When I later learned that I would have to face Cracker Jack and his team for the heralded Exclaim! Cup I felt the anxiety flooding in.

Based on our previous year, when we were blown out in every game, some Flying Vees hadn't harboured a lot of confidence that we would make the final. They had booked their flights home early on Easter Sunday afternoon, before the final was scheduled to happen, meaning we were going to be short a few players. Making matters worse, with such an incredible amount of hockey in such a short time, we had several injuries to deal with: our captain John Silver had broken his finger in Game 2 but had it frozen and was still playing; and one of our best goal scorers, Cabo Wabo, had hurt his knee in a collision in the semifinal but was willing to keep playing. My knee was holding up, but I tried to keep moving between games, fearful that if I rested I would seize up like the Tin Man in a rainstorm.

I showed up at the arena about an hour before the Exclaim! Cup championship. The weather was mild and spring-like, so I decided to loosen up and do a warm-up and some stretching on the other side of the field, three hundred feet from the entrance of the rink. I was jogging on the spot, doing jumping jacks and, in what I've been told from a distance looks like "jazz hands," loosening up my arms. Then I heard someone shout at me. "Hi Grant!"

I turned around and squinted. It was Corky "Cracker Jack" McCracken, over at the entrance of the rink with a couple of his teammates, hockey bag over one shoulder, sticks in his hand. He and his teammates were laughing. "What the fuck are you doing over there? Is that some sort of Richard Simmons dancing goalie routine or what?" While they laughed their way into the rink, I immediately stopped my warm-up and stared down into the grass in humiliation. Cracker Jack was trying his jockular best to throw me off my "game." It was already working.

Our dressing room, usually boisterous and crackling with energy, had a pensiveness that we had never experienced. The injured guys iced and wrapped their sore parts. Too many players were missing. My stomach felt like a Celtic knot. From where we sat nervously lacing skates, we could hear that the arena was packed with fans eager to watch the Easter Sunday final, with rink rock blaring. It was the kind of energy I would usually love to be a part of.

I've always believed that the unspoken code (maybe an actual rule?) of the on-ice hockey warm-up is that each team is to warm up in its own end of the rink. At no time should another player cross the centre line to enter the other team's zone except maybe, and only maybe, to chase a wayward puck. Cracker Jack decided to rewrite this age-old point of hockey etiquette by doing laps of the entire rink during warm-up, skating through our end of the rink to the surprise and confusion of our players. I was stretching along the sideboards near the players' bench on our side of centre, trying to ignore him. Cracker Jack leaned down and loudly slapped his stick on the ice directly in front of my face, like a butcher chopping steaks. "You ready, Lawrence? You ready?"

I ignored him, looking away, wondering if I might puke with anxiety right through the grill of my mask. Luckily, my old pal Nick "Lock-Eye" Thomas saw it all and charged at Cracker Jack, cross-checking him back across the centre line. Cracker Jack spun on his skates and swung at Nick with his stick, both yelling at each other, until the captains of the respective teams and various other players from both sides pulled them apart. It was guys exactly like Cracker Jack who made me want to have nothing to do with sports in the first place and yet here I was, in my early thirties, still having to deal with people like him, and at the Exclaim! Hockey Summit of the Arts of all places.

After a tentative first few minutes, midway through the first period their best player came down the ice one-on-one with one of our defencemen. The Corndog cut across the high slot and shot the puck low and hard, beating me on the glove side. 1–0 Corndogs. Cracker Jack assisted on the goal. As I collected myself in the crease he skated by and hissed at me, "If you're gonna serve us up goals like that, this is going to be easy." The second period was scoreless, but on one particular rush, Cracker Jack took the opportunity to crash the net as hard as he could, supposedly chasing a loose puck. He drove me into the back of the net, but the puck stayed out. I was able to get a few whacks of my blocker into the back of Cracker Jack's helmet without the ref noticing.

"What the fuck is wrong with you?" screamed Cracker Jack, swinging back at me with his stick as the Vees defence dragged him out of the net. The score was still a perilous 1–0 for the Corndogs, well into the third period. We were pounding the puck on their net, but their goalie, a tall, Gumby-like guy, stopped everything. With just five minutes to play, there was a turnover at our blue line and one of the Corndogs' weakest players found the puck on his stick and whacked at it. The shot was an off-speed knuckler that fluttered right over my blocker and into the top corner of the net.

This guy must never score because the Corndogs poured off their bench and mobbed him at centre ice, dog-piling on him as if it were an overtime goal. It may as well have been. As the clock ticked down, there would be no beer-league Flying Vees miracle during this final. When the buzzer sounded the Calgary Corndogs won the championship game 2–0.

Back in our end, we gathered and gave them three limp cheers, then lined up for the handshake at centre ice. To each Corndog player I muttered either "Good game," or "Congratulations." I saw Cracker Jack smirking ear to ear, shouting backhanded compliments to every Flying Vee who shook his hand. The handshake is supposed to represent the sportsmanship of the game. No matter what bad blood there may be during the game, it stays in the game. The handshake is supposed to wipe the slate clean. Staring at the gleaming, smarmy face of the victorious Cracker Jack, I saw a flip card Rolodex of every bully in a hockey jacket who had ever teased me, shot me, concussed me, slapped me, punched me or crashed my goalie crease. I thought to myself, "What would Tiger Williams do in this situation?"

At the very moment Cracker Jack and I were to meet in the handshake line of the Exclaim! Hockey Summit of the Arts championship—he the winner and I the loser—I committed one of the cardinal sins of sports. Instead of reaching for Cracker Jack's outstretched hand, I smacked both of my hands into his chest and shoved him back, barking "YOU'RE AN ASSHOLE!" It was loud enough for the entire packed rink to hear. Then, to the horror of my teammates, I went yard sale. I tossed my blocker and glove to the side, pulled my mask up over my head and charged at him, fists balled, like I had seen Dan "The Man" Cloutier do so many times. I managed to get a hold of Cracker Jack's jersey when someone grabbed hold of me and yanked me back. It was one of our forwards, "Flowin'" Kevin Rowan. I spun around on my skates, got loose from Flo-Ro's grip and charged at Cracker Jack again.

The crowd in the stands was now on its feet, raining down a blurred cacophony of surprise, amusement and disgust. Cracker Jack was screaming at me, trying to get at me just as hard as I was trying to get at him. His teammates were holding him back while mine blocked me. Gloves and sticks flew into the air as other Flying Vees grabbed other Corndogs. It was a mob of pushing, shoving and yelling at centre ice. The ref streaked back onto the ice, blowing his whistle in a steady scream like a raging kettle on the boil. The crowd continued to holler down incomprehensible noise. John "The Silver Screen" Silver wrestled me to the ice. "COOL IT!"

The Flying Vees were herded toward our gate so the Corndogs could receive their championship trophy. My teammates pushed their way into our dressing room, exhausted and bitter from defeat, and embarrassed by my actions. I kept going, waddling down the hallway and collapsing into a nook beside the janitor's mop bucket. I was a heap of sweat, stench and goalie equipment. I broke the code. I had lowered myself to Cracker Jack's level and gone against everything the Hockey Summit was trying to achieve: *sportsmanship, fun, safety, creative expression, inclusion, empathy*. Somehow, even though my hockey team had defied the odds and made it into two championships in the space of a month in two different cities on two different sides of the country, I felt like an epic loser. It was just as Nick had warned . . . my actions made me into the jerk I was trying to avoid. I had lost my temper at the most inappropriate time imaginable. I had to redeem myself.

25

LOUIE, LOUIE

THE SUMMER FOLLOWING those two Flying Vees finals, the Vancouver Canucks would make one of the most gargantuan trades in the history of the team, and they would make it with the man who had almost destroyed the team years earlier: Iron Mike Keenan. After getting turfed from Vancouver, and a short stint with the Boston Bruins, he had landed on his feet first as the head coach, then as the general manager of the Florida Panthers. Trade trigger-happy as ever, it didn't take long for Iron Mike to swing a huge deal with the Canucks. Swapping rain boots for flips-flops was Vancouver power forward Todd "The Uzi" Bertuzzi, along with a defenceman and an expendable goalie. Headed the other way from Florida was the all-star goalie Roberto "Bobby Lu" Luongo.

Most Canucks fans, including myself, freaked out with joy at the news. Not only were we getting arguably the best young goalie in the NHL, we were also offloading the oversized baggage of Bertuzzi. Two years earlier, Todd Bertuzzi, who had emerged into a star after landing in Vancouver in a trade for Trevor Linden, was involved in one of the ugliest on-ice incidents in Canucks history. While attempting to defend the honour of Canucks captain Markus Naslund, Bertuzzi went after marginal Colorado Avalanche forward Steve Moore, who had bodychecked Naslund in the face earlier in the season. Moore wouldn't fight Bertuzzi, so the massive winger stalked Moore down at centre ice and attacked him from behind, slugging Moore with a right hook in the side of the face, then drove Moore face down onto the ice. The 230-pound Bertuzzi came down on top of him. Other players from both teams piled on top of them. When the bodies were eventually removed from the dog pile, Moore lay motionless, arms akimbo.

I watched the game and was extremely conflicted by the incident. On the one hand, Moore had injured our captain and one of our players was trying to make him answer for it. Retribution and standing up for your teammates, especially your captain, is a tradition as old as the NHL itself. On the other hand, wasn't Bertuzzi's attack on Moore the exact type of thuggery that churned my stomach? How could I in good conscience say "good riddance" to Steve Moore? Moore was an agitator, a breed of NHL player who often infuriated the other team by on-ice actions often referred to as "cheap shots." Moore definitely didn't want to fight Bertuzzi, likely because Moore had already fought earlier in the game with another Canucks forward, and who else but a heavyweight would willingly want to fight a hulk like Bertuzzi?

It was later determined that Steve Moore suffered a broken neck, concussion, and facial cuts in the attack and subsequent dog pile. Moore never played another NHL game and the incident hung over the Canucks like a curse. Once Bertuzzi served his long suspension, his once dazzling offensive numbers and on-ice power forward dominance were never the same. He was hounded by the media before and after every game. During the games, fans in rinks around the NHL relentlessly booed him. The eventual assault charges and lawsuits that followed were a major distraction. So when Bertuzzi was finally traded for Luongo, many fans saw the trade as a double-win. We had rid ourselves of the Bertuzzi albatross and Vancouver's years of revolving goalies were finally over. It had been almost eight years since "Captain" Kirk McLean got booted out of town by Iron Mike, which led to a ridiculous eighteen different goaltenders trying to be the main man since then. The goalie who came closest to being a regular for any length of time was Dan "The Man" Cloutier, a situation that didn't end well.

Roberto Luongo would finally be the Canucks' main man. With his six-foot-three frame, long Roman nose, dark skin and slicked-back black hair, he strode into town with his head held high like a Caesar, ready to save our team from the attacking Huns on the frozen battlefield. And that is exactly what Bobby Lu did. At the end of his first season with the Canucks, he backstopped the team to forty-seven wins, phasering into obliteration Captain Kirk's team record of thirty-eight victories in one season. Most of Luongo's victories for the Canucks were low-scoring games, with finals of 2–1, 3–1 and 1–0. The goal scoring might have been down, but Vancouver fans didn't care . . . We were all watching the goalie gladiator at the other end of the ice, between the pipes, acrobatically stopping almost every puck that came his way. His #1 jerseys disappeared from store shelves as fast as the Canucks' goals-against average shrunk to one of the lowest in the league.

Luongo quickly became a Vancouver folk hero. Radio commentator Tommy Larscheid coined the phrase, "Bingo bango bongo, you can't beat Luongo!" The crowd let out a low and loud "Luuuuuuuuuuuuuuuuuuu" every time Bobby Lu made a great save (a sporting tradition borrowed from BC Lions fans, who pioneered the same rallying cry many years earlier for legendary kicker Lui Passaglia). Eventually, the growing Canucks fan army would show up at other arenas throughout the league and the "Luuuuuuuuu" call followed. During Luongo's first season with the Canucks, somehow our Flying Vees band was invited to perform our "rink rock" live, between the whistles of an actual Canucks game, high in the rafters of the Canucks' arena. While we rocked out in thirty-second spurts, we were often put on the Jumbotron. Each time I couldn't

Amazingly, by some bizarre twist of fate and a friend on the inside, the Flying Vees band got to perform our set of "rink rock classics" at a Canucks game high in the rafters of GM Place. Nick, his Flying Vee guitar, and the rest of the band would blast out our tunes between the stoppages in play, and each time, I'd eagerly peer down onto the ice to see if Roberto Luongo took any notice.

help but hope Luongo was looking up, rocking through his mask along with us.

The end of Luongo's first season saw the team finish with their highest points total in club history, launching them back into the playoffs and into a Texas rattlesnake pit in Game 1 against the Dallas Stars, which went to an awe-inspiring four overtime periods with the score tied at 4–4. Canucks centre Henrik "Hank" Sedin finally scored just as the game was about to go into a fifth overtime, but the real saviour was Luongo, who made an unbelievable seventy-two stops over the course of the seven periods of playoff hockey. He was one save shy of the all-time league record owned by Kelly Hrudey.

The series against the Dallas Stars went the full seven games, including three overtime tilts, with the Canucks finally winning Game 7 by a score of 4–1. It was a glorious, exhausting series win. The Canucks' next series against the Anaheim Ducks also included three overtime matches, two of them double overtimes, one of which included a bizarre incident that required Luongo to temporarily leave a game due to an extreme case of overtime diarrhea. I could relate. And even though the Anaheim Ducks eventually flushed the Canucks to go on to win the Stanley Cup, one thing was very clear: Roberto Luongo was no crappy goalie.

26

SNOWED IN

AN EXPERIENCE FEW lifelong Vancouverites have ever had is the Canadian winter rite of passage of playing hockey outdoors. I had only ever skated outside a couple of times growing up in Vancouver, during the few rare freak cold snaps when Lost Lagoon in Stanley Park froze over. A friend from another team tipped off the Flying Vees to an outdoor hockey tournament at the Apex Mountain Resort, a ski hill near Penticton, BC. The yearly outdoor hockey tournament began as an event for firefighters but had branched out to allow regular amateur men's and women's teams, drawing squads from all over BC and the US Pacific Northwest. Soon, the Apex Shootout Tournament became a yearly summit for the Vancouver Flying Vees, replacing the Hockey Summit of the Arts in Toronto as a more viable and affordable hockey experience.

The winter drive from soggy Vancouver barrelled us through the Fraser Valley, up into the Coast Mountain Range, through snowy Manning Park and into the Similkameen Valley. Eventually, we'd take the turn-off just past Keremeos, and like Scatman Crothers we'd urgently drive up a winding, snow-packed mountain road framed by towering trees. We'd roll into the village on top of

It was always a huge thrill for the Vancouver Flying Vees to take part in the Apex Mountain outdoor hockey tournament in the snowy interior of BC. Playing hockey outdoors was a rite of passage that few West Coast kids had ever experienced growing up, so when I first skated out onto that winter wonderland rink surrounded by snow-covered trees and slope-roofed chalets, it felt as if I had glided into the pages of *The Hockey Sweater*.

the mountain at nightfall, often in the softly falling snow, past picturesque, steep-roofed ski chalets nestled in thickets of pine trees. Snow clung to their branches like milk on an upper lip. Apex Mountain village would eventually reveal itself at the end of the snowy road in a twinkling display of ski-in-ski-out post-and-beam wooden lodges and chalets. The frosty wonderland and thin mountain air made us loopy for hockey.

We would step out of the van into sub-zero temperatures and feel the crunch of fresh snow under our inappropriate Converse sneakers. We could see the bright lights flooding the ice rink and hear the telltale signs of hockey: the swish and slice of blades on the frozen sheet, the clacking of sticks, the tweet of the ref's whistle, the shouts for passes. We clamoured over the snowbank and trudged to the dressing room, a heated trailer beside the rink where we all excitedly strapped on our gear, few of us really having

The Flying Vees were always so overjoyed to be playing hockey outdoors on Apex Mountain that we would take the partying to new heights... and lows. Pictured: Jeremy "Bomber" Bidnall, Scotty "The Talker" Walker, Grant "Kingpin" Lawrence, Kellen "Knockout" Neault, Bodhi "Salt Spring Sniper" Jones, Chris "Nitzy" Mizzoni, Ken "Goal-a-Game" Hegan, "Young" Greg Fordham, John "The Silver Screen" Silver, "Diamond" Roy Greig.

any idea what it would feel like to play hockey outside. When I eventually stepped out onto the ice, into the elements of a real Canadian winter surrounded by trees covered in snow, cozy chalets and dark, towering mountains, I felt like I had skated into the pages of *The Hockey Sweater*. It was truly a winter classic. Of course, in classic Flying Vees fashion, that first year at Apex we got trounced in all three games, but we had a fantastic time and made good on our vow to return.

Every year we've participated, the Flying Vees have stayed in a big, three-level chalet outfitted with two hot tubs and large enough to house our whole team for the weekend. Our lovingly obnoxious teammate Larry would often arrive to the tournament later than the rest of us. Larry would fishtail into the village at full speed in his giant SUV, music blaring. Pot smoke would billow into the cold night air when another Vees player in the backseat cracked the window just enough to toss empty tallboy beer cans and 7-Eleven burrito wrappers out into the snowbank. Larry would skid to a sideways stop and jump out of his SUV, leaving the door open, the stereo on, and the engine running. Larry would be so excited to get to Apex that he'd be stripping off his clothes as he ran across the snow and into the chalet. By the time he had leapt up the three flights of stairs to the hot tub, he'd be completely naked. He'd plunge into the tub, which usually contained a couple of new players who hadn't yet met Larry. Then he'd shout something along the lines of "Evening boys! We ready for some hockey or what?!"

In a two-minute stumble from our chalet, we'd be at a massive ski lodge that served as the one-stop shop for all our needs: a general store, a restaurant, and a classic ski-resort bar called the Gunbarrel Saloon. Inside the saloon, the sound of swooshing nylon ski pants and clacking foosball tables mixed happily with loud rock music and rambunctious conversation. We could hear accents throughout the fully toqued clientele that ranged from full-blown Canadian hoser to Australian, British, German, Japanese and beyond. The log walls were covered in aging mountain artifacts: stuffed heads of moose and elk stared out forlornly as if resigned to the many bras and panties that hung from their once-majestic antlers. Their mounted heads were surrounded by vintage sets of skis, snowshoes, hockey sticks and road signs. Suspended from the ceiling above the dance floor was an old chairlift, which drunk couples would haul themselves up into at the height of the night and make out for all to witness and cheer on.

I was never sure if it was the altitude, the excitement of being there, or just Larry's enthusiasm rubbing off on all of us, but the Vancouver Flying Vees partied like Chris Farley at the Apex outdoor hockey tournament. One year, our team posted a 3–0 shutout in a minus-fifteen-degree blizzard, beating the local team of liftees, ski instructors and bartenders. To celebrate, we pretty much re-enacted a cross between *Hot Dog: The Movie* and *Roadhouse*. While some other teams chose to celebrate by eating hallucinogenic mushrooms and wandering into the snowy forest, we opted instead to join Larry for a celebratory naked hot tub back at the chalet, followed by a night at the jam-packed Gunbarrel Saloon, table-dancing to the blaring cover band. It was during one of Nick's more suggestive table dances that the very biggest hockey enforcer in the entire bar took issue with the way our Pavel Bure lookalike was dirty dancing with his highly coveted CBC Radio 3 scarf around various girls' necks.

When the affronted big fellow demanded Nick put an end to the dance, Nick threw his scarf around the dude's neck and tried to draw him up onto the table while pumping his crotch in the jock's face. When the jock recoiled, Nick dumped a half-full pint of beer over his head and soaked him. Predictably, the hockey goon was livid, and chased Nick through the bar like a raging bull after a rodeo clown. Some of his teammates joined the chase, charging right into our team in a full-on confrontation. The beer-soaked enforcer leapt over several people and punched Nick directly in the face (I was blissfully ignorant of this entire episode, dancing wildly by myself in the front of the stage to the cover band The Pids as they did a spot-on version of the Violent Femmes' "Blister in the Sun").

As a result of the melee, Nick and "Young" Greg (one of our new defencemen) were grabbed by the bouncers and thrown out of the Gunbarrel head-first into a snowbank. Kicked out of the saloon but still amped to party, they went in search of Apex Mountain's rumoured, legendary "party igloo," a massive ice cave seemingly plucked from planet Hoth. No wampas were in this cave, just partying ski bums. While Nick and Young Greg were trying to find the forest path to the ice cave, a Kenny Powers–like shirtless drunk on a snowmobile roared up beside them and offered the guys a lift yelling the phrase, "Get the fuck on if you dare!" Without hesitation, Nick and Young Greg immediately climbed aboard, took off and within twenty feet they flipped the snowmobile down an embankment into a thicket of trees.

Hours later, we found Nick and Young Greg in that astoundingly cavernous, maze-like ice cave the size of a large house,

packed with revellers in various states of undress. They were all
dancing to booming tunes spun by a shirtless, Jesus-lookalike DJ.
Nick and Young Greg were in the middle of the throng of bouncing
neon ski bunnies, one with a bottle of tequila, another a bottle of
whiskey. When Darwin "Galapagos" Green and I eventually stumbled from the ice cave at about 4 a.m. to hit the sack back at the
chalet, we hitched a ride with a one-eyed hippie who told us to hop
into the back of his pickup truck and "sit over the rear axle to hold
me down." He then proceeded to wildly fishtail and skid his way up
the hill, our weight seemingly doing nothing. We held on for dear
life, and made it back to the chalet before sunrise to get some sleep
before the game later that morning.

Shaking off our formidable hangovers, when we arrived at the
outdoor rink it was much colder than we had ever experienced,
hovering somewhere around minus-twenty degrees. It was so
cold that guys needed to wear woollen long underwear under their
hockey pants and toques under their helmets. My water bottle
froze in minutes. It was our final game of the tournament, and as
cold and hungover as I was, I couldn't help but get caught up in the
crisp beauty of the day, the rare winter sunshine bursting through
the trees, a gorgeous cobalt blue sky overheard. The ice felt hard
and fast as I made a couple of loops around our end to loosen up
with my teammates. I glided toward the net to receive some warm-
up shots. I tried to never look at the other team to remain focused
on the warm-up, but I couldn't help it. I cast a couple of glances
down the ice at the other team, the Chelsea Daggers. They were
a huge bunch of guys, mostly firemen and rescue workers, who
dwarfed our art-fart roster.

It couldn't be. I stiffened up faster than my water bottle as
pucks bounced off my chest protector and face-mask. I strained
and squinted in the sunshine, trying to convince myself that I had
to be mistaken, that I was psyching myself out. It was him. Down
at the other end of the ice was none other than Angus "The Anvil"
McFadden, the enormous skinhead who had so many years ago

punched me in the stomach, stolen my beer and had sex with my girlfriend. Angus the Anvil was still huge, but a lot of what used to be in his shoulders and chest now swayed around his hips and stomach. I found myself reverting back to my high school self, wanting to roll into a ball and disappear, to get as far away from that beautiful outdoor rink as I possibly could. I tried to push my goalie mask further down my face. I looked around for a place to hide. On an ice rink, there is none. As I discovered during "shirts and skins" in gym class, inside my goalie equipment is about as close to being in a panic room as it gets.

Somehow, some way, because anything can happen on an outdoor rink, by the end of the first period we were keeping pace, with the score 1–1. I had made a couple of big saves including a pad-stacker stop on a two-on-nothing that brought on cheers from the bundled-up onlookers with the Irish coffees at the side of the rink. By the end of the second period, we were tied 2–2. Angus the Anvil was one of the best players on the ice and still as nasty as Bill Sikes, but he hadn't managed to score. And then . . . the unthinkable. At the start of the third period, Angus the Anvil got a clear-cut break-away from the Chelsea Daggers' end of the rink.

He was barrelling down the middle of the ice, head down like a charging moose. I felt myself freeze up with fear, my teeth chattering, my kneecaps rattling in their sockets. Shaking off a formidable ice-cave hangover, Young Greg raced after him up the ice, digging his stick blade into the Anvil's gut. The Anvil felt the stick and collapsed onto the ice like King Kong. I breathed a sigh of relief, but quickly kicked into high-adrenalin alarm when the Marc the Referee's arm shot up and the whistle blew. A teenage nemesis had been awarded a penalty shot on me in a 2–2 hockey game on a snowy mountaintop in British Columbia.

Marc the Ref placed the puck at centre ice and Angus circled it a couple of times like a great white shark eyeing up prey. Then he charged, slicing hard down the ice at me. I forced myself to skate out to challenge him, as strongly recommended in *Fuhr on*

211

Goaltending. Angus looked up and saw the anonymous little goalie coming out to meet him. He deftly deked to the backhand, lifting the puck onto the outer curve of his stick blade, whipping it into the air toward the top corner of the net. I threw my body out in the direction of the puck. I felt a *whap* on my blocker before collapsing face down onto the ice. My team erupted on the bench. I made the save. Angus shot me an icy, oblivious glare and lumbered back down the rink.

The game surged on, and the score remained 2–2 until there was less than five minutes to play. Then, in a chaotic scramble in their end, Brian "Lattatude" Latta whacked the puck hard along the ice in the high slot. I had the perfect view. It skidded along the chipped ice surface through an armoury of skate blades . . . including the goalie's. The Flying Vees were in the lead 3–2. I couldn't breathe. I convinced myself I had altitude sickness. Three minutes to go. We were so close. My muscles were going into uncontrollable spasms. And then, like *Groundhog Day* meets *Slapshot II*, the nightmare happened. Again.

Angus the Anvil got *another* clear-cut breakaway. This time, it was John "The Silver Screen" Silver who was able to catch up and haul the Anvil down. Another penalty shot. My bowels felt like they were going to pull a Luongo deep within my goalie gear. The Anvil came at me again, steam pouring from his flaring nostrils into the dry mountain air. Then the thought struck me . . . who gets a chance at vengeance like this twenty years later?

Angus leaned hard to the forehand this time, which I bit on, but then the big bastard faked, pulled up and deked hard to the backhand, and this time I knew he had me. The puck was airborne. I stretched out like John Travolta in *Saturday Night Fever* in a frantic, extended jumping jack. Every joint, muscle and tendon in my body felt like it was being elongated by a medieval torture device. I dropped my stick and heard it clatter to the ice. This time my palm faced open in my blocker. I stretched. I shut my eyes. I winced. I cried. The tip of my middle finger felt a sharp stinging

It's been called "the most exciting play in hockey": the penalty shot. On the outdoor rink high atop the snowy mountain of Apex, BC, I faced many a penalty shooter over the years, including going head to head against one of my arch rival bullies from high school.

sensation through the wet, coarse brown leather of my blocker's gloved hand. It was the very middle finger I had wanted to give The Bully for my entire life.

The puck had grazed the tip of my middle digit just enough to deflect over the crossbar. Angus, soiler of my first "girlfriend," smashed his stick against the boards in rage. I lay on the ice in a euphoric state as Marc the Ref nonchalantly signalled "no goal." Hearing the sound of the final buzzer on that crisp, cold, sunny mountaintop was one of the single greatest moments of my entire life. The Flying Vees won. The Bully lost. In sixty minutes of outdoor hockey I felt I had exorcised demons that had haunted me since high school. I had maintained my cool and kept within the code. I was mobbed by my teammates in the crease as I held my hands high over my head and whooped in victory.

Once we finished celebrating, we lined up for the post-game customary handshake with the other team. We skated through the lineup, exchanging the phrase "good game," "good game," "good game," over and over again. I couldn't wait to come face to face with Angus, rubbing his face in the defeat and my penalty shot saves. I saw Angus a few players ahead, towering above everyone else, shoulders slumped, face sullen, belly swaying from side to

The Vancouver Flying Vees at the end of another great weekend at the Apex Mountain outdoor hockey tournament. Playing hockey outdoors in sub-zero temperatures and falling snow was one of the most exhilarating sporting experiences I have ever had. Back row L–R: Ted "Hockey Bag" Cochrane, Saleem "The Dream" Dar, Rich "Candy Man" Bon, "Young" Greg Fordham, Kristian "Oly" Olsen, Paul "the Deker" Needham. Front row: Nick "Lock-Eye" Thomas, Chris "Nitzy" Mizzoni, Grant Lawrence, Scotty "The Talker" Walker, Jeremy "Bomber" Bidnall, "Flowin'" Kevin Rowan. (Not pictured: Larry, who slept through this game back at the chalet.)

side in his Chelsea Daggers jersey. Defeated. I shook Angus's huge mitt and said two words to him: "good game."

Back in the heated trailer we used as a locker room, I excitedly told the players who the penalty shooter was and what those saves had meant to me. Scott "Cabo Wabo" Cabianca put down his can of Black Label and belched. "Well, now it feels zlike we just won the whole fuckin' tournament!" Tossing me a partially frozen can of beer, he added with a wink, "Revenge is best served on ice, eh?"

LIKE
LIGHTNING

W HEN I WAS first introduced to Canadian singer-songwriter Jill Barber, it was on a busy patio on College Street
in Toronto. We didn't know each other, but we were both
invited to a dinner to celebrate a mutual friend's birthday. Jill sat
directly across from me. I was immediately smitten, taken aback
at how cute she looked in her snap-button shirt, corduroy jacket
and jeans. We all traded stories and at one point, I mentioned
hockey. Jill asked if I played. I told her yes, I played, and that I was
a goalie.

Years later, when Jill and I were happily married, she admitted she had felt an odd flicker in her tummy when I told her I was
a goaltender. She saw it as some sort of premonition, because goalies run in Jill's family. In the 1950s Jill's dad was a gangly, geeky
goaltender growing up in tiny Roblin, Manitoba, where it would be
minus-thirty degrees *inside* the arena. He wore no helmet or mask,
just a homemade knit toque on his head. His feet were stuffed into
leather skates that quickly felt like burning blocks of ice. If he
could stand playing long enough, his skates actually did freeze to
his feet, and were screamingly painful to remove.

When his team would travel to away-games in prairie towns like Russell, Grandview, and Gilbert Plains, he and his teammates would crowd into the covered back of the coach's half-ton truck, which was equipped with a little woodstove bolted to the floor. His feet were so cold that he'd push them as close as he could toward the glowing cast-iron potbelly of the stove, routinely burning both the bottom of his boots and singeing his socks. Jill's dad retired from goaltending at age twelve when he was forced to wear gigantic, clunky Buddy Holly glasses, but he has remained a lifelong student and fan of the goaltending position, the Toronto Maple Leafs and the good ol' hockey game.

Following in his dad's skating strides, Jill's brother Matthew also became a goalie at an early age. Tall and thin like his father, Matt immediately excelled at the position. His Mississauga teams dominated the opposition, winning tournaments around Ontario and upstate New York. Matt was scouted by Brown University, but felt a consistent mid-teens tug away from the game and quit competitive hockey at age seventeen. It would be music, not hockey, that would become his career and passion.

Years later, Matt's love for music and hockey would bodycheck each other in a happy collision at the Juno Awards. The year Matt was nominated for an award, he was invited to play goal in the Juno Cup, the annual hockey game that pitted the Rockers (a team of nominated musicians who also played hockey, always captained by Blue Rodeo's Jim Cuddy) against a team of retired NHLers, including legends like Lanny McDonald, Paul Coffey, Bob Probert and ex-Canucks Cliff Ronning and Gino Odjick. For as long as the Juno Cup had existed, the NHL Greats had handily triumphed over the Rockers. But the Juno Cup wasn't about winning or losing, or so the Rockers told themselves; it was about living out a Canadian fantasy of skating on the same ice surface as their hockey heroes.

To play in the game Matt dug out his old equipment, including the same pads he wore as a teenager, thoroughly moth-eaten but still usable. By all accounts, Matthew Barber the goalie was

216

a butterfly sensation in the Juno Cup, stopping NHL Great after NHL Great. A member of the rock band 54-40 scored to tie the game in the last second, much to the annoyance of the NHL Greats who were still as competitive as ever, especially against a bunch of skinny musicians. The Juno Cup's first-ever shootout would be needed to decide a winner.

After five intense shootout rounds that saw Matt allow the first shot taken by Cliff Ronning but then make a series of sensational stops against ex-NHLers Mark Napier, Gino Odjick, Dave Babych and Troy Crowder, the Rockers had managed to edge ahead by scoring twice. It all came down to a final pairing: Lanny McDonald, one of the most famous NHL Greats of all time, versus Matthew Barber, the soft-spoken singer-songwriter goalie. If Lanny could score, the shootout would keep going. If Matt made the save, the Rockers would emerge victorious for the first time ever.

Lanny slowly skated to centre where the puck waited for him. He gathered it up on the blade of his stick and streaked straight down the ice, head up and helmetless toward Matt. Lanny's famous once-red, now-greying moustache was flapping in the wind just like it did when he won the Stanley Cup with the Calgary Flames, his huge hands gripping his stick, the puck on the blade. The NHL legend faked backhand, then deked like lightning to the forehand. Lanny had Matt beat along the ice with a yawning cage to keep the game alive for the NHL Greats. But . . . *NO!?!* Somehow, Matt lunged back, did the splits like Chuck Berry and stretched out his glove hand along the goal line.

The puck deflected off his arm and slid harmlessly into the cor- 217 ner. The Rockers rolled off the bench to mob Matt as Lanny "The Moustache" McDonald looked back and wondered who the hell that quiet, lanky goalie in the moth-eaten pads was. Matt didn't end up winning a Juno Award that year, but he did win the Juno Cup.

His sister Jill's rose-coloured memories of her father and brother as goalies came to a quick halt once she moved in with me in Vancouver. She was disgusted to discover that I was in the habit

I was certainly thrilled to meet Lanny "The Moustache" McDonald, one of hockey's all-time greatest players and characters, at the Juno Awards in Vancouver. His good graces quickly came to a halt when I rubbed it in that my goalie brother-in-law, Matthew Barber, had stopped him cold earlier that evening in the shootout, allowing the Rockers to beat the NHL Greats for the first time in the history of the annual Juno Cup hockey game.

of drying out my goalie pads by sticking them in the oven and setting it on bake with the door open. Also, because we lived in such a small apartment, when I returned home from games I would spread my other gear throughout our living room to dry, which according to Jill made our apartment smell like back-alley urine.

Once, Jill found me rooting through my monstrous goalie bag looking for a piece of equipment that I needed to fix. She let out a sudden shriek, pointing at the mess. "What are my panties doing in your goalie bag?" she demanded. Sure enough, when I looked to where she was pointing, a pair of her black lace panties were amongst my stinky goalie gear. I told Jill the nervous truth: I had no clue how her panties got into my hockey bag. "Oh really?" she questioned with knowing, hands-on-her-hips, accusatory sarcasm in her voice. "You tell me why my panties are in your hockey bag this instant!" Jill was absolutely convinced the members of the Flying Vees were involved in some sort of sick, ritualistic panty raid, where each Vee was challenged to sneak a pair of his wife's or girlfriend's underwear into our locker room to be passed around, worn, sniffed, traded or whatever other perversion male hockey players might do to female underwear. No matter how hard I tried, I could not convince Jill the most likely culprit to blame for her panties winding up in my goalie bag was static cling.

28

IN THE BELLY
OF THE DRAGON

THANKS TO THE steady foundation of Roberto Luongo in net, the Vancouver Canucks had finally built up a juggernaut of a hockey team. The team returned to their 1970s colours of blue, green, and white, and to the thrill of many fans, brought back their original stick-in-rink logo. The once teased and tormented twins Henrik and Daniel Sedin had become the best one-two scoring punch in the league, leading scoring races, breaking Canucks records and redefining how the NHL game could be played in the offensive zone with Harlem Globetrotters-like possession, seeing-eye slap-passes and goals, goals, goals. The team owned the regular season, shooting down all comers and winning all sorts of awards, but repeatedly ran into trouble in the playoffs—mostly in the form of the Chicago Blackhawks. Two years in a row, the Canucks made it through the first round only to meet and be shot down by the Blackhawks in devastating fashion. In 2010, just months after Luongo and Team Canada had won Olympic hockey gold on Vancouver ice, the Blackhawks beat the Canucks four games to two and went on to win the Stanley Cup.

One year later, the Canucks finally beat the Blackhawks in the playoffs, in an epic seven-game series that saw the Canucks go up three games to none, only to have the Hawks talon their way back in. The series went to overtime in the seventh game, when Canucks forward Alex "The Arrow" Burrows leapt onto a turn-over at the Chicago blue line and took a golf swing at a rolling puck. I thought the puck hit the metal joint where the crossbar met the post and wouldn't count, but the red goal light blazed to life behind the net. Burrows threw himself into a hysterical cele-bration as the Canucks poured onto the ice to rejoice. The crowd in the arena went ballistic, but I was still fearful it wasn't a goal. I couldn't let myself believe it, even after I saw replay after replay. Roberto Luongo and the Canucks finally slayed their dragon; they were moving on.

And so began another otherworldly Stanley Cup run for the Vancouver Canucks, during which I would repeatedly experience several selfish, serendipitous occurrences that seemed to indicate this would finally be *the year*:

› The Canucks were turning forty, and I was also turning forty. *It had to be a sign.*

› I met both of my Canucks' previous Stanley Cup Final goalie heroes that spring on separate occasions. "Captain" Kirk McLean was a guest on a TV talk show that I was also on, and "King" Rich-ard Brodeur was a celebrity guest at a one-day hockey tournament the Flying Vees participated in. They were both great guys and it was a huge thrill to meet them. *It had to be a sign.*

› At a charity dinner, by sheer fluke I managed to win a Canucks stick signed by the entire team. *It had to be a sign.*

› Before a Canucks playoff game on *Hockey Night in Canada*, host Ron MacLean gave my wife Jill a shout-out that was seen by mil-lions of viewers across the country. *It had to be a sign.*

› I had become unlikely Twitter pals with beloved Canadian chil-dren's entertainer Raffi, bonding online over our love and passion

When I met "Captain" Kirk McLean, one of my all-time favourite goaltending heroes in the spring of 2010 during the Canucks' fortieth anniversary season, I took it as a sign that the Canucks were bound to do well in the upcoming playoffs, and maybe even go all the way to the Stanley Cup finals. No Canucks team had done it since McLean back-stopped the team in 1994.

for the Canucks. It was his *The Corner Grocery Store* record that our class had listened to during the Canucks' first trip to the Stanley Cup Final. *It had to be a sign.*

› The NHL announced that the Atlanta Thrashers would be relocating to Winnipeg and would once again be known as the Winnipeg Jets. *It had to be a sign* that the Stanley Cup was also coming back to Canada for the first time since 1993.

The Canucks' next opponent was the Nashville Predators, a team that featured the sasquatch-like defenceman Shea Weber, who sported a hillbilly beard that was more *Hee Haw* than hockey. Over the course of the spring of 2011, I was constantly on the move for various reasons, which forced me to leave my preferred fortress-of-solitude viewing perch in my apartment and watch the games anywhere and everywhere I could. I took in one game against Nashville in a disgusting fleabag hotel room on Vancouver Island down the street from where my wife Jill was playing a gig. While crackhead arguments raged in the hallway, I had to stand for three hours holding the antenna in order to get a picture, until the game was over and the Canucks had won.

The Canucks dispatched the Predators in six games to move on to the conference finals for the first time since 1994, and they'd do it against Neil Young's favourite team, the San Jose Sharks. On May 24, 2011, I was in Desolation Sound and simply had to see Game 5 of the Western Conference Final between the Canucks and the Sharks. Our cabin didn't have any electricity let alone a television, so I hopped in our boat *Big Buck$* and roared across the inlets toward a famous Desolation Sound landmark: the Cougar Lady's little log cabin. It was now owned and lovingly restored by the Vallance family, who ran Powell River Sea Kayak out of the historic location. The Vallances were ardent Canucks fans and had rigged up a satellite dish to watch Game 5.

The Sharks looked like they had the game won until Canucks forward Ryan Kesler, who had been a monster for the Canucks in the playoffs, miraculously scored to tie the game with just thirteen seconds left in the third period. The eighteen thousand-plus fans in the Canucks' rink went into a frenzy and so did the five people watching in the Cougar Lady's cabin in the West Coast wilderness. The game then stretched into a gut-twisting double overtime, until a bizarre play finally ended it. The puck looked as if it was being shot deep into the Sharks zone, behind their net, but somehow it disappeared from view for just about everybody including players, fans and commentators. Every player on the ice whipped their heads around searching for the puck, except for one: Canucks bulldog defenceman Kevin "Boom Boom" Bieksa saw that the puck had hit a stanchion on the glass and bounced into the high slot. He stepped into a slapshot and pounded a knuckler past the Sharks netminder who was still searching for the puck and never saw a thing. Jubilation shook the century-old logs of the Cougar Lady's cabin. The Canucks were finally headed back to the Stanley Cup Final a long seventeen years *to the day* they were last ushered in back in 1994, also on a double overtime goal by Greg "Gus" Adams against the Toronto Maple Leafs. *It had to be a sign.*

We had to wait impatiently to see which team the Canucks would face from the far-off Eastern Conference—either the Boston Bruins or the Tampa Bay Lightning, who were engaged in a long, drawn-out seven-game series. Most pundits suggested the Tampa Bay Lightning would be the better choice for the Canucks as they were a similar team, built on speed and goal scoring, but with dubious defence and goaltending. I agreed. The Boston Bruins were a more frightening prospect. Physically, they were a mammoth team, none more towering than team captain Zdeno "Zed" Chara, the tallest man to ever play in the history of the NHL at six-foot-nine and 255 pounds. The Boston Bruins were goons who could skate. Sure enough, they beat the Tampa Bay Lightning in the seventh game to move on to face the Vancouver Canucks in the 2011 Stanley Cup Final.

The puck finally dropped in Vancouver on June 1. To the orgasmic delight of Canucks fans around the world, the Canucks won Game 1 by a score of 1–0, beating what everyone said was an exhausted Bruins team that had already played two series that spring that had gone the seven-game distance before flying all the way from Boston to Vancouver.

On the night that Game 2 of the Final went down, I was on the wrong side of the country attending the Joe Burke Literary Festival on Wolfe Island, just outside of Kingston, Ontario. It was a festival curated by my friend, mentor and hockey fanatic Dave Bidini. Dave explained to me that the festival was held at a venue called the Duck Shed, which I assumed was a hip name for a venue or hall paying tribute to the island's duck-hunting traditions. I was surprised to arrive at an actual duck shed. It smelled like dirty blankets and engine oil, was no bigger than a one-car garage, filled with wooden bunk beds, various car engine parts, hubcaps, a potbellied stove, tin cans full of shotgun shells, and an array of mismatched chairs. A TV with rabbit ears was apparently going to provide us with Game 2 of the Stanley Cup Final after the festival readings wrapped up. The TV looked like it had been hauled out of the junkyard that day. I was skeptical.

The authors used the duck shed's wooden deck as their stage to read from, while attendees gathered on blankets on the grass that lay between the deck and the duck pond beyond. At the end of the festival the authors and various local hosers were led by Dave into the dusty confines of the tiny duck shed. We found various folding chairs, cracked open our beer and crowded around the TV to watch the Stanley Cup Final on *Hockey Night in Canada*. As I looked around the peculiar space I found myself in, I had to rack my brain to think if I had ever done anything that felt more Canadian than in that moment. To my left was singer-songwriter Sarah Harmer. To my right was bestselling novelist Joseph Boyden. Dave reached over and pulled the power knob. The TV flickered to life and the scene of the rink back home in Vancouver blazed white across the screen, illuminating our happy faces in the darkened duck shed. Whenever one of the local Wolfe Island hosers farted loud enough for everyone to hear, they'd mutter, "Wow, the bullfrogs sure are cranky tonight, eh?"

We watched an incredible hockey game with exceptional goal-tending at both ends. By the time the horn sounded for the end of the third stanza, the score was tied 2–2, and we were drunk, which seemed only fitting because there was no way a night like this, in the deep dark woods at the head of the St. Lawrence River, could end just yet. Overtime. Being the only diehard Canucks fan in attendance, I made sure I was seated in my fraying nylon deck chair as soon as the puck dropped for the extra frame. Many had not settled in, and missed the icy magic that was about to unfurl. Just eleven seconds into overtime, Alex "The Arrow" Burrows

I watched Game 2 of the Vancouver Canucks vs. Boston Bruins Stanley Cup Final in the unexpected location of an unheated, plywood duck-hunting shed on Wolfe Island, Ontario. I was stuffed into a fraying lawn chair, staring at a TV with a rabbit ears antenna, surrounded by a league of extraordinary Canadians, including authors Dave Bidini, Joseph Boyden and Tanis Rideout, musicians Sarah Harmer and Selina Martin, and many other loud, boisterous, talented people.

hopped on a turnover, drawing Bruins goalie Tim "The Tank" Thomas way out of his crease. Burrows faked a slapshot, then circled the net and just barely slid the puck into the gaping cage for a wraparound goal and overtime victory. The Bruins were stunned. The Canucks now held a commanding 2–0 lead over the supposedly big, bad Boston Bruins in the Stanley Cup Final. I was ecstatic, and partied hard into the rural Ontario night. I'm glad I did, because that would be as good as it would get.

29

THIS CITY'S A MESS

THERE IS AN old saying, which is also the title of a smokin' hot Mitch Ryder album: *Never Kick a Sleeping Dog*. The turning point of the 2011 Stanley Cup Final seemed to spin on an American dime in the first period of Game 3, the first game of the series in the Boston Garden. On an early rush by the Bruins, Canucks defenceman Aaron "Romeo" Rome stayed with his check. Romeo stepped up at the Canucks' blue line to lay a devastating open-ice hit on one of the Bruins' best, Nathan Horton, who had scored the game-winning goals in both of the Bruins' previous two game 7s in the 2011 playoffs. The hit was totally explosive and vicious, and nothing NHL fans hadn't seen before from the New Jersey Devils' Scott Stevens years earlier. But head shots and concussions had become a huge concern in the NHL, and this hit on Horton appeared to be "late" (Horton had passed the puck a split second earlier). It also appeared to be a "blindside" hit, and appeared that Rome had left his feet to land his shoulder into Horton's face, making direct contact with his chin. Horton, a big man himself at over six feet and 230 pounds, flew backward, violently hitting the ice with the back of his head, meaning both the front and back of his head had received major impacts in less than a second.

As Rome skated away unscathed, Horton lay flat out on his back, his head pulled into his shoulders like a turtle, his left arm strangely outstretched as if checking the wind, his left knee bent upward. His chest rose and fell in his black Bruins uniform like an accordion as he gasped for shallow breath. His eyes, half shut and glazed over, looked straight up. Horton was carefully removed from the ice on a stretcher while rage frothed down from the stands in Boston Garden and the Bruins themselves visibly fumed with trembling anger on their own bench. The Canucks looked confused, not knowing what the hit would mean. I paced the living room in my apartment, detecting a very distinct feeling of unease creep into the game.

Horton was diagnosed with a severe concussion and would miss the rest of the series. Rome was penalized and tossed from the game, then suspended for the remainder of the Final. The Bruins suddenly reared up and attacked the Canucks in all aspects of the game: physically, emotionally and with goal after goal. The Bruins would win that Game 3 by a ridiculous score of 8–1. Luongo and the entire team seemingly played dead during the carnage. The Bruins would also win Game 4, 4–0. The Canucks managed to come back in Game 5, usually the pivotal game in a long series, by a score of 1–0, which put them one win away from the Stanley Cup, but they would have to go back to Boston to do it.

Since the hit on Horton, the Bruins had absolutely mauled the Canucks, physically crushing them at every opportunity. Earlier in the series, Dan "The Hammer" Hamhuis, arguably the Canucks' steadiest defenceman, got the worst of a hip check he threw on one of the Bruins' largest players and hadn't played since. Then Canucks speedy forward Mason "Everybody Loves" Raymond was bent over and driven into the corner boards by a hulking Bruins defenceman seconds into Game 6. The crushing hit was enough to break Raymond's back and force him onto the operating table, into a body cast and out of the series. There was no penalty on the play. Ryan Kesler, arguably the Canucks' MVP of the playoffs, was injured but still playing. Every Bruin was smacking every Canuck at every opportunity, before and after the play, including goalie Tim Thomas, who levelled Canucks captain Henrik Sedin flat on his back in front of the Bruins net. No penalty.

In one of the most sickening scenes of Game 6 and the entire series, Bruins agitator Brad "The Boston Rat" Marchand was allowed to speed-bag Canucks leading scorer Daniel Sedin in the face with four gloved left jabs after a whistle. Marc the Referee saw the entire thing and yet . . . no penalty. I shivered at the scene, a display of unchecked, seemingly sanctioned bullying in front of an impressionable audience of millions. The Canucks lost Game 6 by a devastating score of 5–2.

Back in Vancouver, ever since the first round of the playoffs, the CBC had been inviting fans down to our outdoor plaza to enjoy the game on our big screen. As the Canucks' success in the playoffs continued, more and more fans began to gather at the CBC. Eventually, so many fans were showing up that the City of Vancouver got involved. Trusting the fans would behave based on the fresh and positive experiences from the Winter Olympics, the City shut down the streets. Giant screens were rented and placed in the middle of Georgia and Hamilton streets while upward of seventy thousand supposed hockey fans gathered for each game in the warm sunshine of May and June.

On the night of Game 7, Wednesday June 15, 2011, I was in a lonely, generic, sterilized hotel room in Toronto. The room smelled of industrial cleaning agents and stale air. I could have watched at a crowded bar or with my Barber goalies-in-law, but I felt the need to watch Game 7 in my own personal solitude. I sat at the foot of the hotel room bed, my face three feet from the TV screen. My mood was sombre but expectant, and distantly hopeful. All the Canucks had to do was win one game. I thought of Mom and Dad watching back at home, and what this victory would mean to them.

The Canucks did not and could not win. They were spent and broken. They did manage several fine early chances but couldn't score on Tim "The Tank" Thomas. The Boston Bruins won the game 4–0. In turn, they won their first Stanley Cup since the Bobby Orr–led Bruins of 1972, and they did it in front of the Vancouver Canucks and their fans. High in the rafters to see it all was Cam "Bam Bam" Neely, now president of the Boston Bruins, traded away by the Canucks so many years earlier. Since the Aaron Rome hit early in Game 3, the Bruins had scored twenty-one goals, the Canucks just four. I stared wide-eyed and slumped over, empty beer bottles strewn about the sterile hotel room floor, watching the Bruins celebrate in the Canucks' home rink. The Stanley Cup would remain with an American team as it had since 1994, the last time the Canucks were in the final.

Back in Vancouver, an estimated 100,000 people had gathered wearing every possible kind of Canucks merchandise. As the game wore on and the Canucks couldn't score, tensions amongst the crowd ran dangerously high. There was a negative crackle in the warm June evening. Even though there were alcohol checkpoints surrounding the designated "fan zone," many rabble-rousers snuck past the cops with copious amounts of booze intact. It was a gorgeous, cloudless night, but the mood was quickly becoming angry. Fans drowned their sorrows as the game unfolded on the giant screens in front of them. When they were finished with their tallboy cans of beer or mickeys of vodka they began throwing their empties at the screen in frustration. Some now approximated the crowd at over 150,000.

Near the end of the third period with the Stanley Cup looking most definitely lost, behaviour on the street began to spiral. By the time the game was over it was only 7:45 p.m. in Vancouver and still sunny. *Lord of the Flies*–like mayhem quickly broke out in the heart of downtown Vancouver. Unbelievably, a truck was set on fire in front of the main post office on Georgia Street. I watched with blank numbness the post-game reports switching from hockey to the scenes of a riot unfolding directly in front of my workplace at

CBC Vancouver. Billowing columns of cauldron-black smoke were rising from the city's downtown core in the clear evening sky as car after car was overturned by the masses and set ablaze. If the wind switched directions, acidic black smoke smelling of burnt plastic, garbage and gasoline choked the crowd as if they were on the wrong side of a banger bonfire.

All told, seventeen cars were torched, including several unattended cop cars. The rampaging crowds of mostly young suburbanites stormed up Georgia Street, smashing windows and looting the Hudson's Bay Company, Future Shop, Sears, London Drugs and Chapters. Thousands of looters poured in and out of the shattered picture windows—drunk kids and idiot adults caught up in the adrenalin rush of anarchy, smashing, grabbing and stealing whatever they could, usually with gleeful smiles plastered across their faces.

A lot had changed since the Stanley Cup riot of 1994. Back then, just a few TV cameras captured the masses on tape. In 2011, media was handheld and widespread. Bystanders and participants alike felt the need to document not only those around them, but also themselves, stealing from stores or cheering triumphantly in front of burning cars. When the rioters finally burned themselves out and dispersed around midnight, the downtown core was a smouldering disaster zone, the damage and theft estimated somewhere north of four million dollars. At least 150 people were injured including nine police officers. Four people showed up at hospitals with stab wounds. Eventually, over 120 people were arrested and hundreds more were charged. Many were convicted and sent to jail.

I was deeply ashamed of my city, and glad to be in Toronto so far from the wreckage. The Canucks had just lost their third Stanley Cup after being up 2–0 and 3–2 in the series. Smelling the smoke and hearing the sirens would have driven me further downward. The next morning, the citizens of Vancouver who actually lived and worked in the city woke up and cleaned up the mess left over from those who tried to destroy it.

One of the seventeen different cars set ablaze in downtown Vancouver on the night the Vancouver Canucks lost Game 7 to the Boston Bruins. This one happens to be directly in front of the Hudson's Bay Company, the very department store where I bought my first hockey sweater decades earlier. CHRISTINE MCAVOY PHOTO

Amazingly, the riot managed to completely distract from the outcome of the actual game. Even sportscasters could talk about nothing but the riot. It was difficult to find post-game coverage, but maybe it wasn't needed. It was obvious the bigger, nastier, more physical team had won from pure intimidation, muscle and talent. Goons who could skate. The theory I feared so much before the series began had come nightmarishly true. It made me wonder how the hell I could have fallen in love with a game where bullies win on its biggest stage.

234   Weeks later in the aftermath of the series, as if sifting through the very rubble of the riot itself, I found one tiny shard of a silver lining. Brad "The Boston Rat" Marchand, public enemy number one in Vancouver, got a tattoo to commemorate his Stanley Cup win. Unfortunately, his tattoo artist wasn't a great speller, permanently tattooing the words *Stanley Cup Champians* on the side of Marchand's torso, continuing the long tradition of weird Boston Bruins spelling mistakes after Cup wins.

30

OUT LIKE A LION

*B*Y YET ANOTHER twist of fate, the Vancouver Flying Vees were
also stabbing deep into the playoffs at the very same time
as the Canucks, but unlike the NHL's *Braveheart*-like battle-
fields of four rounds each with the potential for seven gruelling
games plus untold overtimes, we only had to play four beer-league
hockey games to go all the way. We had lost our first game but won
the next three, the semifinal going into overtime and then a dramatic shootout. As usual, Captain John Silver couldn't watch and
had his head between his knees at the bench. Much to my team's
complete shock and delight, I was able to stop all three shooters.
Mom and Jill saw it too, in the stands cheering us on. The Flying
Vees were once again in a championship final.

I couldn't sleep the night before the final, as I tried to picture
save after save in my head. Then my insecurities would creep in,
allowing goal after goal to slip into my mental imagery as well. I
lay awake in bed in a cold sweat, covers pushed away, while my
peacefully slumbering beautiful wife lay beside me, blissfully
unaware of my idiotic anguish over beer-league hockey. I unrav-
elled like Gollum, manically telling myself I could stop anything,
then cutting myself off with a curt whisper that I couldn't stop a

beach ball. I wondered why I had chosen the lonely end of the rink, where I would be the only one left behind when the play raced to the other end, hoping the puck wouldn't come back but knowing it would; when the puck did come back, and rippled the mesh behind me, it felt even lonelier.

The championship game started well enough. We held our opponents in their end for extended periods of time in the first period, pounding shot after shot toward their goalie, but most of them missed the net. Then, my nightmare came true as an enemy player was able to steal the puck from one of our defencemen for a long, unobstructed, fast-forward breakaway. When he got close enough, he deked me hard to the glove side and I bit on it like a chinook on a Buzz Bomb. The forward was able to dance around me and bonk the puck into the open net for a 1–0 lead. It was crushing. I let in a bad breakaway goal against the flow of play.

Luckily, as the final seconds raced toward the buzzer in the first period, Chris "Nitzy" Mizzoni grabbed the puck in the far corner and lasered a perfect pass onto the blade of Flying Vees forward Jeremy "Bomber" Bidnall, who was parked immediately in front of the goalie. Bomber slammed the puck through the goalie's legs and into the back of the net just as the buzzer sounded. 1–1.

In the second period, my old pal and bandmate Nick "Lock-Eye" Thomas slapped the puck home in the exact same doorstep position for a 2–1 lead, which we would desperately hang on to deep into the third period... then a penalty against Nitzy with under two minutes to go... then the six-on-four man advantage against us... then the point-blank shot in front of our net that I never saw. I looked up at the clock from my frozen position on the ice, my left pad outstretched and flat on the ice, my right leg tucked underneath me. Just 1:21 remained. The other team was hysterically hugging and high-fiving each other three feet in front of me. My left skate stayed pinned to the base of the post. My teammates looked confused and crestfallen. Here we go again.

I didn't see the shot, but I heard the puck CLACK onto the blade of the shooter's stick and I knew he would let it go immediately. I had grown to truly love and appreciate the *sound* of a save. When the puck solidly hit my leg pads it gave out the extremely satisfying *WHUMP*, like a boxer landing a roundhouse punch on the heavy bag. If I missed the puck completely (which was extremely frequent) I'd listen for the other telltale sounds. The post made a *PING*, the crossbar a *CLANK*, the base of the post a *CLUNK*, the glass behind the net a *CLACK* and the boards a *BOOM*. All of those were sweet soul music to a goalie. It was silence that meant trouble. When a puck sailed past me unmolested to bulge the white twine in the back of the net, it was a soundless incubus.

After the puck was shot I didn't hear a thing. My heart sank into my jockstrap while my ears filled with the unwelcome sound of their immediate celebrations. I began to mentally tear myself apart, the familiar fire crackling in my head, telling myself I was useless, too slow and terrible at hockey; that I couldn't stand the pressure in big games like this; that I should never be playing in the first place; that I was ruining the experience for my teammates. The last time the Flying Vees made the final, I had to be pulled out of the game—

"NOOO!!!" screamed an authoritative, female voice. I looked over at Tina the Referee. Her eyes were bright and alert behind her plastic visor. *"NOOOO!!!"* she yelled again, waving her arms from side to side, the universal hockey signal for . . . "no goal." I stared at her from ice level, trying to figure out how I was misinterpreting her signal. "NO GOAL!" Tina the Referee yelled again. "The puck never crossed the goal line!"

The other team charged at her, an angry herd towering over her, yelling down phrases like "Are you serious? That was *in*! What the fuck? Are you blind?"

"NO!" yelled Tina back up at them, skating from her position on the goal line toward my crease. "The puck is under the goalie's pad!" All eyes of every player in the rink and those watching in the stands stared down at me. Like a mother goose caring for an egg, I very, very carefully lifted my pad straight up. There, lying flat on the ice an inch from the goal line was the puck. No goal. I made the save. Sure, the guy I stopped was probably an assistant manager at Foot Locker by day, but I stopped him. *I made the save.*

At the drop of the puck, the Flying Vees played like a swarm of hornets. Nitzy was forced to watch from the penalty box, his face plastered against the glass with anxiety. Fifty seconds to go. Flying Vees winger Hugh "The Jaw" Baker dropped at the blue line to block a shot with his face. Forty seconds to go. Scotty "The Talker" Walker dove across the ice to poke the puck out across the blue line. Twenty seconds to go. *SMACK.* I stopped a careening slapshot with my blocker. Ten seconds. Vees defenceman "Diamond" Roy Greig slammed his check into the boards and lofted the puck into the air, sliding it into the neutral zone. I held my breath. The blaring final buzzer felt like warm honey being poured into my ears.

I threw my hands and goalie stick in the air, just like I had seen Martin Brodeur do after backstopping Team Canada to the 2002 gold medal in men's hockey at the Winter Olympics in Salt Lake City. I tossed off my sweaty glove and blocker. I pulled my goalie mask off my face and threw it to the ice, whooping with joy. Happy yard sale. I was swarmed by my teammates. I grabbed Nick by the shoulder pads and yelled in his face: "We did it!" Nick scored the game-winning-goal, I made the game-winning save.

THE FLYING VEES

2010/2011 CHAMPIONS

DIVISION FOUR

DUFFERS HOCKEY LEAGUE

Later, I sat slumped in my remaining equipment in our locker room with a giddy, deeply satisfied grin on my face. I was flypaper sticky, having been hosed down by Black Label beer and cheap champagne. While I watched my teammates noisily celebrating throughout our private cinder-block clubhouse, I glanced down

The Vancouver Flying Vees held on to win our second championship by the perilously close, nausea-inducing score of 2–1. It's a moment I never would have imagined myself experiencing during the first 30 years of my life. Rear L–R: "Flowin'" Kevin Rowan, John "The Silver Screen" Silver, Brian "Lattatude" Latta, "Young" Greg Fordham, Bruce "Pounds" Dyck, Hugh "Jaws" Baker, "Diamond" Roy Greig, Geoff "The Dandy" Kehrig. Front L–R: Nick "Lock-Eye" Thomas, John "The Hammer" Stiver, Grant "Kingpin" Lawrence, Scotty "The Talker" Walker, Jeremy "Bomber" Bidnall, Chris "Nitzy" Mizzoni.

at my beat-up old goalie skates and was reminded of the first time Mom shoved my feet into those tiny torturous black skates against my screaming protests. I thought about how the very sight of a locker room or the smell of a hockey rink used to send a nervous chill up my spine. I thought about King Richard, Captain Kirk and Bobby Lu, my goaltender heroes.

239

I would always have a conflicted relationship with the game of hockey for all its dirty, pugilistic flaws offset by its speed, creativity and beauty, but when Captain John Silver thrust that tarnished beer-league championship trophy into my lap, my personal battle with the game of hockey was over. The perpetually flawed Canucks hadn't yet won the Stanley Cup, but I still loved them. And I was still a gimpy, small, lopsided goaltender who always made the first move, who flopped like a wounded moth and let in way too many goals. It didn't matter, because at that moment I felt like Indiana Jones cradling the rarest of idols. I tilted the dirty cup toward my lips and let the metallic taste of Black Label beer pour down my throat. I held the trophy aloft, whooped, and passed it over to Nick. I couldn't wipe the smile off my face, and I couldn't wait for the next hockey season to begin.

Joyfully celebrating the beer-league hockey championship with Chris "Nitzy" Mizzoni. And with that, the demons of my sporting past were exorcised. Here's to many further adventures on ice with my friends and teammates on the Vancouver Flying Vees.

★ ★ ★

The END

*"The greatest feeling a goalie can have
is to have played well and know
you've really contributed to the cause
when your team has won the game."*

JEFF HACKETT, *NHL goalie, 1988–2004*

OVERTIME

★ ★ ★ ★

RECOMMENDED READING

THERE IS A long, bruising and colourful history of puck-lit that strongly influenced this book. First and foremost, I owe much of my rediscovery of hockey, and my interest in writing about it, to my friend and mentor Dave Bidini. He not only inspired me with his books such as *On a Cold Road*, *Tropic of Hockey*, *The Best Game You Can Name*, *A Wild Stab For It* and others, but also flat-out suggested the idea to me for this book. Thanks for that, Dave, and for all you've done to open up the game for so many others like me, for better or for worse.

When it comes to goaltending, my favourite how-to manual is the downright casual *Fuhr on Goaltending* by Grant Fuhr, featuring Grant on the cover in his Oilers uniform in an amazing knee-drop kick-save. Also helping me understand the position was the similarly titled but somewhat more philosophical *On Goaltending* by the innovator Jacques "Jake the Snake" Plante. I was impressed that Plante included "strength of character" and "personality" high on his list as must-have traits for a goaltender. I have also never forgotten his amazing "fraction of a second" reaction rule between saves and goals (never give up on a play no matter how out of position you are).

When it comes to great goalie biographies, my favourite is *Shut Out: The Legend of Terry Sawchuk* by Brian Kendall. Sawchuk seemed so damaged—on the outside by pucks repeatedly smashing his unmasked face in, and on the inside from depression and alcoholism. This book aptly explains the story behind hockey's legendary tragic goaltender who died at age forty. Canadian poet Randall Maggs has a beautiful book of poems dedicated to the same goalie entitled *Night Work: The Sawchuk Poems*. I also loved *Beyond The Crease*, the autobiography by the New Jersey Devils' goalie superstar Martin Brodeur (with Damian Cox). Brodeur's hybrid playing style makes him by far my all-time favourite goalie to never wear a Canucks uniform. Ken Dryden's classic *The Game* can get heavy at times, especially near the end, but I found the book invaluable when analyzing the mindset of the goaltender ("goaltending is not fun"). *The Game* strongly reinforces the notion that there is room on the ice for both the smashers and the thinkers.

One of the great raconteurs of Canadian hockey history is the ever-generous Ron MacLean, host of *Hockey Night in Canada*. He tells his own story in *Cornered* (with Kirstie McLellan Day), including coming clean on his televised critique of Canucks forward Alex "The Arrow" Burrows. CBC broadcaster, goalie, author, Buffalo Sabres superfan and ex-sportscaster Kevin Sylvester tells the satirical story of what Canada would have been like had Russia won the 1972 Summit Series in the hilarious and disturbing book *Shadrin Has Scored for Russia: The Day Canadian Hockey Died*.

Helping me understand the faces behind the fists of the hockey fighters, goons, agitators, rebels and party animals was a stack of "sin bin" books. The early benchmark for the genre is *I've Got to Be Me*, the outrageous 1972 autobiography of hockey's Derek "The Turk" Sanderson of the Boston Bruins (with Stan Fischler). If the stories are to be believed, "The Turk" was basically the Austin Powers of the NHL. I also loved the raw, unfiltered, often hilarious passion found within *Tiger: A Hockey Story* by Tiger Williams (with James Lawton). Love him or hate him, Dave "Tiger" Williams was one of the all-time characters of the NHL, who always told it like he saw it. The league could use a lot more character players like Tiger Williams. A tragic tale of a beloved hockey heavyweight is *Tough Guy: My Life on the Edge* by Bob Probert (with Kirstie McLellan Day). Probert died before the book was even published; it's a riveting portrayal of what the "goon" goes through on a daily basis. My all-time favourite hockey book happens to be written by one of the all-time arch-enemies of the Vancouver Canucks: *Playing with Fire* by Theo Fleury (also with Kirstie McLellan Day), one of the most brutally honest stories you'll ever read: hockey or otherwise. I had a chance to meet Theo Fleury and Bob Probert on separate occasions. Both were very giving, kind individuals who happily indulged me with their stories about playing against the Canucks. Books on the Canucks themselves are few and far between (hence Dave Bidini's suggestion that I write this one) but the best of the few is *Canucks at 40: Our Game, Our Stories, Our Passion* by Greg Douglas and Grant Kerr.

And finally . . . check out *Clancy with the Puck*, the children's book written and illustrated by the Vancouver Flying Vees' own Chris "Nitzy" Mizzoni. You can also enjoy his obsessive and entertaining hockey blog: nitzyshockeyden.blogspot.ca.

RECOMMENDED
LISTENING

S WAS THE case with my first book, my love of rock 'n' roll
music is woven throughout this book, starting with the title,
a ferocious, driving, heartfelt song by the Tragically Hip. My
humble appreciation goes out to the Tragically Hip's lead singer
and songwriter Gord Downie (a fellow goalie) for his permission
to use this song title. You can find "The Lonely End of the Rink"—
the song—on the Tragically Hip's album *World Container*. Almost
all of the chapter titles in *The Lonely End of the Rink* are musical tips of the toque, as well. "That Boston Dandy" is a bizarre,
smoky, spoken-word B-side found on Alan Thicke's wawa-heavy
funk rock single "Wondrous Bobby Orr" from 1967. Back then,
future TV dad Alan Thicke was recording under the name "AJ
Thicke." "Canadian Winters" is a whimsical indie-pop song by
the band Maplewood Lane from Grimsby, Ontario. "True Patriot
Love" is a roaring, Elvis Costello-esque protest rocker by one of my
all-time faves, Joel Plaskett. It can be found on his stellar album
Down at the Khyber. "Drunk Teenagers" and "Snowed In" are two
more anthemic Plaskett rockers, from his teenage rock 'n' roll
love triangle concept record *Ashtray Rock*. "Blood on the Ice" is a

two-minute blast of puck rock from the Riverdales, the side-project of legendary Chicago band Screeching Weasel. The song was written during lead singer Ben Weasel's short-lived but total fascination with the Chicago Wolves of the American Hockey League. He even did a hockey zine for the Wolves' fans. The Buffalo Jump is a band from Vancouver. "(I'm Gonna) Run Away" is one of the all-time great rock 'n' roll songs by Joan Jett and the Black Hearts, dedicated here to the Black Hearts hockey club of Toronto.

WHEN IT COMES to defining "puck rock," the Hanson Brothers are pretty much the end-all be-all, and I mentioned several of their titles in the book, including their greatest song ever, "(He Looked a Lot Like) Tiger Williams," in which the Hanson Brothers predict that if there is a god above, he will probably look a lot like Tiger Williams. "Total Goombah!" is the last song from their stellar debut album *Gross Misconduct*, and if you can find them, *Johnny Hanson Presents Puck Rock Volumes 1 and 2* are both full-throttle mid-1990s musical tributes to the frozen game from an offensive attack of misshapen bands. The Smugglers' inglorious and almost-fateful "Our Stanley Cup" is on Volume 1. One of the best parts of both compilations is the inspired band logos designed as hockey crests in the album artwork. As for hockey players who also play music, Camp Radio is a blazing rock 'n' roll power trio made up of members of the Ottawa Songbird Millionaires, featuring my old pal Chris Page on lead vocals, guitar and defence.

"How Darwinian" is a song by Vancouver troubadour Dan Mangan, who once proudly sang "O Canada" on the ice at the start of a Canucks game, just a few feet from Roberto Luongo. "Crash Years" is a song by the New Pornographers, one of the best Canadian bands of all time. "Let's Wreck the Party" is a D.O.A. blast from the band's 1985 "stadium rock sell-out" album of the same name (I had no idea of the criticism and thought the album was pretty damn good when I eventually found it). "School Days (Hail, Hail Rock 'n' Roll")" is just one of the stack of anthems that became the blueprints of rock 'n' roll, found on one of the greatest song collections ever assembled: *The Great Twenty-Eight* by Chuck Berry, chronicling his string of non-stop hit singles for Chess Records from 1955 to 1965.

Some of my favourite Canadian bands come from the tiny garden province of Prince Edward Island. "Heroes of the Sidewalk" is a potato-fuelled fist-pumper by Two Hours Traffic, one of the island's best-ever musical exports. "Grab Me by the Lapel" is a ferocious fuzz-soaked garage rock pounder by the North Lakes, also from PEI.

Continuing in the wacky world of novelty hockey records, "Hockey Sock Rock" is yet another Alan Thicke–penned, goofy *Happy Days*-type tune sung by various members of the 1979 New York Rangers. On the flipside, the Los Angeles Kings take on what is actually a pretty great pop tune called "Please Forgive My Misconduct (Last Night)", also written by Alan Thicke. "Main Offender" is an incredibly powerful single by the Hives, who outrageously beat us in a ball hockey game we challenged them to our on home turf in Vancouver. "Northern Wish" is a classic song by Dave Bidini's band, Rheostatics. "The Buzz in My Flesh" is not only one of my all-time favourite song titles, but simply a great Fleetwood Mac–like pop workout from a very underrated Canadian band called Young Galaxy. "Took Me By Surprise" is a swingin' jazz pop number by my wife, Jill Barber. The song can be found on her radiant, award-winning album *Mischievous Moon*.

I've long argued that Sloan are the Beatles of Canada. Bassist Chris Murphy can not only sing like a bird and write great songs, he also captains some sort of hockey team every year at the Hockey Summit of the Arts. "Everything You've Done Wrong" (written by Sloan's Patrick Pentland) is from Sloan's bestselling record, *One Chord to Another*. Nardwuar the Human Serviette has introduced me to lots of mind-blowing music over the years, for which I am forever grateful. His starting point was the Sonics' searing version of the classic Northwest frat-rock anthem "Louie, Louie."

"Like Lightning" is a striking song by brother-in-law/goalie/ singer-songwriter Matthew Barber. "In the Belly of the Dragon" is a song by Halifax singer-songwriter Jenn Grant from her album *The Beautiful Wild*. It's a beautiful record that I listened to repeatedly while writing this book. "This City's a Mess" isn't about the Stanley Cup Riots, but it certainly fits, and was written and performed by Vancouver heroes Said The Whale. "Out Like a Lion" is a lovely duet, my favourite arrangement in music, by the exceptional musical husband-and-wife team of Luke Doucet and Melissa McLelland, otherwise known as Whitehorse. That song is from their brilliantly named album *The Fate of the World Depends on This Kiss*. I love all of this music, and almost all of the Canadian selections are available for you to hear on a playlist (and hopefully buy) at music.cbc.ca/profile/Grant-Lawrence.

Oh . . . and don't forget about the Evaporators, and of course, the Smugglers.

THANK YOU

J ILL BARBER AND Joshua Lawrence, Jean, Garth and Heather Lawrence, Dave Bidini, Gord Downie and the Tragically Hip, Samantha Haywood and the Transatlantic Agency, Nick Thomas, everyone who has ever played on the Vancouver Flying Vees Hockey Club, The Smugglers, Ron MacLean, Kevin Sylvester, Angie Abdou, Boyd Devereaux, Geoff Kehrig, everyone at Douglas and McIntyre and Harbour Publishing, Silas White, Derek Fairbridge, Patricia Wolfe, Naomi MacDougall, Christy Nyiri, Ken Beattie and Killbeat Music, Christine "CMac" McAvoy, Lee "Shotgun" Hower, Steve Pratt and everyone at CBC Music and Radio 3, the blog community of CBC Radio 3, Jo-Ann Roberts, *All Points West, Radio West, On the Coast, Definitely Not the Opera*, Bob Kronbauer and VancouverIsAwesome.com, Paul Clarke, Tom Goodwin, the Good Times Hockey League of the Arts, Chris Murphy, the Ottawa Songbird Millionaires, the Halifax–Dartmouth Ferries, the Morningstars, the Jokers, the Parkdale Hockey Lads, Charlene Jaggers and Duffers Hockey League, Marc Tougas and the Apex Shootout Outdoor Hockey Tournament, Apex Accommodations, Sarah Harmer,

253

the Greig family, Garry Monahan, Kyle Fogden, Rob Zifarelli, Adam Countryman, Rob Thornton, and Jack Ross of the Agency Group, Patrick Sambrook, Jian Ghomeshi, Trena White, Dave "The Vancouver Flying Vees' #1 Fan" Thomas, Ken Kelley, Bill and Sam Baker, Barry Needham, Fiona Forbes and *The Rush*, Darryl and Ann Barber, Darrell and Anita Dick, Val Mason, Michael Eckford, Barb Rees, Grant Galbraith, Human Alghabi, Zulu Records, Outside Music, Lindsey Love, Rick Thaddeus, Charlie Demers, Francois Marchand, Cory Ashworth, Tamara Stanners and everyone at the *Peak*, Shannon Behan, Rum and Randy Iwata, David Myles, Jon Bartlett, KJ Jansen, Said the Whale, Michael Bernard Fitzgerald, Ben Bouchard, Brigs, Del Barber, Belle Plaine, Andy Swan, Powell River Sea Kayak, Shelagh Rogers, Wayne and Lucy Brown, Yukon Dave White, Theo Fleury, Brian, Joyce, Matthew Barber and Alexis Taylor, Lizzy Karp and Rain City Chronicles, Museum of Vancouver, Nardwuar the Human Serviette, Virginia Clark, the Hanson Brothers, Anne DeGrace, Mark Mattson, Nancy's Bakery, Phillips Brewing, Galiano Island Literary Festival, Joe Burke Literary Festival, Sunshine Coast Festival of the Written Arts, Denman Island Readers and Writers Festival, North Shore Writers Festival, Home County Folk Festival, Regina Folk Festival, Vancouver Folk Music Festival, West Vancouver Memorial Library, Kootenay Library Federation, Shuswap Writers Festival, Powell River Writers' Conference, Shivering Songs Festival, Laundromat Espresso Bar, Word On The Street, Communitea Café, FRED, the Drake Hotel, BC Book Prizes, Writers' Trust of Canada, Hilary Weston, Wilfrid Laurier University, the Flame, "Bad" Karen Skadsheim and Townsite Brewing... and the bookstores: Breakwater, Pollen Sweaters, 32 Books, Black Bond, Coho, Bluewaters, Galiano Island Books, Blackberry, Mosaic, Munro's, Salt Spring Books, Mulberry Bush, Pages, McNally Robinson, Mermaid Tales, Armchair, Books and Company, Curious Coho, Type, LaVerne's Grill, Coast Princess, Talewind, Tanner's, Bonanza, Volume One, Bolen, Café Books, Bookmark, Dave's Book Bar, Jennie's

Book Garden, Collected Works, Crockett, Lotus, Laughing Oyster, Otter, Polar Peak, UBC Bookstore, Abraxas, Blue Heron, Hager, Mac's Fireweed, Nanaimo Maps and Charts, Coles, Bookingham Palace, Marnie's, Talewind, Chapters, Hooked on Books, People's Co-Op, the Refuge Cove Store and Gallery, and the BC Ferries Passages Gift Shop.

To contact the author, please write or send a postcard:

Grant Lawrence
700 Hamilton Street
Vancouver, BC
Canada V6B 4A2

grant.lawrence@cbc.ca
www.grantlawrence.ca